中传学者文库编委会

主　任： 廖祥忠　张树庭
副主任： 蔺海波　李　众　刘守训　李新军　王　晖
　　　　　杨　懿　柴剑平

成　员（按姓氏笔画排序）：

王廷信　王栋晗　王晓红　王　雷　文春英
龙小农　付　龙　叶　龙　刘东建　刘剑波
任孟山　李怀亮　李　舒　张绍华　张　晶
张根兴　张毓强　林卫国　郑　月　金　炜
金雪涛　周建新　庞　亮　赵新利　徐红梅
贾秀清　高晓虹　隋　岩　喻　梅　熊澄宇

中传学者文库
1954-2024

主编／柴剑平　执行主编／龙小农　副主编／张毓强　周建新

文化科技发展探索
蒋伟自选集

蒋伟　著

中国传媒大学出版社
·北京·

图书在版编目（CIP）数据

文化科技发展探索：蒋伟自选集/蒋伟著.－－北京：中国传媒大学出版社，2024.8.

（中传学者文库/柴剑平主编）.

ISBN 978-7-5657-3776-3

Ⅰ.G12-53

中国国家版本馆 CIP 数据核字第 2024Y2F989 号

文化科技发展探索：蒋伟自选集
WENHUA KEJI FAZHAN TANSUO: JIANG WEI ZIXUANJI

著　　者	蒋　伟
责任编辑	杨小薇
封面设计	锋尚设计
责任印制	李志鹏

出版发行	中国传媒大学出版社			
社　　址	北京市朝阳区定福庄东街 1 号	邮　编	100024	
电　　话	86-10-65450528　65450532	传　真	65779405	
网　　址	http://cucp.cuc.edu.cn			
经　　销	全国新华书店			
印　　刷	北京中科印刷有限公司			
开　　本	710mm×1000mm　1/16			
印　　张	16.75			
字　　数	279 千字			
版　　次	2024 年 8 月第 1 版			
印　　次	2024 年 8 月第 1 次印刷			
书　　号	ISBN 978-7-5657-3776-3/G·3776	定　价	84.00 元	

本社法律顾问：北京嘉润律师事务所　郭建平

总　序

媒介是人类社会交流和传播的基本工具。从口语时代到印刷时代，再经电子时代至今天的数智时代，媒介形态加速演变、融合程度深入发展，媒介已然成为现代社会运行的基础设施和操作系统。今天，人类已经迈入媒介社会，万物皆媒、人人皆媒，无媒介不社会、无传播不治理。今天，无论我们怎么用力于信息传播的研究、怎么重视信息传播人才的培养都不为过。

中国传媒大学（其前身为北京广播学院）作为新中国第一所信息传播类院校，自1954年创建伊始，即与媒介形态演变合律同拍、与国家发展同频共振，努力探索中国特色信息传播人才培养模式、构建中国信息传播类学科自主知识体系，执信息传播人才培养之牛耳、发信息传播研究之先声，被誉为"中国广播电视及传媒人才摇篮""信息传播领域知名学府"。

追溯中传肇始发轫之起源、瞩望中传砥砺跨越之未来，可谓创业维艰而其命维新。昔日中传因广播而起，因电视而兴，因网络而盛，今天和未来必乘风破浪、蓄势而上，因人工智能而强。在这期间，每一种媒介兴起，中传均吸引一批志于学、问于道、勤于术的

 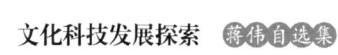

学者汇聚于此,切磋学术、传道授业,立时代之潮头,回应社会需求,成为学界翘楚、行业中坚,遂有今日中传学术研究之森然气象,已历七秩而弦歌不断,将传百世亦风华正茂。

自新时代以来,中传坚守为党育人、为国育才初心,励精图治、勠力前行,秉承"系统治理、创新图强、交叉融合、特色发展"的办学理念,牢牢把握高等教育发展大势、传媒业态发展趋势,瞄准"智能传媒"和"国际一流"两大主攻方向,以世界为坐标、以未来为向度,完成了全面布局和系统升级,正在蹄疾步稳、高质量推动学校从传统高等教育向未来高等教育跨越、从传统传媒教育向智能传媒教育跨越、从国内一流向世界一流跨越,全力建设中国特色、世界一流传媒大学。

中国特色、世界一流,在于有大先生扎根中国大地,汇聚古今、融通中外;在于有大先生执教黉门,学高为师、身正为范;在于有大先生躬耕杏坛,敦品积学、启智润心。习近平总书记更强调,高校教师要立志成为大先生,在教书育人和科研创新上不断创造新业绩。中传广大教师素来以做大先生为毕生职志,努力成为新时代"经师"与"人师"的统一者,做真学问、立高品行,践履"立德树人"使命。

2024岁在甲辰,欣逢中传建校70华诞,学校特邀约部分学者钩玄勒要、增删批阅,遴选已公开刊发的论文汇编成集,出版"中传学者文库",意在呈现学校在学科建设、科学研究、服务行业实践等方面的最新成果,赓续中传文脉,谱写时代新声。

文库汇聚老中青三代学者,资深学者渊渟岳峙、阐幽抉微;中年学者沉潜蓄势、厚积薄发;青年学者踌躇满志、未来可期。文库与五十周年校庆所出版的"北广学者文库"相承接,大致可勾勒中传知识生产薪火相传、三代辉映之概貌，反映中传在构建中国特色新闻传播类、传媒艺术类、传媒技术类学科体系、学术体系和话语体系方面的耕耘与收获，窥见中国特色信息传播类学科知识体系构建的发展脉络与轨迹。

这一构建过程，虽筚路蓝缕，却步履铿锵；虽垦荒拓野，亦四方辐辏。一批肇始于中传，交叉融合、具有中国特色的学科，如播音主持艺术学、广播电视艺术学、传媒艺术学、数字媒体艺术学、政治传播学等，从涓涓细流汇入滔滔江河，从中传走向全国，展现了中传学者构建中国自主知识体系的学术想象力和创新力。文库展示的虽然是历史，实则是呈现今天；看似是总结过去，实则是召唤未来。与其说这套文库的出版，是对既有学术成果的展示，毋宁说是对未来学术创新的邀约。

回首过往，七秩芳华。我们深知，唯有将马克思主义基本原理与中华优秀传统文化相结合，才能推动中华学术创造性转化和创新性发展，推动中国自主知识体系的构建。我们深知，唯有准确把握媒介形态演变的脉动、深刻认知媒介形态变革所产生的影响，才能推动中国信息传播类学科自主知识体系的构建与时俱进。

展望未来，星辰大海。我们深知，以人工智能为代表的产业和科技革命正迅疾而来，媒介生态正在加速重构，教育形态正在全面重塑，大学之使命与价值正在被重新定义；我们深知，唯有"胸怀国之大者"、面向世界科技前沿、面向经济主战场、面向国家重大需求，才能确保中传始终屹立于中国乃至世界传媒教育发展之潮头。

如何应对人工智能带来的深刻变革，对中传而言是一场要么"冲顶"、要么"灭顶"的"兴亡之战"。我们坚信，不管前方是雄关漫道，还是荆棘满途，唯有勇敢直面"教育强国，中传何为？"这一核心命题，奋力书写"智能传媒教育，中传师生有为！"的精彩答卷，才能化危为机，奋力开创人工智能时代中传智能传媒教育新纪元。

功不唐捐，芳华七秩；风帆正举，赓续创新。

是为序。

第十四届全国政协委员，中国传媒大学党委书记、教授、博士生导师

目 录

第一部分　文化与科技融合

国家级文化科技融合示范基地发展水平的评价体系设计 ········· 003
文化科技的主要概念及相互关系 ········· 012
中国文化科技发展与融合40年（1978—2018） ········· 023
关于"推进文化与科技融合"的一点思考 ········· 046
虚实融合放大演艺魅力 ········· 053

第二部分　视听技术

视听觉融合效应及其信息融合处理方法综论 ········· 057
A Study of Visual Attention Elements with Experiment Analysis Based on Composition ········· 066
The Association Between Timbre of Musical Sound and Texture ········· 080
A Study of Color-Emotion Image Set Construction and Feature Analysis ········· 093
Analysis and Modelling of Timbre Perception Features in Musical Sounds ········· 105
Human Perceptual Responses to Multiple Colors: A Study of Multicolor Perceptual Features Modelling ········· 135

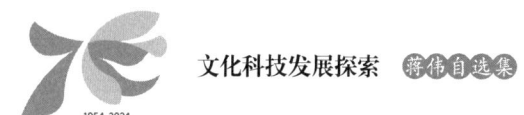

第三部分　研究报告

科技进步与文化建设研究（节选） ································ 165

文化科技创新活动的评价、评估与统计问题研究 ················ 172

"十三五"时期科技与文化融合发展的新趋势及其对文化发展的影响 ········· 197

工业和信息化部、文化和旅游部文化装备发展行动计划（2018—2020 年）···· 206

"十四五"城镇化与城市发展领域战略科技研究（节选） ··········· 217

第四部分　讲话发言

开创"十二五"文化科技发展新局面的相关考虑 ·················· 233

对接国家新需求，推动科研迈向文化科技领域 ··················· 242

文化阵地的新载体与新服务

　　——论云文化馆的新担当与新征程 ······················· 245

数字体育专业委员会工作任务及聚焦方向的一些考虑 ············· 248

推进文化与科技的融合，把握好研发团队的建设 ················· 251

数字化赋能与激发文化创新 ···································· 254

第一部分
文化与科技融合

国家级文化科技融合示范基地发展水平的评价体系设计*

一、引言

文化与科技融合是当下经济发展的热点话题，自 20 世纪 80 年代起，欧美发达国家就开始了文化与科技融合发展的讨论，从全球文化竞争格局来看，我国文化科技发展相对滞后。当前，推进文化科技创新已成为深化文化体制改革、推动社会主义文化大发展、大繁荣的重要任务之一。我国已进入全面建设小康社会的关键时期和深化改革开放、加快转变经济发展方式的攻坚时期，文化科技发展正面临重大的战略机遇。

在中央政府的高度重视下，文化与科技融合产业在全国掀起新一轮发展浪潮。各地文化产业园区、文化创意产业研究中心蓬勃兴起，推动了文化产业系统化、区域化、集群化发展，同时也在构建优良的人才培养平台、促进产业配套升级、提升产业发展层次等方面发挥了重要作用。2012 年 5 月，科技部、中宣部、文化和旅游部、国家新闻出版广电总局、新闻出版总署五部门联合发布了首批国家级文化和科技融合示范基地，是贯彻落实党的十七届六中全会精神的一项重要举措，旨在进一步发挥文化和科技相互促进的作用，更好地引导和推动各地文化和科技融合，增强文化产业领域科技实力和自主创新能力，促进我国文化产业持续健康快速发展。

文化科技融合示范基地是文化企业及相关机构的聚集区域，是文化产业的载体，其内聚集着各类文化和科技融合型企业，一大批文化科技复合型人才，以及专业孵化器、中介服务机构、科研院所等相关机构，是探索文化科技产业集群式发展、创新链和产业链互动集合的新模式的重要载体，产生集约效应和集聚效应。开展文化科技融合示范基地评价工作，总体目的是准确了解与把握文化科技融合创新的发展现状和总体进展，重点考量文化科技的融合创新对文化发展的成效，为相关决策者（各级政府等）制订相关政策、措施、目标和规划提供依据；使相关参与者及时了解自身的发展水平和发展潜力，

---

* 本文原载于《第九届中国科技政策与管理学术年会论文集》2013 年，与张龙菲、郑成琳、刘美合作。收入本书时有改动。

通过对比明确自身的优势，清醒认识自己的劣势，激发文化科技融合创新的积极性，并借鉴他人的先进经验实现自身的快速成长和跨越式发展。

由于首批文化科技融合示范基地的认定时间还不久，因此目前还没有针对该问题的研究成果。本文是从文化科技融合的特点出发，结合我国目前的国情和文化科技发展形势，借鉴了其他类似问题的研究方法，并选择性运用到该评价问题上，最终形成了较为合理的、可实施性强的研究成果，即适用于文化科技融合示范基地的评价指标体系。

二、文化科技融合示范基地发展水平的评价体系设计

文化科技融合示范基地建立的目的主要有以下几点：一是加速技术、人才、资金、政策等要素聚集，促进文化科技成果产业化；二是加快推动文化科技产业新兴业态的形成和发展，促进区域产业结构调整和优化升级；三是加强文化科技产业集群建设，探索集群式创新发展的新模式，切实发挥示范、辐射、带动作用。文化科技融合示范基地作为一项重要的政策手段，是国家的政策工具，对文化科技融合示范基地的评价定位于"政策评价"，强调目的性，强调其对国家导向目标的实现程度和实际融合产出效果。通过对文化与科技融合示范基地的评估，从区域层面对文化科技创新活动发展水平进行了解和把握，明确开展文化科技创新活动的切入点和关键环节，从而为各地推进文化科技融合提供方向性指导。

（一）文化科技融合示范基地发展水平的评价体系设计原则

根据我国文化与科技融合的现状，充分考虑文化与科技融合的主要特征，在探索融合评价指标体系和评价标准时，具体评价原则如下：

1. 科学性原则：指标体系的设计必须建立在科学的基础上，要客观真实地反映示范基地文化与科技融合发展的内在规律，同时结合必要的专项调查和考证，定性、定量相结合。

2. 可比性原则：一套指标体系是对多个评价对象的文化科技融合状况进行综合评价，因此，该指标体系的设计必须充分考虑到其各自统计指标的差异，在具体指标选择上，文化科技融合状况评价体系的评价指标必须是他们各自共有的指标含义，统计口径和范围尽可能保持一致，保证指标的可比性。

3. 可操作性原则：指标的设计要在较准确地反映评价目标的基础上，尽可能选取具有共性的综合性指标，在基本满足评价要求和给出决策所需信息的前提下，应尽量减少指标个数，突出重点指标，使指标体系简单明了，评价指标的数据便于收集和整理，定量指标可直接量化，定性指标也能间接赋值量化，具有可行性和可操作性，能够与现行统计方法相衔接。

4. 相对独立性原则：由于文化科技融合的内涵与外延非常丰富，描述文化科技融合创新水平的指标之间常常存在信息重叠的现象。因此，在选择指标时，应尽可能选择具有相对独立性的指标，以具有纵向、横向可比性的相对指标为主，提高评价的准确性和科学性。

5. 系统性原则：评价指标体系应能从系统的角度，全面、综合地反映被评价对象的总体情况，评价指标体系内部的各指标之间要有一定的逻辑关系，不但要涵盖文化科技融合示范基地的主要特征，还要能反映其现状和发展。不是指标的简单堆积，而应是统一的有机整体。

（二）文化科技融合示范基地发展水平的评价体系框架构建

基于"政策评价"的定位，要设计出一套科学合理的评价体系，首先是对评价对象的认识和研究。在文化科技融合示范基地内，与开展文化科技融合工作相关的主体主要包括三种类型：融合的推动者（政府、中介机构），融合的需求者（企业），融合的服务提供者（高校、科研院所）。基地内的企业是融合的主体，是融合的需求方。区域主管部门（政府）为企业进行文化科技融合创新活动提供硬件、网络等基础和环境保障，中介机构提供资源的协调、人才的培训等。高校、科研院所为企业开展文化科技创新活动提供信息、技术、整体解决方案等支撑和服务。以上三种类型相关方共同努力，通过开展文化科技融合创新工作促进基地内企业竞争力的提升、产业结构的优化升级、人均劳动生产率的提高，以及区域整体经济和社会效益及竞争力的不断提升，最终实现社会主义文化的大繁荣、大发展。

在了解文化科技融合示范基地内参与文化科技融合活动的几项主体后，就可以确定评价的方向及评价体系的大致框架。借鉴国内外对其他各种形式融合发展水平的评估指标体系设计和开展评估工作的经验，同时通过对示范基地文化科技融合发展规律的探讨和研究，可以发现，融合环境、融合深度和融合成效三个要素与基地文化科技融合工作最为相关。

融合环境是文化科技融合示范基地内各企业、机构和单位应用科技的前提条件，文化和科技融合的发展水平在良好的基础环境保障中得到进一步提升和优化。融合深度是示范基地内各单位应用科技提升其研发设计、生产管理、商务流通等业务的能力和水平，文化科技融合促进文化产品质量提升、经营管理的精细化、商务流通的有效等，最终会直接或间接地导致基地本身、基地内企业以及文化产业和文化发展产生重要效益（融合成效）。融合环境、融合深度、融合成效三个方面的相互作用，构成了示范基地文化科技融合的发展模式。因此，确定融合环境、融合深度和融合成效三个目标层。

目标层确定之后，围绕三个目标层，分析各个目标层的评价相关因素，延伸并综合分类后，可得出准测层。在本指标体系结构中，每个目标层分别下设两个准测层，即基

地建设、产业结构、创新投入、创新成果、融合成效和文化贡献,共计六项。准测层再延伸研究,分析各个相关影响因素,并经过推敲和筛选,便得到统计指标层。

(三)文化科技融合示范基地发展水平的评价体系指标设置

根据上述研究结论以及评价指标、评价体系的概念,并结合文化科技融合示范基地发展水平评价体系自身的目的,确定了评价指标体系。该指标体系包括一级指标3个,二级指标6个,三级指标35个。指标的选取遵循定量与定性相结合的原则,定量指标和定性指标结合使用既可以使评价具有客观性,便于数学模型处理,又可弥补单纯定量指标评价的不足及数据本身存在的某些缺陷。指标体系详细设置如表1所示。

表1　文化科技融合示范基地发展水平评价指标体系

一级指标	二级指标	三级指标
融合环境	基地建设	基础设施建设
		基地管理体制和监管能力
		基地发展规划
		公共服务平台建设
		人才队伍建设
	产业结构	特色产业集聚度
		主导产业首位度
		每百户单位中文化科技企业数
		每百户单位中科技服务机构(中介机构)数
		与高校共建研究中心(研究所、实验室)数
融合深度	创新投入	每百户企业拥有研发机构数
		每千人拥有研发人员数
		研发经费支出占园区生产总值的比重
		文化科技企业孵化器面积
		在孵文化科技企业数
		发明专利数
	创新成果	省级以上名牌产品数
		重大文化科技创新项目实施数量
		拥有著名、驰名商标数
		文化新产品年产出量

续表

一级指标	二级指标	三级指标
融合成效	绩效产出	基地技工贸总收入
		总资产利润率
		单位面积的资产总额
		文化产业产值利税率
	绩效产出	单位工业增加值能耗、新鲜水耗
		文化科技产品销售收入占产品总销售收入的比重
		文化产业增加值占地区 GDP 比重
		基地内文化科技型企业的发展水平和趋势
		文化产业总产值
		科技贡献率
	文化贡献	对文化产业的带动作用
		文化事业服务能力
		文化领域共性关键技术研究贡献
		对传统文化产业优化升级的促进作用
		对新兴文化产业培育和发展的推动作用

三、评价体系指标的含义及说明

融合环境指的是示范基地能够为推进文化科技融合提供的基础设施环境、政策资金环境、创新服务环境、产业支撑环境等，衡量基地文化科技融合的基本资源保障情况。因此该一级指标包括基地建设和产业结构两个二级指标，其中基地建设主要衡量基地的软硬件条件及建设情况，而产业结构主要指基地的文化产业结构，即文化产业行业在分工基础上的行业间的相互联系与比例关系，包括资源的配置状态以及行业间相互依存和相互制约的关系，反映文化产业发展水平。具体统计指标的选取如下：

1. 基础设施建设：反映基地知识传播能力和信息化建设水平，体现对基地开展文化科技融合活动的基础支持作用。考量因素包括交通、供水供电、商业服务、技术服务、园林绿化、环境保护等市政公用工程设施和公共生活服务设施等。

2. 基地管理体制和监管能力：反映基地管理体制的科学性、有效性以及整体运行效率。考量因素包括基地管理体制是否顺畅、管委会领导班子和干部队伍是否健全、有关经济管理权限赋予是否到位等。

3. 基地发展规划：主要包括产业园区的发展战略规划、项目概念规划、总体发展规

划、产业发展规划以及项目详细规划。

4. 公共服务平台建设：包括公共技术服务、投融资交易、知识产权、品牌培育、人才培训等文化科技融合服务机构是否健全，综合信息服务平台是否建立健全，文化科技创新成果的发布和产权交易是否有便捷高效的渠道，以及是否引进专利代理、投融资、猎头等服务公司。

5. 人才队伍建设：提倡加强人才队伍建设，目的在于为推动文化和科技融合、加快建设示范基地提供智力支撑。考量因素主要包括人才引进措施及优惠政策、发挥各类人才作用的发展环境等。

6. 特色产业集聚度：指基地内特色产业工业总产值占基地工业总产值的比重。有学者提议对文化科技融合示范基地实施"特色文化科技提升计划"。即加强对地方特色文化的高新技术应用产品开发，引导和形成一批有规模的特色文化产业创新集群。该指标正是反映特色产业在基地内的集聚程度，有益于推动基地特色产业发展。

7. 主导产业首位度：反映基地主导产业在所有国家融合示范基地中该产业的集中程度和重要性。

8. 每百户单位中文化科技企业数：指经认定的文化科技型企业占基地单位规模的比重。从企业数量上反映基地文化科技融合的发展水平。

9. 每百户单位中科技服务机构（中介机构）数：指为企业开展技术评估、技术咨询、技术服务、技术转移、软件开发、工业设计、专利代理和科技信息等服务的各类科技中介机构以及以中小企业和文化科技项目为主要投资对象的创业投资机构数量。

10. 与高校共建研究中心（研究所、实验室）数：指基地内企业与高校、科研院所等单位签订了产学研合作协议、实体化运行的机构数。反映基地的产学研结合水平。

融合深度指的是基地的发展水平，是衡量基地文化科技融合水平的重要内容。科技极大地影响着文化的发展，科技创新是文化发展的强大引擎，是科技发展的强力支撑，科技创新可以直接反映基地文化科技融合的发展程度，因此设立包括创新投入和创新成果两个二级指标。其下属三级指标分别为：

1. 每百户企业拥有研发机构数：包括重大创新平台、科研院所、文化科技企业研发中心、重点（工程）实验室、产业技术创新战略联盟和中试基地、引进共建的创新载体和企业技术中心等。反映基地实施研发的硬件条件水平。

2. 每千人拥有研发人员数：指基地内的研究人员、技术人员和辅助人员。研究人员是指主要从事研究开发的专业人员，技术人员是指在研究人员指导下参与具体研发工作的人员，辅助人员是指参与研发的熟练技工。从技术人员的规模角度反映基地的创新能力。

3. 研发经费支出占园区生产总值的比重：反映基地对研发和技术创新的重视程度以及投入能力。

4. 文化科技企业孵化器面积：指经认定的文化科技企业孵化器建筑面积。反映基地对创业企业的扶持能力。

5. 在孵文化科技企业数：经认定的文化科技企业孵化器内的企业数。反映创业企业的活跃程度。

6. 发明专利数：指基地拥有的经认定的发明专利的数量。反映基地知识创造和产出状况。

7. 省级以上名牌产品数：指基地内企业获得由省级及以上名牌战略推进委员会授予，且在证书有效期内的名牌产品。

8. 重大文化科技创新项目实施数量：反映基地对国家发展导向的响应程度。

9. 拥有著名、驰名商标数：指基地内企业由省级及以上工商行政管理部门认定，且在认定有效期内的著名、驰名商标。

10. 文化新产品年产出量：指每年基地内企业获得国家及省相关部门确认或认定的文化新产品数量。直接反映文化产出的能力。

融合成效指的是融合直接或间接带来的竞争力、经济和社会效益的影响，对文化建设和文化发展的贡献，是评价体系的核心部分。考察基地通过实施文化科技融合之后产业结构比例优化、整体经济效益提升、创新能力提升以及集约化发展的情况。因此下设绩效产出和文化贡献两个最具共性的二级指标。其下属三级指标分别为：

1. 基地技工贸总收入：指生产产品销售收入、技术性收入和与本基地产品相关的商品销售收入、其他业务收入、营业收入等各种收入的总和。

2. 总资产利润率：即利润总额与总资产年平均额之比，又称总资产收益率。反映了基地利用全部经济资源的获利能力。

3. 单位面积的资产总额：资产总额与基地实际占地面积之比。反映基地总的资产规模和密集状态。

4. 文化产业产值利税率：指基地内已实现的利润、税金总额（包括利润总额、产品销售税金及附加和应交增值税）占同期全部工业总产值的百分比。反映基地文化产业的效率和贡献。

5. 单位工业增加值能耗、新鲜水耗：反映基地内企业对资源的利用效率，考察该指标有益于促进经济增长向集约内涵式发展。能耗指基地内用于生产、生活的煤、电、油等能源的消耗（包括生产取暖、降温用能）。水耗指基地内用于生产和生活的新鲜水量（生活用水单独计量且生活污水不与工业废水混排的除外），它等于企业从城市自来水取用的水量和企业自备水用量之和。

6. 文化科技产品销售收入占产品总销售收入的比重：该指标为产出的绩效性指标。反映基地内企业将文化转化为商品的能力和基地文化科技创新能力。

7. 文化产业增加值占地区GDP比重：反映了文化产业在区域内的重要性和影响力。

8. 基地内文化科技型企业的发展水平和趋势（定性）：如每年新增文化科技型企业数、骨干企业数、龙头企业数、上市企业数等。反映了文化科技融合基地内部企业发展的影响。

9. 文化产业总产值：反映文化产业的直接经济效益。

10. 科技贡献率：包括科技人员占文化产业从业人员的比例、科技投入占文化产业总投入的比例、拥有自主知识产权的文化产品占文化产品的比例、科技型文化项目占文化产业总项目的比例。

11. 对文化产业的带动作用：对产业的示范带动作用是基地应具备的基本作用，整体评价基地对产业发展的辐射带动作用。

12. 文化事业服务能力：包括文化资源传承与保护、公共文化服务建设以及文化市场管理方面的能力。

13. 文化领域共性关键技术研究贡献：包括文化内容创作、生产、管理、传播与消费等文化产业发展的共性关键技术研究成果，文化资源保护开发共享、知识产权保护、文化安全监管、文化诚信评价等文化管理共性技术的研究成果，文化艺术、广播影视、新闻出版、网络文化等行业关键设备与集成系统的研制成果。

14. 对传统文化产业优化升级的促进作用：包括对文化艺术、广播影视、新闻出版领域的研究及对行业发展的推动作用。

15. 对新兴文化产业培育和发展的推动作用：包括推动创意设计、网络文化以及文化科技与相关产业融合发展方面的作用。

四、结论

文化科技融合示范基地作为推动文化与科技融合必不可少的组成元素，普遍具有一定代表性，通过对其进行融合发展水平的评价工作，将使融合活动的各个参与主体具有更明确的发展规划和目标任务，不断壮大规模，使基地功能全面激活，不断提高自主创新能力并增强基地内企业集团的竞争实力，扩大品牌影响力，切实为全国文化与科技融合产业的发展起到标杆作用，使我国文化与科技融合产业持续保持健康向上、蓬勃发展的良好态势。

参考文献

[1] 科技部. 国家文化科技创新工程实施纲要 [Z]. 2012.

[2] 白国庆. 文化科技融合与城市创新发展 [Z]. 2011.

[3] 陈磊. 首批认定国家级文化和科技融合示范基地公布 [N]. 科技日报，2012-05-19.

[4] 胡惠林. 文化产业学 [M]. 北京：高等教育出版社，2006.
[5] 于平. 文化与科技融合的自主创新和协同发展 [R]. 北京：社会科学文献出版社，2013: 2-6.
[6] 西安市科技局，西安市委宣传部，西安市文广新局. 西安市国家级文化和科技融合示范基地建设实施方案 [Z]. 2012.

文化科技的主要概念及相互关系*

近期,文化科技司正在组织编制"文化科技创新体系建设纲要"和"相关行动计划",目前处在意见征求与论证阶段,了解与把握"文化科技""文化科技创新""文化科技创新体系"等相关概念与内涵,特别是了解与把握他们之间的相互关系,是做好相关编制工作的基础。

文化科技工作涉及面较广,是国家科技工作的重要组成部分,又是新时期国家鼓励的重要发展领域,在理论和实践两个层面都极具探索性和挑战性。

一、文化和科技的概念

(一)文化及文化的内涵

由于文化本身具有的多样性和复杂性,很难给文化下一个准确的、清晰的定义。自20世纪初以来,不少哲学家、社会学家、人类学家、历史学家和语言学家一直努力,试图从各自学科的角度来界定文化的概念。然而,迄今为止仍没有获得一个公认的、令人满意的定义。据统计,有关"文化"的各种不同的定义有200多种。不同的学科对文化有着不同的理解。但是几乎各种论著都指出:文化的含义有广义与狭义之分。《中国大百科全书》的社会学卷说:"广义的文化是指人类创造的一切物质产品和精神产品的总和。狭义的文化专指语言、文学、艺术及一切意识形态在内的精神产品。"由此定义可以看出,文化的广义含义是人类在社会历史发展过程中所创造的物质财富和精神财富的总和,它包括物质文化、制度与社会文化和精神文化三个方面,或可认为它包括经济、政治、文化三者。狭义的文化是指意识形态所创造的精神财富,包括宗教、信仰、风俗习惯、道德情操、学术思想、文学艺术、科学技术、各种制度等。有了这个认知,我们就可以进一步弄清楚它的内涵,即它的本质。因此,文化的内涵就是:文化是人类的精神活动及其产品,是经济和政治的反映,归根到底是人类物质活动的反映。

文化的外延则不是很容易弄清楚的,无法把文化所具有的具体的分子一一指陈出来,唯一的办法只能是根据其内涵来分门别类地列举其各个组成部分。因为文化是一类社会

---

* 本文原载于2016年5月《文化科技工作通讯》(内刊),收入本书时有改动。

现象，是人们长期创造形成的产物。这样，我们就可以把文化的外延表述为若干类文化现象。为了对文化的外延有一个比较具体的理解，有学者用以下的文化现象来说明文化的外延问题：第一类文化现象就是科学技术（这里指的主要是自然科学技术），它是一个社会的物质生产水平的直接反映并直接推动生产的发展，为了发展我国的生产，我国应大力发展我国的科学技术。第二类的文化现象是经济思想和经济理论。第三类文化现象是政治法律思想和理论。第四类文化现象是语言文字。第五类文化现象是道德伦理观念、善恶标准和道德伦理理论。第六类文化现象是宗教现象。第七类文化现象是文学艺术。第八类文化现象是哲学和社会学说。第九类文化现象是教育和教育思想。第十类文化现象是新闻出版事业。第十一类文化现象是公共文化设施及其活动。第十二类文化现象是民间文化。以上所谈十二个领域都是作为现实的经济政治之反映的文化现象，除此之外，我国的文化当然还包括古代遗留下来的文化因素，即传统文化因素，以及从国外传播进来的文化因素，特别是西方文化因素。

（二）科技及科技的内涵

科技是科学与技术的简称。科学指研究自然现象及其规律的自然科学。技术泛指根据自然科学原理生产实践经验，为某一实际目的而协同组成的各种工具、设备、技术和工艺体系，但不包括与社会科学相应的技术内容。科学与技术是辩证统一体。

"科学"一词，在西方源于拉丁文 Scientia，其本义为"学问或知识"，表示探究事物而获得知识的概念。科学的内涵和外延是随着科学本身的发展和人们对科学认识的不断深化而发展变化的。首先，科学是一个完整的知识体系，即运用定理、原理、定律等把零散的知识进行总体上的描述，有计划地发展以及研究。科学也是自然、社会和思维的知识体系集合体，即它本身有一套完整的认识、思维和解决问题的理论与方法，通过人们掌握、利用而发展着，起到改变客观世界的作用。其次，科学是一种创造性的智力活动，反映了客观世界的规律性，经历了反复实践、反复认识和反复检验的过程。苏联 1953 年出版的《大百科全书》对科学如此定义："科学是在社会实践基础上历史地形成的和不断发展着的关于自然、社会和思维及其发展规律的知识体系。科学是对现实世界规律的不断深入认识的过程，同时也是不断创造的过程。"

"技术"一词来源于古希腊语 Techne（艺术、技巧）和 Logos（言词、说话）的结合，意思为完美的技艺和演讲。1615 年，英国的巴克爵士创造了 Technology 一词，即完美而实用的技艺。我国古代没有"技术"一词，把有经验、有技巧的人称为"工"，而"工"的特长就是"巧"，所谓"巧"就是"技术"。对于技术一词的概念，到目前为止还没有一个统一认识。国外主要有两种不同的看法，形成两大派别。其一是最早提出技术概念的法国启蒙思想家、《百科全书》主编狄德罗。他认为，技术是"为某一目的的共同协作组成的各种工具和规则的体系",即包括两个部分：一是工具,二是规则。另一派是以苏联科学院科学史研究所达尼雪夫斯基为首的,他提出,"技术是社会生产体系中的劳动手段""技术是解决社会上发生的实际问题而发展起来的劳动手段体系"。

我国学者对技术的定义有广义和狭义之分。狭义的定义将技术限制在工程学的范围内,如机械技术、电子技术、化工技术、建筑技术；广义的定义将技术定义为"人类在为自身生存和社会发展所进行的实践活动中,为了达到预期目的而根据客观规律对自然、社会进行调节、控制、改造的知识、技能、手段、规则方法的集合"。我国出版的新版《现代汉语词典》(第5版)(2005)指出:"技术是人类在认识自然和利用自然的过程中积累起来并在劳动中体现出来的经验和知识,泛指操作方面的技巧。"《新华词典》(2004)定义技术为"进行生产活动或其他活动的知识技巧和操作技巧"。而《现代汉语辞海》(2003)将技术定义为两方面：一是生产劳动中的经验和知识；二是技术装备,生产上用的各种机械、仪器、仪表、工具等设备。

二、文化与科技的关系

（一）文化与科技有着非常密切的互为支撑和互相影响的关系

当了解了文化和科技的概念后,我们需要进一步分析文化与科技的关系,以便准确地定义文化科技的概念。文化与科技有着非常密切的互为支撑和互相影响的关系,两者相容相生,不断融合促进。不论是精神文化、社会文化还是物质文化,都明显存在着科学技术的应用和实践,从某种意义上说,把文化与科技割裂开来看,是犯了"二分法"的错误,文化与科技是不可分割的。

（二）科技是文化的重要内容

文化是人类所创造的物质财富和精神财富的总和,反映了一定时期物质文明和精神文明的水平和特点。科学技术作为社会智力发展的一个方面,既是文化的重要内容之一,也是文化的重要体现形式。

（三）文化发展为科技发展建立了重要基础

人类物质财富和精神财富是互相促进的发展领域,没有社会文化水平的整体提升,科技也难以获得发展的土壤和应用的空间。文化的发展不但为科技发展提供了必要的环境条件,也影响着技术的选择与发展路径,进而对社会发展产生新的影响。

（四）科技发展为文化发展提供了重要支撑和手段

正是有了电影、电视、互联网等技术的发展，文化才有了更多的表现形式和传播手段。新闻出版、广播电视电影、传统文化保护、艺术等文化服务行业的提升，新的文化服务形式和业态的形成，都需要科技的支撑、引领。

（五）科技的应用无时不在塑造着社会文化的形态，影响着大众文化的变迁

高新技术的发展直接影响着社会文化及其发展演变。同时，科技与文化结合，才能充分体现以人为本、可持续发展的理念，有效推动新技术的转化应用，促进和塑造社会物质文明向着健康的方向发展。

（六）文化和科技融合既是目的也是手段

综上，准确理解与把握好文化与科技的关系，对于促进文化发展与繁荣和加强文化与科技的有机结合，有着重要意义。目前常用的"文化与科技融合"一词，既高度体现了文化与科技的关系及其意义，又反映出来新时期文化和科技工作共同面临的新机遇、新挑战，同时还表达了党和国家对文化科技工作的新要求。

三、文化科技的内涵及面向

（一）文化科技的内涵

文化科技在学术研究领域是一个不断发展的概念，其内涵与外延与国家在一定时期的经济和社会发展背景密切相关。理解其内涵首先要正确认识文化科技概念提出的时代背景，其次要考虑我国基本国情、技术发展水平现状和战略目标，最后要把握不同层级政府的职责定位、公共文化服务和文化产业的特点。总的来说，文化科技的本质是一种服务于社会意识形态的特殊工具(手段)。其特殊是因为它具有动态特点和时代特色，不同时代表达不同的文化，其作用不同，服务对象不同。就宏观层面而言，文化科技就是通过将各类文化元素、内容、形式和服务，与科学技术的原理、理论、方法和手段的有机结合，提升有关产品（含服务）的价值与品质，形成新的内容、形式、功能与服务，更好地满足人民文化需求。

（二）文化科技的外延

如果说文化科技是一种服务于社会意识形态的特殊工具，那么我们可以从文化科技服务或研究的对象来介绍文化科技的外延。根据文化科技相关的国家政策以及国家文化

发展战略，我们认为文化科技应该主要关注社会文化和精神文化两个层面的相关科学技术，而不是将文化科技的着力点放在物质文化这个更为物化和宽泛的层面上进行考虑。而在社会文化的层面上，我们也不应该重点考虑诸如法律、政策、政府机构等具备强制性色彩的社会架构所带来的各种文化物化产物。因此，我们认为，文化科技所关注的对象就是"服务于意识形态，有助于意识形态，特别是有助于非强制、非结构化的意识形态的表现、表示、表达、传播、影响、传递、认知、理解、认同相关的物化文化形式及内容发展的各类科学技术"。文化科技的研究对象有着以下几层含义：

第一层，文化科技的功能和作用必须是有助于意识形态的。这就意味着直接的物质文化中所蕴含的科技，由于其最终的功能或并非弘扬意识形态，因此可能并不是文化科技所需要进行研究和处理的对象。比如，任何工业产品的制作，其实也蕴含了相应的文化成分，形成其独特的工业产品文化，但是这种文化往往是从实用角度、从消费角度进行考虑，并没有同上层建筑的意识形态有明显的关联，即使在其中添加了很多新的科技元素和科技成分，这种产品所关注的科技，依然不能够看成是文化科技的组成部分。但是，在文艺演出、电影、网络文化的创作、演出、制作中，内容明显传递着创作者、制作者和管理者的思想，同整个社会环境中的价值观念、审美观念、思维方式、道德伦理紧密关联，而科学技术的运用，能够明显改善其中蕴含的意识形态元素在表现、表示、表达、传播、影响方面取得的效果。此时，我们从目的论的角度看，是否是文化科技，首先要看其是否是有助于意识形态的传播和影响。

第二层，文化科技必须依托相应物质化的文化载体，而不能孤立存在。由于科技是个实际存在，是改造自然世界的方法，是形而下的。而文化本身则是来自人文世界和精神世界的东西，是形而上的，物质只是文化的一种表象。那么文化科技就必须首先符合科技存在的客观规律，认定其存在具体的物质形式，这样才可以避免将文化科技的着力点转入形而上的领域。由此，诸如艺术形态的系统论等科学理论体系的梳理和建立，并不应属于文化科学需要主动研究的范畴，只有当艺术形态的方法论能够指导艺术内容创作的物化和最终实体化时，这种科学理论才能够成为文化科技的主要研究内容。因此，文化科技的对象研究还主要是针对"物"或"实体"的研究，而不是针对更深层次的形而上的研究。

第三层，文化科技对非强制、非结构化意识形态的物质形式产生作用。意识形态的物化形态有很多种，政府体制和结构就是属于结构化的意识形态的物质化表现，而像法律就是意识形态的强制部分，对于各类法律的物化形式，比如法具、刑具、警具的科技化，则不属于文化科技需要研究的对象和范围。而像国家机关、行政机构、管理体制等物质存在，虽然其属于意识形态的物质化表现，但是由于其已经相对系统化、结构化，也不属于文化科技所研究的部分。文化科技所涵盖的文化领域，应该是文学、艺术、科学、旅游、新闻、出版等意识形态相对宽泛的领域，而不是类似法律、行政之类的已经强制化、结构化的东西。

（三）文化科技创新

"创新"的英文为 innovation，该词的原意为"更新，创造新的东西或改变"，该词源于古拉丁语 innovore。20 世纪 60 年代，美国学者华尔特·罗斯托提出"起飞六阶段理论"，将"技术创新"提高到"创新"的主导地位。21 世纪之后，世界各国普遍将科技创新上升为国家整体发展战略。总之，在创新驱动的各个维度和层面中，科技创新具有动力维度的决定性。

科技创新是"科学技术是第一生产力"思想的根本体现与实现途径，"创新驱动发展"是我国科技发展的根本任务，实现创新驱动发展最根本的是要依靠科技。文化建设与发展的动力是"科技进步"和"体制机制改革"，文化科技创新是两个内生动力之一，所以我们常说"文化科技创新是文化建设的引擎"。2012 年 7 月中共中央发布的《关于深化科技体制改革加快国家创新体系建设的意见》要求"加强文化科技创新"，2016 年 5 月中共中央国务院发布的《国家创新驱动发展战略纲要》要求"科技创新与文化创新相结合"，文化科技创新对于提升我国文化建设、构建创新型国家和文化强国，特别是全面建成小康社会、实现社会主义现代化和中华民族伟大复兴的"中国梦"都具有极端重要的战略意义。"十二五"以来，文化科技创新成为国家文化发展战略的支撑，成为我国提高自主创新能力、建设创新型国家的关键。

（四）新时期文化科技创新的主要面向

一是围绕文化建设与发展的重点领域和优先主题，开展重大公益性技术前期预研，开展国家标准和文化行业重要技术标准研究，开展涉及文化行业全局性、方向性、公共安全性的相关检验检测与评价技术研究；

二是围绕文化科技基础性工作，开展科学考察与调查、科技资料整编和科学典籍志书图籍编研、标准物质与科学规范研制等科学活动；

三是围绕增强文化艺术的创造力、表现力和感染力，开展针对提升文艺作品创作、创意协同、艺术表现、受众互动和展演展映展播展览等效能的共性关键技术的研究；

四是围绕扩大文化传播的有效覆盖与公共文化产品的服务效益，开展文化遗产传承、文化资源利用、对外文化交流、知识产权保护、文化安全监管、文化贸易等公共文化服务领域的共性与共享技术研究；

五是围绕促进我国新兴文化产业高新技术的发展和传统文化产业的技术更新，开展文化与科技融合发展的应急性、培育性、前瞻性技术研究和集成创新研究；

六是围绕演艺业、娱乐业、动漫业、游戏业、文化旅游业、艺术品业、工艺美术业、

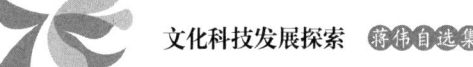

文化会展业、创意设计业、网络文化业、数字文化服务业等重点文化产业和公共文化服务与传播渠道建设,开展重要技术装备和重大系统平台的应用基础研究与前瞻性技术研究;

七是围绕促进文化与科技的结合与融合发展,开展对国家和行业重大文化科技问题的评议研究和文化科技软科学研究。

四、文化科技创新体系的内涵及建设

(一)国家创新体系与科技创新体系的内涵

国家创新体系是立足于国家发展战略层面而构建的满足国家发展、提高国家核心竞争力的完整的、有机的、系统的创新整体,它在一定程度上反映了国家发展的整体实力、持续力与综合实力。针对具有中国特色的国家创新体系的界定,2006年国务院颁布的《国家中长期科学和技术发展规划纲要(2006—2020年)》给出了较为权威的界定:"国家创新体系是以政府为主导、充分发挥市场配置资源的基础性作用、各类科技创新主体紧密联系和有效互动的社会系统。"国家创新体系是由各种创新主体构成的有机的网络系统;当前在我国国家创新体系中,政府、高等院校、企业、科技中介是创新的主体,要突出技术创新体系、知识创新体系、国防科技创新体系、区域创新体系以及科技中介服务体系、制度创新体系等功能,创新资源、创新环境、国际互动、创新机制保障等环境要素则调控与制约着国家创新体系能否顺利实施和能否取得成效的关键。总而言之,我们可以简单地理解为:国家创新体系大约等同于国家科技创新体系。

科技创新体系是科技创新过程中的系列支撑条件,是科技创新的主要组成力量,是引领科技创新的核心动力源。科技创新体系的组成要素可以分为如下几大方面:第一,科技创新的主体。即科技创新的推动者,主要包括政府、企业、高等院校、科研院所、科技中介组织以及其他组织等;第二,科技创新的基础平台。即科技创新过程所需要的各种基础研究设施以及各种物资保障等,主要包括实验室、研究基地、研发中心、科技产业园区、协同创新平台以及各种科研项目等。第三,科技创新人员。即完成科技创新的人才因素,主要包括专职科研人员、高等学校教师、企业研发人员以及其他研究人员等。第四,科技创新成果。即上述科技创新的科研人员利用科技创新平台而研发的高质量创新型科技成果,主要包括论文、著作、专利以及其他各种基础性和实用性新技术等。第五,科技创新成果的转化。即实现科技创新成果推广、转化或产业化的过程,主要包括科技创新成果的转化机制等。

综上,科技创新体系不是一个独立存在的单一个体,而是一个由多种要素组成的有机的系统,这一系统包含了创新的主体、平台、人员、成果以及成果转化等;当然科技创新体系还存在于社会发展的宏观环境当中,必须与之融合并相互促进。

（二）文化科技创新体系及特征

在科技创新的概念体系中，文化科技创新体系是其下位概念，文化科技创新体系是国家科技创新体系的重要组成部分。文化科技创新体系是指在文化领域，由企业、科研院所、高等院校、科技中介组织以及其他科研与服务机构等相关组织构成的，开展知识创新、技术创新、区域创新、科技中介服务以及机制创新等相关活动的有机网络系统，这一系统肩负了创新国家文化科技和提升国家文化软实力的使命与责任。文化科技创新体系具有一定的层次结构和整体功能。

文化科技创新体系的特征主要表现在三个方面：

一是多主体性。文化科技创新体系的多主体性主要是针对创新的组织者而言的，这些科技创新的主体主要包括企业、高等院校、科研院所以及其他科研与服务组织等；除此以外，这些组织联合成立的研发中心、科技示范园区、重点实验室、重点研究基地等也都是科技创新的主要实施者。

二是协同性。协同性即强调文化科技创新体系的系统性、有机性、互动性等，即在文化科技创新体系中所有的要素都是相互影响、相互支撑而构成的有序的统一体。在新形势下，文化科技创新如火如荼，仅靠单一组织的推动很难完成一项高质量的科技创新活动，需要组织与组织间的协同与合作，发挥各自的资源优势，使组织间的创新活动凝聚成合力，共同促进文化科技创新的可持续发展。

三是跨行业性和多学科交融性。全球已经进入了信息化、数字化时代，大数据、云计算、虚拟现实、移动互联网、物联网等重要技术的逐步产业化，将对当今及未来的生产生活方式产生革命性影响，加速了文化生产方式及发展模式的变革，开创了文化传播传承方式的新革命，促进了文化消费与接受方式的新变革，文化科技创新的内容十分广泛，呈现出了跨行业、多部门、多学科、复合性的特征，更加需要重视各创新驱动要素和创新资源的有效配置。

（三）文化科技创新体系建设的定位

文化科技创新体系建设的定位应该是面向国家、区域和文化行业发展的需求，全面提高科学技术对文化发展的支撑能力。面向国家就是要结合国家科技创新体系（国家创新体系）的建设，将文化科技创新体系放在国家科技创新体系的视野下，发展面向国家文化发展战略的文化科技，加强文化与科技融合，努力完善科技对文化建设的支撑作用。面向区域就是要在区域科技创新体系建设的基础上，使文化科技创新体系与区域科技创新体系相结合，发展面向区域需求的文化科技，满足区域公共文化和文化产业发展对文化科技的需求，突破区域发展的瓶颈。面向行业发展就是要将文化科技创新体系作为促进文化建设的内生动力，科技创新直接面向国家文化发展主战场，通过体制机制创新，激发文化科技人员的积极性,满足文化建设对科技的需求。

从微观层面来看,构建文化科技创新体系主要在于发挥如下功能:

一是文化科技创新平台的搭建功能。通过文化科技创新体系,能够更为有效地、更为便利地进行文化科技交流、文化创新主体的互动、文化科技人才的聚集与合作等。

二是文化科技需求与成果的培育功能。通过文化科技创新体系,能够更加有效地将先进适用的科技知识和技术应用于文化发展实践,对接文化发展实践的科技需求,规划相关研究项目,引导文化科技工作者应用相关前沿科技知识和技术,进行科技知识与成果向实践应用转化等;能够更加有效地丰富文化科技理论并研发文化科技领域的技术、方法、手段等,能够更加有效地设计合理的研究项目、扶持资金、考核评价政策,助推文化科技创新主体和人才可持续性地进行文化科技活动等。

三是文化科技成果的转移转化功能。通过文化科技创新体系,能够更为有效地进行文化科技成果的传播、转移、转化、应用、市场开发等,包括提供文化科技成果展示窗口,搭建文化科技工作者与文化实践工作者之间合作与沟通的桥梁,提供文化科技成果与行业、企业合作应用的渠道,保护文化科技成果知识产权的权益等。

(四)文化科技创新体系的发展要求

从总体上看,国家及文化和旅游部推动与完善文化科技创新体系建设,其目的主要为:支持文化科技发展,降低文化科技创新成本,提供制度、法律和物质方面的保障,促进区域和行业创新,提高文化科技对文化事业与文化产业的支撑能力。

为了保障文化科技创新体系的健康发展,政府在构建与加强文化科技创新体系建设中遵循的原则主要为:

一是充分发挥政府的引导作用。引导创新要素向文化建设与发展集聚,强调文化科技创新中的协同与融合、技术集成;围绕文化科技发展,重点突破,明确产出,推动文化技术创新及文化发展方式转变;鼓励创新主体立足于文化建设与发展的科技需求和文化科技自身发展,合理运用市场机制集聚创新资源,搭建不同创新主体的协同创新平台,发展各主体自主创新能力,培育优秀科技成果,提升发展竞争力。

二是坚持正确导向,协同发展。以促进自主创新为导向,协调创新主体关系,大力发展基于文化建设需求的科技创新活动,明确发展的方向和方式,使不同利益主体在协同创新中得到发展,最终实现共赢;协同创新要以管理体制和机制改革为引领,改变"分散、封闭、低效"的管理和发展现状,进一步释放文化科技人才、科研机构、科研组织等的活力,通过系统的改革设计,围绕文化建设和文化科技发展需求,不断增强不同创新主体之间的协作与互动,以更好地促进创新要素的高效集成,提升各创新主体的自我创新能力。

三是坚持结构优化和重点突出并举。在文化科技创新体系的建设过程中,要根据需求不断优化体系结构,从体制机制创新上解决文化科研协作不够、科技资源开放共享制度不健全和竞争过度等问题;鼓励创建工程技术中心、重点实验室、科技条件平台、企业技术中心等文化科技创新基地和技术创新服务平台,重点解决自主创新能力不足的问题。

四是坚持尊重人才和注重实践能力相统一。

五是加强政策引导和政策倾斜。鼓励文化科技创新主体的形成,努力形成市场选择的机制;鼓励构建符合区域和产业发展需求的科技创新体制机制;创新管理模式和奖励机制,使不同科技创新主体在发展中实现利益的最大化;在财政、金融、投融资、股权激励、政府采购等相关政策方面加大支持力度。

五、文化科技发展的目标、任务、手段及工作重点

由于文化科技服务于意识形态,服务于文化发展,因此必须要以文化大发展大繁荣的根本任务作为文化科技发展的根本任务,文化内容的物化形式承载文化科技,文化内容在生产、创作、传播时也必须遵守这一根本原则。因此,满足人民群众日益增长的精神文化需求,也是文化科技所必须要完成的根本任务。所有文化科技发展的形式、内容、状态,都必须满足人民群众的文化需求,这种需求既包括数量上的需求,也包括了质量上的需求。文化科技满足文化需求中的数量需求,主要是面向文化事业领域的科技需求,提供更具备普遍性、基本性、根本性的文化需求,而文化科技满足文化需求中的质量需求,则主要是要面对文化发展中的科技需求,提供创新性、差异性、独特性的科技需求。

(一)新时期文化科技发展的总体目标

新时期文化科技发展的总体目标是:按照建设社会主义文化强国和增强国家文化软实力的总体要求,牢固树立以人民为中心的工作导向,发挥科技对文化创新的驱动作用,文化科技创新体系基本完备,自主创新能力大幅提升,科技竞争力显著增强,文化重点领域的核心关键技术取得突破性进展,文化科技基础环境条件得到改善,科技资源与文化资源的共享明显增强,文化行业标准化体系相对完善,文化与科技融合在深度和广度上取得实质性进展,有力支撑和引领文化事业和文化产业的发展。

(二)文化科技发展的核心任务

在文化和科技的创新活动中,无论是创新者,还是用于创新的知识、方法和思维模式都有很大的不同,在促进文化与科技自身发展的同时,建立和完善有利于两类资源开展协同创新的机制,是促进文化与科技融合,实现两类创新资源协同、共生、互用的前

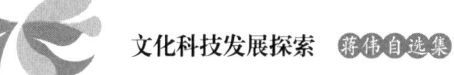

提。从更有利于国家文化建设和经济、社会发展的高度，确定创新目标，促进文化与科技创新要素的有效互动与结合，提升创新效率，提高创新质量，实现我国精神文明和物质文明的共同繁荣与发展，是文化科技发展的核心任务。

（三）文化科技发展的主要手段

从宏观层面来讲，发展文化科技的主要手段是强化文化科技创新体系的建设。从中观层面来讲，发展文化科技的主要手段是有效实现文化与科技的深度融合。关键是遵循文化发展与科技创新的一般规律。

（四）当前促进文化科技创新的工作重点

一是建立、完善有利于文化与科技创新要素有机结合的协同创新机制以及支撑平台，加快建立健全以企业为主体、市场为导向、产学研相结合的文化技术创新体系，加强复合型人才培育，促进文化与科技领域相关创新资源的有效整合与协同互动。

二是不断提高文化创新对于先进技术的集成应用能力。首先应进一步加强与文化应用关系密切的重点科技领域自身的发展，为解决文化对科技的需求问题奠定更扎实的基础，提供更多的可能和手段。同时应不断提升有利于加强文化创作力、表现力和传播力的信息、材料、装备等领域先进技术的创新与集成应用能力，注重以技术进步激发文化创意，以文化产品的创新促进技术的成熟和应用创新，促进文化服务新形式、新产品、新模式、新业态的形成。加强对文化科技发展全创新链的系统推进，促进文化产业集聚，培育新型文化服务业态，提升文化服务能力。

三是加强先进文化建设对于物质文化创新的引导作用。通过文化与科技融合，强化有关技术选择、应用以及相关产品、系统开发与先进文化、理念结合的意识和能力，提高具有科技与文化融合特点的物质文化的创新能力。

四是充分发挥科技对于先进文化建设的促进作用。加速文化科技自身发展，既是实现文化大发展大繁荣的重要目标，也是发挥科技对于文化的支撑作用的基础。而加强以科技为内容的多种形式文化产品的创制和传播，不但有利于培育科学精神、传播科技知识、提升公民科学素养、倡导科学生活方式、培育崇尚科学的创新文化、提升自主创新能力，也是文化建设和文化产业发展的重要内容。

五是通过文化与科技融合创新，为民族文化拓展更多的载体以及表现、传播形式，提升中华文化的感染力和对外传播能力。

中国文化科技发展与融合40年（1978—2018）[*]

一、引言

从党的十七大提出推动"文化大发展大繁荣"到十八大明确"建设文化强国"，再到十九大强调要"坚定文化自信"，文化在国民经济与社会发展中的重要性日益提升。从"四位一体"到"五位一体"的总体布局更新，"文化建设是灵魂"，已然成为社会主义事业总体布局的重要组成部分。

坚定不移地推进文化科技进步和文化创新，是加快文化发展的强大动力之一。坚定不移地推进文化与科技的融合，是更加自觉、更加主动、更加自信地推动社会主义现代化强国建设的客观要求，是实现新阶段文化发展目标的必由之路，是文化科技工作的核心。

近40年来，我国文化与科技融合总体上呈由缓慢上升至快速攀升的态势，其发展由内外动力共同驱动，既得益于文化繁荣发展又源于科技支撑引领，主要表现在三个方面：一是全球新科技革命和产业变革的"大势"与我国转方式调结构的"大事"形成历史性交汇，对文化科技工作提出了更高的要求；二是文化科技不仅是推动新形势下文化发展的重要动力，也成为促进文化创新发展的重要力量；三是从文化科技自身发展来看，我国文化科技创新呈现领跑、并跑、跟跑"三跑"并存格局，建设社会主义文化强国需要进一步提升自主创新能力。

二、文化科技概念的提出与深化

文化为体、科技为酶。近40年来，文化科技在文化领域中的综合创新应用，极为深刻地影响并改变着文化发展的环境、业态、格局。例如，大量的文化艺术活动，尤其是在以北京奥运会开幕式、G20峰会开幕文化活动等为代表的许多备受瞩目的大型文艺演出中，文化科技所带来的震撼效果引发了社会的广泛关注和观众的啧啧赞叹，被传为

---

[*] 本文原载于《中国文化发展（1978—2018）》第11章，2018年，收入本书时有改动。

美谈。

进入 21 世纪之前，人们通常是按行业科技来理解文化科技的，如艺术科技、电影科技、广播电视科技等。进入 21 世纪后，文化科技的概念及内涵发生了深刻的变迁，传统的行业科技概念被逐步淡化，文化科技已经全面融入文化创作、生产、传播、服务、消费以及文化服务与模式创新、文化内容与形式创新、文化产业升级与业态创新、文化市场监管与服务创新等全链条中。

（一）文化与科技的关系

要实现文化强国的发展目标靠什么？最根本是依靠两大动力，一要靠推进文化体制改革与机制创新，二要靠文化科技进步和文化创新的有力支撑。

1. 文化与科技有着非常密切的互为支撑和互相影响的关系。两者相容相生，不断融合促进。不论是精神文化、社会文化还是物质文化，都明显存在着科学技术的应用和实践，从某种意义上说，把文化与科技割裂开来看，是犯了"二分法"的错误，文化与科技是不可分割的。

2. 科技是文化的重要内容。文化是人类所创造的物质财富和精神财富的总和，反映了一定时期物质文明和精神文明的水平和特点。科学技术作为社会智力发展的一个方面，既是文化的重要内容之一，也是文化的重要体现形式。

3. 文化发展为科技发展奠定了重要基础。人类物质财富和精神财富是互相促进的发展领域，没有社会文化水平的整体提升，科技也难以获得发展的土壤和应用的空间。文化的发展不但为科技发展提供了必要的环境条件，也影响着技术的选择与发展路径，进而对社会发展产生新的影响。

4. 科技发展为文化发展提供了重要支撑和手段。正是有了电影、电视、互联网等技术的发展，文化有了更多的表现形式、传播手段和消费方式。新闻出版、广播电视电影、传统文化保护、艺术等文化服务行业的提升，新的文化服务形式和业态的形成，都需要科技的支撑、引领。

5. 科技的应用无时不在塑造着社会文化的形态，影响着大众文化的变迁。高新技术的发展直接影响着社会文化及其发展演变。同时，科技与文化结合，才能充分体现以人为本、可持续发展的理念，有效推动新技术的转化应用，促进社会物质文明向着健康的方向发展。

6. 文化与科技的融合既是目的也是手段。准确理解与把握好文化与科技的关系，对于促进文化发展与繁荣和加强文化与科技的有机结合，有着极其重要的意义。目前常用的"文化与科技融合"一词，既高度体现了文化与科技的关系及其意义，又反映出来新时期文化和科技工作共同面临的新机遇、新挑战，同时还表达了党和国家对文化科技工作的新要求。

（二）文化科技的定义及内涵外延

由于文化科技本身具有的多样性和复杂性，很难给文化科技下一个准确的、清晰的定义，40 年文化科技的实践过程，也是人们不断凝练文化科技的定义及内涵外延的过程。2017 年的首届文化科技学术会议（The 1st Conference on Culture-oriented Science & Technology in 2017）给文化科技下了一个相对受到大众认可的定义。

1. **文化科技的定义**。文化科技是将现代科学技术的理论和方法应用于文化创新发展的一门综合性学科或专门领域，一般特指能够直接服务、参与、支撑文化内容表现和再现的相关科学技术。它面向文化创作、生产、传播、服务、消费及再生产的各个环节，着力为文化发展提供精致、准确、高品质的支撑。

2. **文化科技的定位**。文化科技要以服从与服务于文化发展的需求与需要为先导，融合美学、艺术学以及声学、光学、电子、电气、机械、信息、材料、测控、计算等工程技术，推进文化科技自身的发展与进步，服务于文化内容的表现与呈现、受众的感知与消费以及政府施政的管理与服务等。

3. **文化科技的内涵**。文化科技在学术研究与应用实践领域是一个不断发展的概念，其内涵与外延与国家在一定时期的经济和社会发展背景密切相关。理解其内涵首先要正确认识文化科技概念提出的时代背景，其次要考虑我国基本国情、技术发展水平现状和战略目标，再次要把握不同层级政府的职责定位以及文化产品创作生产、公共文化服务、文化市场监管、文化产业、文化遗产保护传承的特点。总的来说，文化科技的本质是一种服务于社会意识形态的特殊工具（手段）。其特殊是因为它具有动态特点和时代特色，不同时代表达不同的文化，其作用不同，服务对象不同。就宏观层面而言，文化科技就是通过将各类文化元素、内容、形式和服务，与科学技术的原理、理论、方法和手段的有机结合，提升有关产品（含服务）的价值与品质，形成新的内容、形式、功能与服务，更好地满足人民文化需求。

4. **文化科技的外延**。如果说文化科技是一种服务于社会意识形态的特殊工具（手段），那么人们可以从文化科技服务或研究的对象来理解文化科技的外延。根据文化科技相关的国家政策以及国家文化发展战略，文化科技应该主要关注社会文化和精神文化两个层面的相关科学技术，而不是将文化科技的着力点放在物质文化这个更为物化和宽泛的层面上进行考虑。而在社会文化的层面上，我们也不应该重点考虑诸如法律、政策、政府机构等具备强制性色彩的社会架构所带来的各种文化物化产物。因此可以认为，文化科技所关注的对象就是"服务于意识形态，有助于非强制、非结构化的意识形态的表现、表示、表达、传播、影响、传递、认知、理解、认同相关的物化文化形式及内容发展的各类科学技术"。

三、文化科技创新体系的概念

2006年国务院颁布的《国家中长期科学和技术发展规划纲要（2006—2020年）》中明确表示："国家创新体系是以政府为主导、充分发挥市场配置资源的基础性作用、各类科技创新主体紧密联系和有效互动的社会系统。"总而言之，我们可以简单地将其理解为：国家创新体系大约等同于国家科技创新体系。文化科技创新体系是国家科技创新体系的重要组成部分。

（一）科技创新体系的组成要素

科技创新体系是科技创新过程中的系列支撑条件，是科技创新的主要组成力量，是引领科技创新的核心动力源。科技创新体系的组成要素可以分为如下几大方面：第一，科技创新的主体。即科技创新的推动者，主要包括政府、企业、高等院校、科研院所、科技中介组织以及其他组织等；第二，科技创新的基础平台。即完成科技创新所需要的各种基础研究设施以及各种物资保障等，主要包括实验室、研究基地、研发中心、科技产业园区、协同创新平台以及各种科研项目等。第三，科技创新人员。即完成科技创新的人才因素，主要包括专职科研人员、高等学校教师、企业研发人员以及其他研究人员等。第四，科技创新成果。即上述从事科技创新的科研人员，利用科技创新平台研发的高质量创新型科技成果，主要包括论文、著作、专利以及其他各种基础性和实用性新技术等。第五，科技创新成果的转化。即实现科技创新成果推广、转化或产业化的过程，主要包括科技创新成果的转化机制等。

综上，科技创新体系不是一个独立存在的单一个体，而是一个由多种要素组成的有机的系统，这一系统包含了创新的主体、平台、人员、成果以及成果转化等；当然科技创新体系还存在于社会发展的宏观环境当中，必须与之融合并相互促进。

（二）文化科技创新体系的内涵

1. 文化科技创新体系的概念。文化科技创新体系是指在文化科技领域，由政府、企业、科研院所、高等院校、科技中介组织以及其他科研与服务机构等相关组织构成的，开展知识创新、技术创新、区域创新、科技服务以及模式创新等相关活动的有机网络系统，这一系统肩负了创新国家文化科技和提升国家文化软实力的使命与责任。文化科技创新体系具有一定的层次结构和整体功能。

2. 文化科技创新体系的定位。文化科技创新体系建设应该是面向国家、区域和文化行业发展的需求，全面提高科学技术对文化发展的支撑能力。面向国家就是要结合国家科技创新体系（国家创新体系）的建设，将文化科技创新体系放在国家科技创新体系的视野下，发展面向国家文化发展战略的文化科技，加强文化与科技融合，发挥科技对文化建设的支撑作用。面向区域就是要在区域科技创新体系建设的基础上，使文化科技创新体系与区域科技创新体系相结合，发展面向区域需求的文化科技，满足区域文化事业与文化产业发展对文化科技的需求，突破区域文化发展的瓶颈。面向行业发展就是要将文化科技创新体系作为促进文化建设的内生动力，科技创新直接面向国家文化发展主战场，通过各创新驱动要素和创新资源的有效配置和体制机制创新，激发文化科技人员的积极性，满足文化建设对科技的需求。

3.文化科技创新体系建设发展的目标与要求。推动与完善文化科技创新体系建设，其目的主要为：支持文化科技发展，降低文化科技创新成本，提供制度、法律和物质方面的保障，促进国家、区域和行业创新，提高文化科技对文化事业与文化产业的支撑能力。政府在构建与加强文化科技创新体系中遵循的原则主要为：一是引导创新要素向文化建设与发展集聚。强调文化科技创新中的协同融合与技术集成，推动文化技术创新及文化发展方式转变。二是坚持正确导向，协同发展。以促进自主创新为导向，大力发展基于文化建设需求的科技创新活动，不断增强不同创新主体之间的协作与互动，以更好地促进创新要素的高效集成，提升各创新主体的自我创新能力。三是坚持结构优化和重点突出并举。根据需求不断优化体系结构，从体制机制创新上解决文化科研协作不够、科技资源开放共享制度不健全和竞争过度等问题，重点解决自主创新能力不足的问题。四是坚持尊重人才和注重实践能力相统一。五是加强政策引导和政策倾斜。

四、文化科技的主要技术框架及代表性技术

近40年来，我国文化科技总体上呈现需求牵引与学术牵引双轮并重发展的特征，特别是进入21世纪以来，应用驱动已经成为文化科技自身进步最主要的动力来源。快速迭代的实践应用导向加速形成了文化科技发展正循环，围绕文化共性技术、文化产品生产技术、文化服务技术、文化传播技术、文化资源技术、传承文化的材料技术和高新技术改造传统文化产业等技术领域，一批高新技术得到持续快速的发展和工程化产业化的推广应用。

（一）文化共性技术

1.语言文字技术

中文、外文及少数民族文字的识别、处理、编码转换与翻译技术；多语种应用支撑

技术；字体设计与生成技术；字库管理技术；支撑古文字、少数民族文字研究的相关技术；支撑书法及绘画研究的相关技术；支撑语言文字类文化资源研究的相关技术；支撑语言文字类文化资源的信息采集、转换、记录、保存的相关技术等。

2. 声音技术

语音识别与合成技术；语音应用技术；多语音应用支撑技术；声乐发音模拟技术；器乐发声技术；音乐（含声乐和器乐）的分析、处理技术；电声信号（单声道、立体声、环绕声等）的拾取、合成、编辑等制作处理技术；支撑声音类文化资源研究的相关技术；支撑声音类文化资源的信息采集、转换、记录、保存的相关技术等。

3. 图形图像技术

基于内容的图形图像检索及管理技术；基于海量图像数据的服务技术；多通道用户界面技术；静态图像、动态图像、视频图像及影视画面的处理技术；裸眼3D内容制作技术；3D图像处理技术；3D模型原创性鉴定技术；2D图形图和3D图形图转换技术；复杂公式图表智能识别转换技术；虚拟现实与现实增强技术；位图矢量化技术和工程文件智能化分层管理技术；支撑图形图像类文化资源的信息采集、转换、记录、保存的相关技术等。

4. 文化内容监管技术

著作权内容登记、传输监督管理技术，包括：作品（出版物、广播影视节目、音像制品、剧目等）登记技术，作品授权的登记与跟踪技术，作品传输的跟踪与审计技术，作品的版权交易登记管理技术，作品内容审核技术，作品内容编目与检索技术、敏感内容检测技术，非法作品与非法内容的追踪、注销、阻断传播、取证技术，作品标识符管理技术，以及新媒体视听节目的监测、监控技术。

5. 版权保护技术

版权管理与保护技术，包括：版权自动生成及跟踪技术，数字加解密技术，数字内容分段控制技术，数字水印技术，数字签名技术，数字指纹技术，内容权利描述及监督执行技术，信任与安全认证技术，连接保护技术，身份鉴别技术，密钥管理技术，多硬件捆绑技术，生产过程的数字版权保护技术，内容交易与分发数字版权保护技术，信息隐藏与提取技术，版权保护可信计数技术，防复印技术，防扫描技术，按需印刷版权保护技术等的应用，系统集成，盗版监控平台和新工艺开发。

文化、文物及文物衍生产品防伪技术，包括：各种介质生产、防伪、压印、压膜、标记技术，介质的标签唯一标识技术等。

6. 检索技术

信息检索技术，包括基于文本、图像、音频、视频的基础检索技术，海量检索技术（分布式检索技术），多媒体加工及索引技术，基于语义的内容检索技术，异构多媒体数据组合检索技术，复合媒体检索技术，并行跨媒体检索技术，模糊检索，过滤和排序，交互检索技术，多维导航技术，音视频电影资料编目技术，音视频电影关键信息提取技术，高效音视频电影内容检索和内容导视技术等的应用、系统集成和新工艺开发。

7. 标准化技术

文化领域标准研制与标准化技术，包括：语言文字、内容采集、创作、制作、工艺、集成、交换、分发、发行、放映、播出、传输、传播、发射、接收、质量、服务、物流、装潢、印刷、版式和格式、文化资源保护、安全与监测等自主知识产权的高新技术及应用的标准化。

（二）文化产品生产技术

1. 图书、报纸、期刊

内容采集与处理技术，包括：自然语言处理技术，本体处理技术，自动摘要技术，概念空间处理技术，结构层次识别技术，自动标引技术，主题筛选技术，内容过滤技术，多媒体信息的多卡、多码流采集技术，自动采集、自定义压缩、传输与还原技术，非标数据过滤清洗技术，内容挖掘技术，高质量内容采集技术、在线采编（分布）技术等的应用、系统集成和新工艺开发。

面向出版的内容结构化编辑加工及专业领域深加工技术，包括：结构化与非结构化内容管理，基于结构化内容的创作、编辑评审工具，资源结构化、工业化加工技术，基于XML的可视化编辑、标引技术，基于XML的公式、图、表技术，修改痕迹跟踪技术、版本回滚，可视化模板制作、灵活组件的引擎等的应用、系统集成和新工艺开发。

知识组织管理技术，包括：知识识别、提取、归并、关联、类聚、推送、共享技术，知识库建构与进化工具，知识系统自洽技术，基于同义词和主题词的索引词技术的应用、系统集成和新工艺开发。

内容制作技术，包括：跨媒介的内容重组与版式再造技术，创意效果的设计与制作技术（展现版面设计、封面及外观设计等），基于XML的排版技术，交互式科技排版、校验技术，自动排版技术，集群排版技术，中外文混排技术，多种文档格式转换技术，模板生成技术等的应用、系统集成和新工艺开发。

协同编辑管理技术，包括：选题管理技术，采编业务的流程控制技术，数字化编辑、审校、批注、自动比对技术，自动留痕与编审技术，配图流程控制技术，统计分析、评价技术，版本跟踪与控制、内容数据分类标注系统（按照知识检索、需求的重要性对不同颗粒度的内容进行智能标注），多分类文档存储管理系统，按需出版系统的专业构建技术的应用、系统集成和新工艺开发。

2. 音像制品与电子出版物

音像制品与电子出版物的制作、复制、出版技术，包括：高清晰度视频节目编辑、多种语言文字字幕生成、多语种声像同步合成应用技术；支持各种主流的光盘格式、音视频编码和数字版权保护系统的高清晰度光盘节目编著系统（Authoring Systems），具有自主知识产权的光盘格式、音视频编码系统和数字版权保护系统（如 DKAA 等）。

音像制品与电子出版物的只读介质（如 CD/DVD）或其他有形介质（如磁带、硬盘、半导体存储器件、磁条等）的内容版权保护技术及管理系统，以及该内容在网络传播时的保护系统转换技术。个性化的和小众的音像制品与电子出版物标识及管理系统。

音像制品与电子出版物产品样盘、样带外观质量检测，内容质量检查设备、仪器和技术的集成和应用。

3. 电影

电影拍摄、采集、处理和终端显示应用技术，包括：音视频处理技术，虚拟场景技术，灯光技术，电影的 JPEG2000 编码/解码技术，数字电影播放器，高清晰度和高深度色彩数字摄影技术，新光源投影技术，基础运动（拍摄）典型场景数据和拍摄轨迹获取与制作技术，动作捕捉技术，运动轨迹控制技术，三维立体图像的采集，虚拟场景模型建立技术等的应用，系统集成和新工艺开发。

电影编辑与制作应用技术，包括：非线性编辑技术，音频处理技术，数字中间片制作技术，电影特技制作技术（电脑特效与三维动画技术），多影像融合技术，数字 3D 电影制作技术，数字动漫，数字存储技术，素材编辑、合成和特技效果处理，配音及混合录音等后期制作技术应用。

特种电影制作和放映应用技术，包括：巨幕、穹幕、环幕和 4 维动感等制作和放映技术应用。

4. 广播电视节目

广播电视节目生产技术，包括：高清/标清摄像技术，高清/标清录像技术，录音调音技术，灯光照明技术，转播车技术，演播室技术，虚拟演播室技术，自动收录技术，非线性编辑技术，图文包装技术，特效技术，动画技术，字幕制作技术，切换矩阵技术，总控系统，信号调度技术，硬盘播出技术，监视和测试技术，故障检查，远程网络报道技术，远程转播技术，在线广播电视媒体资产管理技术等的应用、系统集成和新工艺开发。

适用于数字广播电视、移动多媒体广播（CMMB）形态的节目开发，包括：推送式视音频技术，点播式视音频技术，数据广播服务等。支持数字广播电视的各种类终端产品和技术；支持手机电视、车载电视、MP3、MP4 等移动多媒体广播终端的产品及技术。

5. 动漫、游戏产品

动漫、游戏设计与制作技术，包括：动漫公共技术平台及其支撑技术，动漫自动设计技术、渲染技术，动画设计技术，动画后期处理技术，动画生产技术，游戏引擎技术等的应用、系统集成和新工艺开发，动作捕捉系统，三维扫描系统，动画实时录制系统，二维无纸动画系统，动漫特效合成系统的应用、系统集成和新工艺开发。

6. 美术工艺作品

美术作品创作、生产技术，包括：美术创作的专用智能化机械、设备，美术创作空间技术应用及生产工艺，文物的仿古、复旧、高保真复制技术应用。

反映民族文化和再现文化遗产的工艺美术品制造工艺、生产技术，包括具有民族传统和地域特色的剪纸、绘画、陶瓷、泥塑、雕刻、编织等民间工艺美术作品。

7. 表演艺术剧目

反映民族传统文化的表演艺术剧目及生产技术，包括：民族艺术剧目、民族传统戏曲、曲艺、杂技的剧目及生产、集成技术；反映民风民俗、反映民族历史、传统节日的剧目及生产、集成技术；对民族文化、地域文化、民间文化、民俗文化具有深度传播作用的文化旅游表演项目及其集成技术，以及分布式表演艺术创作系统及其支撑技术。

8. 娱乐产品

以传播民族文化为主的创新型游览、游戏、游乐项目及其支撑技术；创新型文化娱乐产品及其开发技术（含数字娱乐产品）；支撑娱乐新业态的核心技术与集成技术（包括利用三维虚拟技术生产的新型文化娱乐产品、交互式娱乐技术）。新型卡拉OK点播技术（含VOD产品及技术）；歌舞娱乐创新型产品及其核心技术；利于传播民族文化的旅游纪念品及其开发技术。

（三）文化服务技术

1. 重大文化服务工程

重大文化服务工程支撑技术，包括：宽带广电建设工程，广播影视数字化提升工程，数字出版创新工程，艺术呈现技术提升工程，国家珍贵文化和自然遗产保护利用工程，文物数字资源共享工程，非物质文化遗产保护与传承工程，中华文化资源数据库建设工程，中国古代典籍整理工程，民族民间文化典藏与传播工程，传统工艺振兴工程等支撑技术。

2. 公共文化服务

公共文化技术平台及其支撑技术，包括：国家文化发展基金技术支撑平台，中国文化产业投资资金技术支撑平台，文化产业发展专项基金技术支撑平台，公共文化投资监控平台，译制技术支撑平台，国家出版物信用管理查验系统。

公共文化服务平台及其支撑技术，包括：有线广播电视服务平台，地面广播电视服务平台，卫星广播服务平台，移动多媒体广播服务平台，演出院线服务平台，电影院线服务平台，电影放映服务平台，文化资源共享网络服务平台，按需出版服务平台等。

支撑图书馆、博物馆等公共文化单位采、编、藏及检索服务的计算机集成管理系统；

支撑图书馆参考咨询服务、图书馆 RFID 的应用技术；文献资源数字化技术，网络资源采集技术，内容组织与管理技术，内容分发与聚合技术。

公共文化场所技术应用，包括：公共文化设施专用设备及其生产技术，藏品库、文物整理库的环境保护技术，针对舞美制作、电影电视拍摄、艺术作品后期制作、舞台演出等研发的智能化机械，流动综合文化服务车及支撑技术（流动演出、流动图书）。

3. 文化演出服务

支撑戏剧、戏曲演出形式、艺术表现的舞台技术。

舞台音响技术。用于舞台表演的专用音响设备、控制设备及系统集成技术，包括剧场及临时搭建舞台专用音箱、拾音、扩音产品及其制造技术，舞台音响系统集成与服务，矩阵控制系统和主动降噪技术应用及其设备，实质性改变声学性能的设备、器材加工生产技术和生产工艺，群众文化专用低耗能音响设备。

舞台灯光技术。用于舞台效果的舞台灯具、控制系统及舞台灯光通信系统的专用设备及系统集成技术，包括针对舞台效果研发的专用舞台灯、效果器、天幕投影设备、舞美显示设备等产品及新型舞台灯具制造技术，舞台高亮度长寿命新型光源及其技术，新一代舞台灯光传输协议与灯光网络技术、电磁兼容技术。

舞台机械技术。安装在舞台演出空间、用于舞台演出的专用机械设备及其系统集成技术，包括控制技术，现代舞台机械制造、安装、服务技术，舞台吊杆专用电机产品及其生产加工技术。

舞台监督监控技术。专门用于舞台与大型文化活动监督的监督台、监控台及其系统集成技术；具有舞台安全、舞台监督、数据库功能的舞台监督设备及其制造技术；适用于舞台通信的系统集成技术，包括语音及视频数字合成组网技术。

环境声学技术。适用于剧场、录音棚、排练厅、演播室、摄影棚的声学环境营造技术及其加工工艺、生产技术（包括声场设计、加工、建造技术），专门用于剧场声学条件的座椅设计、工艺、生产技术。

大型临时搭建舞台。适合于安全、高效、快速搭建临时舞台的专用设备及技术。

4. 广播电视服务

广播电视内容集成平台服务，包括综合应用视音频编码、采集转码、内容集成分发、节目交换交易、复用加密、数字版权保护、用户管理、运营支撑、质量监测监控、安全运营等技术，为各种传输媒介提供广播电视节目的服务。

有线广播电视网络服务，包括基于有线电视网络的前端编/解码、复用、加扰、调制、传输、接收、机顶盒、用户管理、运营支撑、业务配置和管理、综合网络管理、数字版权保护、用户认证、计费系统、质量监测监控、自动播出、安全播出等技术的集成应用，面向用户提供模拟电视和数字高清/标清电视，数字声音广播、推送点播、时移播放、视频点播、双向互动业务、数据广播、紧急广播、在线游戏、家庭网络、宽带数据接入、客服呼叫等服务。

无线广播电视网络服务，包括基于地面、卫星广播电视网络的前端编/解码、复用、加扰、调制、发射、组网、接收、机顶盒、用户管理、运营支撑、业务配置和管理、综合网络管理、数字版权保护、用户认证、计费系统、质量监测监控、自动播出、安全播出等技术的集成应用，面向用户提供模拟电视和数字高清/标清电视，移动多媒体广播电视、调幅中/短波广播、调频广播、数字声音广播、推送点播、时移播放、视频点播、双向互动业务、数据广播、紧急广播、在线游戏、客服呼叫等服务。

5. 电影服务

城市数字电影院线，包括：综合应用数字放映机，数字电影播放服务器，数字放映管理系统改造传统胶片放映，影院放映票房统计和监管技术，流动电影服务技术，电影衍生产品服务技术，仿真影院设备及技术，影院建筑环境技术，长寿命高亮度低温投影光源技术。

6. 新闻出版服务

文化出版内容服务技术，包括：内容按需更新技术，受众管理技术，受众交互技术，售后信息分析与反馈技术、权利认证、需求识别、选择推送、信息抓取等技术。

在线出版服务，包括：在线工具书，在线大众读物，在线教育产品，在线音视频检索点播，在线原创平台服务、计次、计费、统计管理技术等。纸质数码有声出版（MPR），语音识别文字校正技术，语音知识管理及链接技术，离线阅读新介质、新设备与数字内容捆绑技术等。

7. 展览、展示服务

展品展览展示设计与支撑技术，包括：激光全息技术，分体（整合）展台/展板技术，观众定位跟踪技术，展陈区紫外线控制技术，展陈照度、湿度、温度自动化控制技术，三维互动演示技术，自动解说系统集成技术等。

8. 广告服务

广告服务技术，包括：创意设计、虚拟模拟、电子绘画、图形图像制作、色彩渲染、建模、广告业务流程、广告投放与统计管理、平面与流媒体广告、广告版面管理、户外广告显示、大屏幕广告显示等技术。

（四）文化传播技术

1. 文化传播的安全与监测技术

文化传播体系安全运行保障技术，包括：广播电视安全播出保障技术，图书馆、博物馆、剧院、纪念馆、美术馆安全防护保障技术。

广播电视安全播出与监测监控应用技术，包括：广播电视信号监测和监控技术，广播电视信号质量测评技术，广播电视信号识别技术，广播电视安全播出与安全传输保障技术，网上视音频节目内容监管技术等的应用、系统集成和新工艺开发。

文化市场监控技术平台，包括：网吧监控技术平台，网络文化监控技术平台，曲库管理技术平台，卡拉OK厅监控技术平台，剧场演出监控技术平台，电影放映监控技术平台，非法出版物监控技术平台，在线文化内容监控平台。

文化市场管理信息平台及其支撑技术，包括：生产与流通互联互通信息，文化市场信息统计系统及其支撑技术，影剧院监控体系，文化娱乐场所监控体系，版权交易服务平台。

全国票务公共服务平台，包括：含演艺票务全国联网系统，电影院票务全国联网服务系统，博物馆参观票务联网服务系统，纪念馆参观票务全国联网服务系统，美术馆参观票务全国联网服务系统。

新闻出版物报送系统，包括：内容审读监测、出版物登记、版权交易与代理平台。

2. 演出场所/渠道

演出院线服务，包括：演出中介服务及其现代管理技术，票务连锁服务网络及其支撑技术。

3. 广播电视传输

广播电视传输，包括：有线广播电视、地面广播电视、卫星广播电视、移动多媒体广播电视传输等。

有线广播电视传输技术的应用，包括：有线广播电视前端集成技术，有线广播电视光缆干线传输技术（SDH、DWDM、MSTP、RPR等），有线广播电视光缆/电缆分配技术，有线电视宽带接入技术（PON、DOCSIS、EOC、LAN等），有线电视家庭网关技术，有线电视条件接收技术，有线电视运营支撑技术、中间件技术，有线数字标清/高清电视用户接收技术，有线数字电视交互系统终端技术等的应用、系统集成和新工艺开发。

地面广播电视传输技术的应用，包括：中短波调幅广播及数字化技术，广播调频同步技术，广播调频数字化技术，数字声音广播技术，数字多路微波分配（MMDS）技术，地面电视传输技术、中间件技术，地面广播电视发射技术（天馈线系统、发射天线等），地面电视覆盖组网技术，地面数字标清/高清电视接收技术等的应用、系统集成和新工艺开发。

直播卫星广播电视传输技术的应用，包括：卫星数字电视信道编码调制传输技术，卫星广播电视节目上行/下行传输（卫星地球站系统），直播卫星信道编码调制传输技术（ABS-S）、中间件技术，直播卫星条件接收技术，直播卫星运营支撑技术，直播卫星标清/高清晰度接收技术等的应用、系统集成和新工艺开发。

移动多媒体广播电视传输技术的应用，包括：移动多媒体广播电视信道编码调制传输技术，移动多媒体广播电视复用技术，移动多媒体广播电视电子节目指南技术，移动多媒体广播电视紧急广播技术，移动多媒体广播电视数据广播技术，移动多媒体广播电视条件接收技术，移动多媒体广播电视安全广播技术，移动多媒体广播电视中间件技术，移动多媒体广播电视终端技术，移动多媒体广播电视运营支撑技术，移动多媒体广播电视覆盖组网技术等的应用、系统集成和新工艺开发。

信息网络视听节目传播应用技术，包括：基于互联网的音视频分发技术、高效传输技术（组播技术、P2P等）和质量保障技术等，面向大众提供网上广播、网络电视、网上音视频等业务。

4. 电影发行

电影发行应用技术，包括：电影发行公司和电影院线的电影发行，数字电影城市放映和农村流动放映，电子售票技术，数字电影网络及卫星传输技术，电影数字节目放映授权管理等应用和开发。

5. 出版物发行

出版物供应链管理（SCM）技术，包括：出版发行平台技术，基于码洋折扣的多品种、多形态的出版物订单、仓储、配送、销售系统，多渠道的分销、零售系统，产品信息（含版本、出版单位等）的集成、跟踪、管理系统，基于全行业的出版物销售信息反馈系统，出版物在途跟踪管理系统，客户管理系统，新闻出版业通用ERP系统等。

出版物物流中心关键技术与装备，包括：基于电子商务的出版物配送管理系统，出版物高速存取、分拣系统，快速退货系统，高速输送设备，出版物电子标签（含RFID）应用技术，接触与非接触式识读技术，基于电子标签、语音的出版物拣选技术等。

（五）文化资源开发、存储、保护技术

1. 文化资源开发

文化资源科技支撑平台，包括：文化资源数据库、素材库，文化地图，信息库及其技术应用和开发技术、集成技术、支撑技术。

文化内容再利用技术，包括：文化资源数字化转换技术，文化内容的对象结构管理技术，知识重组与内容重构技术，词表抽取与维护技术，文学典藏作品数字化制作生产的专用产品及其生产技术；支撑数字图书馆，数字博物馆等素材库、资源库的生产技术，数字文化地图的关键技术。

利用虚拟现实技术开发的文化内容产品或建构的公共文化设施，大文化遗产保护区、文化街区、历史名城等公共文化场所；重大历史事件过程仿真技术，美术、声乐、乐器、舞蹈数字仿真技术；考古设备及其技术（含水下考古专用设备及其技术）；具有自动测量、定位的录入设备及虚拟现实技术。

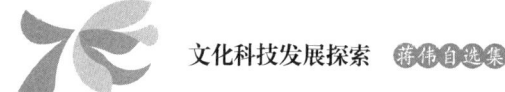

2. 文化资源保存及存储

文化资源，包括音视频节目、电影作品、文艺作品、出版物等。

文化资源存储技术，包括：磁盘/磁盘阵列技术，磁带/磁带库技术，大容量快速固态存储技术，存储控制器技术，蓝光盘技术，编目存储检索，数字内容的迁移、转换、仿真技术，内容与应用的分离技术，介质存储、管理技术，介质保存寿命的检测与评估技术，数据恢复与修复技术，异地灾难备份技术，海量文档存储、恢复管理系统等。

文化资源媒体资产管理技术，包括：内容存储、索引、检索、服务器、多媒体及人机交互、分类管理技术，结构管理技术，属性结构管理技术。

3. 文化资源保护

支撑文献修复与保护的关键技术与设备；智能化脱酸、补浆、防腐、防蛀、防氧化等技术与设备；对纸质、丝绸、土、木、砖、石、陶、瓷、铜等文物介质的保护技术；可移动文物、珍品整体保护保存技术；不可移动文物及其文物缓冲区整体保护保存技术；数字资源存储介质保护技术；考古挖掘技术，包括自然环境下文物挖掘保护技术；文物鉴定技术；文物修复技术（包括历史唱片可干预智能化修复）；抢救性钢丝录音带、唱片拾音无损伤技术；古籍善本保护与修复技术；木刻水印、雕版印刷保护、保存技术；国家文物、重大文化遗址、历史文化名城、世界大文化遗产卫星定位实时检测监控技术；数字资源长期保存技术；藏品存储技术、保存技术。

保护和修复重大不可移动文物的产品、技术及其工程服务；对不可移动文物、文化遗址、文化街区、历史文化名城、世界文化遗产等开发性破坏、保护性破坏、建设性破坏的保护技术。

（六）传承文化的材料技术

1. 文化载体和介质

文化艺术用可再生环保纸（不含木料纸、新型非涂布纸和轻涂纸、轻质瓦楞纸板）、特种纸、电子纸等新型纸的生产技术；仿古纸（包括传统工艺制作的古代书画修复用纸、纸质文物修复用纸等）的制备技术；光盘及原辅材料的制备技术；仿古墨的生产技术等。

2. 艺术专用材料

针对艺术专用品及改进其工艺生产的材料制备技术；针对艺术需要的声学材料的设计、加工、制作、制备等技术。

3. 影视场景和舞台专用材料

用于文化表演艺术场景与视效呈现的专用新型材料、制备工艺等。

4. 印刷新材料

绿色环保数字直接制版材料，数字印刷用油墨、墨水，环保型油墨，特殊印刷材料等制备技术。

5. 文物保护专用材料

文物提取、清洗、固色、黏结、软化、缓蚀、封护等材料的制备技术；文物存放环境的保护技术；用于古籍书画复制的制版和印刷材料开发技术；3D打印文物复制、修复技术及新材料制造技术等。

（七）高新技术改造传统文化产业

1. 电影

传统胶片电影的数字化，包括胶转磁、中间片、数字修复与保护等技术以及采用新技术的制景、烟火、道具等的升级及应用。

电影胶片洗印工艺及设备升级改造技术，包括环保、水处理、药液、自动冲印质量控制技术等应用。

2. 广播电视

传统音视频资料数字化加工技术，包括：电视音像资料的原始介质库存管理技术，音像资料的预处理、上载、转码、提取关键帧、内容编目加工、检索查询、视听审看、远程服务和信息发布、节目资料下载、用户安全认证、工作流技术、音像资料编目技术等的应用、系统集成和新工艺开发。

传统广播电视节目生产流程数字化技术改造，包括：广播电台电视台数字化网络化改造技术，台内网互联互通技术，互联互通接口体系，点对点的互联架构，基于消息总线或中间件的互联架构，基于SOA的双总线集成架构，软件通信接口协议，消息队列接口技术，Web Services接口技术，组件接口技术，视音频编码及文件格式标准，互联互通服务接口规范，数据接口技术等的应用、系统集成和新工艺开发。

有线电视数字化转换、双向化改造，基于有线数字电视技术实现有线电双向、交互、多业务、大容量传输技术应用。

微波线路改造，包括：光纤传输技术，数字调制技术，数字直放站技术，高线性功率放大器技术，大容量高质量传输技术等的应用、系统集成和新工艺开发。

发射台自动化改造，包括：计算机技术，数字回传技术，远程遥控技术，故障诊断技术，光纤传输技术，数据库管理技术，网络智能化技术等的应用、系统集成和新工艺开发。

3. 新闻出版

传统图书数字化加工技术，包括：自动扫描，出版物图像预处理，基于大字符集的文字识别，版面识别与恢复，多层结构的高保真全息数字化文件生成，各种电子文件格式自动转换等。

传统新闻出版生产流程数字化技术改造,包括:传统编辑业务流程再造,内容加工工艺设计与质量控制,在线编辑系统中数据的流转与分发技术,中文数字对象标识符(DOI)、暗纹和二维码编码嵌入、解析技术,内容数据库生产制作技术,报刊数据实时加工、动态更新技术,出版企业信息门户技术。

4. 光盘复制

光盘复制行业的专用及周边设备技术,包括:光盘母盘、子盘复制技术,光盘在线与离线检测、印刷、封装技术,基准盘检测等技术。

专用集成电路芯片开发,包括:多阶光盘、蓝光光盘前后端专用芯片技术,为整机配套的行业共性关键的集成电路产品技术等。

新型超高密度光盘存储技术,包括:全息存储技术,双光子存储技术,近场光存储技术,多维、多阶、多层光存储技术等。

5. 乐器制造

乐器及其器材加工工艺和调试技艺,乐器生产线或自动化生产技术,MIDI系统生产调试技术。

6. 印刷

印刷色彩管理技术,数字化印刷技术,绿色印刷工艺技术,高保真印刷工艺技术,古籍、文物复制印刷设备及应用技术等。

五、文化科技发展的主要进展(1978—2018年)

(一)文化科技创新成为国家推动文化发展的重要任务

国务院2009年9月26日印发《国务院关于印发文化产业振兴规划的通知》(国发〔2009〕30号文),这是我国第一部文化产业专项规划,文中明确要"采用数字、网络等高新技术,大力推动文化产业升级"。2011年10月18日党的十七届六中全会通过的《中共中央关于深化文化体制改革、推动社会主义文化大发展大繁荣若干重大问题的决定》(中发〔2011〕14号文),在"加快发展文化产业"的举措中已经明确要求"推进文化科技创新"和"要发挥文化和科技相互促进的作用,深入实施科技带动战略,增强自主创新能力","文化科技"一词在中央文件中被首次提出。中共中央2012年7月3日印发的《关于深化科技体制改革 加快国家创新体系建设的意见》(中发〔2011〕6号文)再次对文化科技工作提出更高要求,即"加强文化科技创新,推进科技与文化融合,提高科技对文化事业和文化产业发展的支撑能力",该《意见》明确了"文化科技创新"是国家创新体系的组成部分这个核心问题,并将"推进文化科技创新"深化为"加强文化科技创新",将"文化科技创新"的面向由文化产业拓展到了文化发展各领域。科技部等六部委

2012年6月27日联合印发《科技部 中宣部 财政部 文化部 广电总局 新闻出版总署关于印发〈国家文化科技创新工程纲要〉的通知》（国科发高〔2012〕759号文），将文化科技创新纳入了国家科技战略层面。

进入21世纪特别是"十二五"以来，国家层面不断采取积极的文化科技创新举措，科技部在"十二五"国家科技计划中部署了100余项文化科技项目（国家科技支撑计划文化科技专项），在"十三五"国家重点研发计划"现代服务业共性关键技术研发及应用示范"重点专项中对"文化科技"领域做出了部署，中宣部和财政部在"文化产业发展专项资金"中设立"推进文化科技创新和文化传播体系建设"方向，文化和旅游部、新闻广电出版总局等文化部门还设置了"国家文化科技提升计划"等一批文化科技专项。各级地方政府落实国家战略部署，均制订了文化科技计划或设立了相关文化专项资金。这些文化科技类项目的组织实施，有效强化了文化领域基础性和共性关键技术的研究，集中力量解决了一批具有前瞻性、全局性和引领性的重大科技问题，促进了科技创新成果的运用与推广，增强了社会各界参与文化创新的自觉性和主动性，发挥了科技项目的引领带动作用。

（二）文化与科技融合的主要成效

1. 科技进步已经成为文化发展的重要引擎

进入21世纪后，在党和国家的战略决策下，文化与科技融合在广度、高度、深度、跨度四个维度上实现了跨越性的进展，取得了较为丰硕的成效。文化科技创新能力不断增强、体制机制逐步完善、国际影响日益扩大，文化科技发展处于新的起点。

2. 文化科技已成为支撑驱动文化发展的主要力量

适应人民需要的文化产品不断丰富，公共文化网络覆盖面持续扩大，文化产业整体实力显著增强，推动中华文化走向世界的文化开放格局进一步完善。以先进技术为支撑的一批公共文化服务设施、渠道、装备和软件系统被广泛应用，形成一批面向需求的系统化集成解决方案和网络化运营服务平台，数字技术在公共文化内容的呈现形式和数字空间载体建设中起到了显著作用，互联共享的效果也更加明显。以技术创新、业态创新、内容创新和模式创新为主导的文化信息传输服务、文化创意和设计服务等新兴文化产业占比大、增长快，传统文化产业和文化相关产品生产继续保持增长，高新技术引领高端文化专用装备制造的作用明显。文化产品和服务的生产、传播、消费的数字化与网络化发展蓬勃，与相关产业跨界融合发展呈常态，对外文化贸易的进出口结构得到进一步优化。数字技术在物质和非物质文化遗产保护传承领域的开发应用得到持续推进，民族文化资源和特色文化资源的开发利用途径得到进一步拓展。

3. 探索中国特色文化科技发展道路取得重要突破

提高文化科技自主创新能力，构建文化技术支撑体系，实施国家文化科技创新工程和国家文化科技提升计划等科研专项，有效引导和支持了文化科技创新要素向文化建设集聚。形成推动文化科技创新合力，提高科技成果转化应用水平，遴选与认定34个国家级文化与科技融合示范基地，有力推动了新兴文化业态的形成和发展，促进区域产业结构调整和优化升级。提升文化创新能力，遴选与认定了一批文化科技领域的省部级重点实验室，开展文化科技领域应用基础研究，培育和发展我国文化科技服务力量。

4. 数字科技引领的新浪潮，已全面影响文化发展的路径

全球已经融入大数据、工业4.0、网络智能化三大潮流中，信息通信技术、计算机技术、视听表达技术、仿真技术、新材料技术、人工智能技术是推动潮流发展的六大技术。这些技术为文化发展植入了创新基因，已对当今及未来的生产生活方式产生革命性影响，加速了文化生产方式及发展模式的变革，开始了文化传播传承方式的新革命，促进了文化消费与接受方式的新变革。以科技为核心竞争力的一大批新兴文化业态不断应运而生，革命性地改变了我们所处时代的日常文化存在形态，正在持续助推文化服务运营和文化产业链整合的大繁荣。

5. 文化与科技融合呈现加速推进态势，有力驱动了文化创新

我国的文化科技已从"选择性介入"走向"整体融合"，为文化创新驱动力奠定了坚实基础。文化发展不断提出更多的科技诉求，科技发展在文化领域寻找到广泛的应用空间，文化科技整体融合在推进文化创新的同时，不仅形成对文化科技基础研究和科技创新的倒逼机制，而且为文化创新发展提供可持续驱动力量。经过多年持续积累，我国文化科技实力实现整体跃升，与发达国家的差距明显缩小，呈现领跑、并跑、跟跑"三跑"并存格局。文化与科技融合发展在文化管理、文化创意、文化生产、文化展示、文化传播、文化交流、公共文化服务、文化遗产保护等领域将越来越发挥出解放文化生产力和改变文化发展方式的巨大作用。

6. 文化科技的杠杆倍增功能和平台托举功能加速驱动了文化创新向协同发展迈进

我国文化科技的跨越式进步正在助推各级文化行政管理部门积极深化文化科技体制改革，加快实施创新驱动发展战略，加快转变政府职能，不断提高政府文化行政治理效率，推进文化制度运行和文化政策落实的长效化、规范化、精密化和可操作化。以科技创新和模式创新为核心竞争力的各类文化平台正在大量涌现，使文化创意、文化生产、文化消费、文化传播、文化贸易获得了强大的平台托举支撑，资金、技术、人才、信息、项目以及创意环境等关键性要素获得了超过预期的协同效应、聚集效应、漫溢效应、提升效应以及优化配置效应。文化科技的引擎牵引功能进一步放大，在协同创新的文化发展道路上充分显示了其主动性、能动性、导向性和可持续性，以源源不断的牵引力量驱动中国文化建设的各个具体方面。

（三）文化科技发展存在的不足与面临的挑战

近40年文化科技的发展与实践尽管取得了显著的成效，但仍存在一些关键问题，主要表现在如下几个方面。

1. 科技文化工作的体制有待进一步改革完善

文化科技工作还不能完全适应文化建设的形势和需要，国家科技与文化分割的体制性问题还没有从根本上解决，科技与文化建设之间脱节的问题虽有所改善但也尚未根本解决，科技成果转化为文化生产力与文化竞争力的渠道尚不够通畅，无论是科技体制或是文化行业内部体制都有待进一步改革完善。

2. 尚未形成科技支撑文化持续健康发展的长效机制

文化科技与现代科学技术迅猛发展及广泛应用还不相适应，文化科技竞争力相对较弱，文化部门与科技部门在战略层面科技发展的规划、组织、引导、调控等方面的手段还不够丰富，科技队伍整合、科技资源和成果共享问题尚没有得到很好的解决。

3. 文化领域关键技术自给率和科技成果转化率较低

面向文化领域的关键技术自给率和科技成果转化率相对较低；公共文化事业与文化产业中的高新技术比重较小，具有自主知识产权的核心技术的数量和质量都落后于其他行业，文化科技自主创新能力与核心技术供给对文化发展的贡献虽有提高但仍有限。

4. 文化科技投入总量有待大幅度提高

全国文化科技发展还处于不平衡状态，不同区域文化科技水平差别较大，科研力量分散、低水平重复现象仍较严重，文化科技创新平台的综合性和交叉性较差、国际化程度普遍较低，科技转化与服务平台不够完善。各级文化与科技部门的科技投入总量相对不足，科技资金短缺的矛盾依然突出。

5. 文化科技复合型人才匮乏

文化科技的研发力量尤其是高层次创新型科技人才匮乏，成为制约文化科技创新的重要因素。文化科技机构可持续发展能力有待提高，吸引与凝聚全社会文化科技力量的工作有待进一步加强。

6. 文化与科技的融合程度还相对较低

主要表现在：一是文化科技领域原始创新能力不足。尽管取得了一批基础前沿和高科技单点技术研究成果，但仍缺乏引领性的原始创新和系统性的技术集成创新，影响了依靠技术进步和模式引领驱动的文化发展。二是文化科技相关技术研究与集成应用脱节。我国文化和科技两条腿走路，相关科技成果与文化领域实际需求结合不够紧密，使得目前支撑文化领域的专门技术、系统平台及高端装备不足，制约了艺术创作、生产、传播、消费支撑力与保障力的提高。三是面向文化产业发展的共性服务技术支撑平台短缺。亟须建立支撑其转型升级发展的产业共性服务技术集成平台并出台系统解决方案，但技术转移转化渠道不畅，技术资源分散，面向专业应用的共性服务技术集成度不高，也间接影响了文化产业转型升级的进程。

六、新时代文化科技的发展愿景

当前，文化与科技融合发展正处在一个新的历史起点上，文化科技创新在国家发展全局中的战略地位更加突出，文化科技创新迎来了一个空间更加广阔的跨越发展期。

（一）新时代文化科技发展的基本思路

1. 主要思路

紧紧围绕创新驱动发展战略，引导和支持创新要素向文化领域集聚，努力实现文化各领域的科技进步，进一步构建完善以企业为主体、市场为导向、产学研结合的文化技术创新体系，着力加强文化科技创新体系建设，精心组织文化科技创新工程和文化科技重点专项，促进科学技术在文化领域的应用与创新，进一步加强文化资源和文化内容形式的协同运用能力，提高文化领域基础、技术和服务标准，推动文化与科技融合向纵深发展。

到2035年，形成推动文化事业进步、文化产业融合创新、文化管理有序的文化科技创新体系，形成以企业为主体、市场为导向、政产学研用相结合的文化科技技术支撑体系。

2. 指导思想

贯彻党的十九大精神，按照坚定文化自信和建设社会主义文化强国与增强国家文化软实力的总体要求，牢固树立以人民为中心的工作导向，发挥科技对文化创新的驱动作用，加强文化与科技融合，深化文化科技体制机制改革，促进创新资源的合理配置，培育创新主体，增强创新动力，优化创新环境，切实提高科技对现代文化产业体系、现代文化市场体系建设、现代公共文化服务体系构建和文化开放水平提升的驱动支撑能力，推动社会主义文化大繁荣大发展。

3. 基本原则

需求牵引，持续提升。文化是民族凝聚力和创造力的重要源泉，以面向人民需求和面向市场需求为牵引，充分发挥政府在文化科技创新体系和文化技术支撑体系建设中的积极作用，有效聚集、整合和利用相关创新要素资源，推进文化与科技深度融合，着力提升国家文化软实力。

系统规划，统筹推进。改善文化科技创新发展的顶层设计，优化配置文化资源、科技资源和人力资源，强化文化部门与科技部门的联合，统筹项目、基地、人才、政策以及文化科技创新体系建设,从主要依靠科技项目推动转向在工作层面系统全面推动文化科技创新发展。

创新驱动,融合发展。充分调动社会各方面积极性,促进技术创新、业态创新、内容创新、模式创新和管理创新,持续提升中国文化的生产力、创作力、感染力、表现力、传播力和影响力,充分发挥科技进步对文化繁荣发展的支撑驱动作用。

4. 发展目标

(1)在文化资源领域,加速各类民族文化资源的数字化、信息化、网络化进程,发展支持文化资源采集、加工、获取、整备、管理、保护、保存、应用的系列技术与标准,研发与创新一批文化资源的转化技术、表现技术、呈现技术和传播传承系统平台,让中华优秀传统文化活起来。

(2)在文化产业领域,研发一批共性关键技术,创新一批新产品、新服务、新装备和新模式,发展一批文化与装备制造、消费品工业设计、城乡建筑、信息服务、旅游等跨界深度融合的新型业态,增强文化产业整体实力和核心竞争力。

(3)在公共文化服务领域,数字技术支撑文化信息资源共享、数字图书馆、数字博物馆、数字美术馆的作用进一步加强,研发一批公共数字文化资源的加工、供给、分发、保护等关键技术,形成一批面向互联互通及应用的系统化技术解决方案和网络化运营服务平台,创新一批公共文化服务新业务、新渠道、新模式,促进基本公共文化服务标准化、均等化、便捷化。

(4)在文化科技管理领域,文化产业科技方面实现从投资驱动为主向创新驱动为主的转变,公共文化服务科技方面实现以政府投入为主向多元化投融资为主的转变;技术进步方面实现以引进为主向二次创新和自主创新为主的转变;管理模式方面从政府具体管理为主的格局向宏观管理为主的格局转变。

5. 主要愿景

(1)共性支撑技术取得重要突破。重点围绕文化资源互联互通、文化内容版权保护、文化安全监管、文化诚信服务等共性瓶颈技术问题,攻克20—50项关键支撑技术难关,制定100项以上文化服务技术与管理标准规范,构建5—10个网络化管理和科技服务平台。

(2)文化科技驱动支撑作用明显加强。聚焦现代文化市场秩序和现代公共文化服务重点领域,全链条布局,有针对性地研发一批文化产品创意、生产、传播、运营、展示、消费等环节的关键技术和集成应用技术,研制一批文化专用装备,提出一批面向应用的系统化集成解决方案,开发50项以上系统软件并建立系统平台,构建10个左右文化科技创新服务运营平台,创新一批服务模式,培育一批新兴文化业态,在典型文化领域开展一批应用示范,打造10家左右文化服务运营品牌,扶持200家以上规模化文化科技创新型企业。

（3）文化科技创新体系不断完善。积极发展以国家重点实验室、工程技术研究中心、企业技术创新中心和技术创新战略联盟为主体的文化科技创新体系；设立10家左右文化科技领域国家重点实验室和国家工程（技术）研究中心，统筹建设一批各具特色的文化与科技融合示范基地，统筹建设一批各具特色的文化科技融合产业化基地（示范园区），加强文化科技产业发展载体建设，形成文化科技发展良好环境。

（二）新时代文化科技发展的主要任务

1. 发展数字文化资源新优势

支持数字文化资源在采集、加工、获取、整备、管理、保护、保存、应用、传播、表现等全过程链条中相关技术和装备的研发，构建文化资源相关技术支撑平台和基础研发平台，加速文化资源数字化、信息化、网络化进程。支持图书馆藏资源、博物馆藏资源、美术馆藏资源的数据化专用技术研发，加强现代人文艺术学科研究的基础数据支撑；支持民族文化素材的创建、描述、组织、检索、服务与长期保存的技术、标准和装备研发；鼓励记录、保存、展现中国传统生活文化的新方法、新手段、新模式的研究，推动传统文化生活方式在现代生活中的有效保存和二次创新；支持数字文化资源记录与保存介质材料的研发，鼓励传统文化介质的现代复原工艺研究；推动文化资源与信息产业有效对接的模式创新，加快技术层面的文化资源整合与互联互通，着力打通数字化文化资源访问的关键技术环节，实现文化价值与产业应用的有效结合。

2. 推动新型文化业态融合创新

充分运用数字技术、网络技术、智能技术、材料技术，加快文化产业重要装备、材料、工艺、系统、平台的开发和利用，加快传统文化企业的转型升级步伐；促进新兴科技企业向文化领域的渗透，实现传统文化产业领域的颠覆式创新；设立大数据、云计算、虚拟现实、互联网+、人工智能等新兴战略科技在文化领域的创新试点，形成由点带面的示范性应用，强化文化产品（服务）的互动性和体验性，触发文化产业的深刻变革；促进众筹、众包、O2O、社交聚合等互联网成熟商业模式向文化产业领域的渗透，鼓励文化产业的业务融合创新；支持文化与相关产业双向或多向融合发展。

3. 拓展公共文化服务新空间

加快公共文化服务的数字化建设步伐，结合智慧城市、智慧社区、宽带中国等国家重大战略举措，发展技术先进、覆盖广泛、方便快捷的数字化公共文化服务网络与载体；研究制定一批公共文化领域标准规范和服务模式；支持流动文化工作站、移动文化方舱、数字农家书屋等文化下乡的专用设备与装备的研发；鼓励符合我国核心价值观的公共文化内容供给的新呈现、新表现和新揭示的相关技术和标准研究；支持一站式文化服务相关技术、装备、系统与平台的研发；针对博物馆、美术馆、文化馆等重要公共文化设施，开展相应的虚拟化、数字化、智能化特种体验装备研究；鼓励公共文化服务手段创新和新兴公共文化服务业态创新。

4. 培育文化艺术新形态

加快文化艺术创作的集约化、专业化步伐，鼓励创作手段创新，催生与培育文化艺术新形态；支持动漫游戏编辑制作、影视编辑、特效生成处理等专业生产工具和系统的研发；支持舞美、布景、道具、灯光、音响、机械、视效、观演互动等领域的技术与系统研发，鼓励虚拟现实、人机交互、自动控制等先进技术在演艺舞台中的集成应用；支持艺术创作与观众情感间的定量化分析研究；鼓励舞蹈、音乐、美术等编排数字化专用工具和创作工具的研发。

5. 提高政府文化行政治理效率

支持文化施政管理过程中的数据采集、交汇、存储、处理和分析等相关技术与系统的研发；鼓励文物鉴定相关标准规范、参数指标、标准物质、装置装备的研究；开展艺术品的量化估值方法研究，建设相应数据库；针对演出场所、娱乐场所、公共文化设施建设，制定相应规划、验收、评估、公共安全、运营维护等强制性技术标准；推进文化行业相关计量检测和检验技术的研究；展开文化市场监管、文化市场诚信评估、文化内容版权保护等文化管理共性技术研究；支持对文化工作统计制度、指标体系、调查方法的研究，展开文化科技领域的软科学研究。

关于"推进文化与科技融合"的一点思考*

一、党中央的有关部署

从党的十七大提出推动"文化大发展大繁荣"到十八大明确"建设文化强国",再到十九大强调要"坚定文化自信",文化在国民经济与社会发展中的重要性日益提升。从"四位一体"到"五位一体"的总体布局更新,"文化建设是灵魂",已然成为社会主义事业总体布局的重要组成部分。

文化科技创新在文化创新驱动发展中占有核心地位。我国自2012年推动文化与科技融合以来,在创新要素汇聚、创新主体培育、创新动力激发、创新能力提升和创新环境建设等主要层面,已经取得了显著的成效。

1. 党的十七届六中全会提出"要发挥文化和科技相互促进的作用,深入实施科技带动战略,增强自主创新能力"。(2011年10月)

2. 科技部会同中宣部、文化和旅游部等六部委印发《国家文化科技创新工程纲要》,提出"充分发挥科技创新对文化发展的重要引擎作用,深入实施科技带动战略,推进文化科技创新,增强文化领域自主创新能力和文化产业核心竞争力,推动文化产业成为国民经济支柱性产业,繁荣发展社会主义文化"。(2012年6月)

3. 党的十八大报告提出"促进文化和科技融合,发展新型文化业态,提高文化产业规模化、集约化、专业化水平"。(2012年11月)

4. 习近平总书记在亚洲文明对话大会发表主旨演讲时指出"应对挑战、迈向美好未来,既需要经济科技力量,也需要文化文明力量"。(2019年5月)

5. 科技部会同中宣部、文化和旅游部等六部委印发《关于促进文化和科技深度融合的指导意见》。(2019年8月)

6. 习近平总书记在长沙考察时指出:"文化和科技融合,既催生了新的文化业态、延伸了文化产业链,又集聚了大量创新人才,是朝阳产业,大有前途。"(2020年9月)

7.《中共中央关于制定国民经济和社会发展第十四个五年规划和二〇三五年远景目标

---

* 本文原载于2022年7月《文化科技工作通讯》(内刊),收入本书时有改动。

的建议》指出，要"提高社会文明程度""提升公共文化服务水平""健全现代文化产业体系"。（2020年10月）

8. 中共中央办公厅、国务院办公厅印发《关于推进实施国家文化数字化战略的意见》。（2022年5月）

二、战略意义和必要性

1. 党的十九届五中全会首次明确提出"到2035年建成文化强国"的远景目标，并强调在"十四五"时期推进社会主义文化强国建设。

2. 新一轮科技革命正在深度影响和重构文化的形态、结构和价值追求，是新时期文化创新性转化和创造性发展的重要引擎。

3. 文化和科技融合是在现代技术经济环境下文化、科技、商业模式等多种要素综合的文化发展方式变革，是文化力量和科技力量的有机融合。

4. 文化与科技相互促进、融合发展是人类文明发展的最重要特征。

5. 文化数字化、数字文化产业化、文化产业数字化，是新时代我国文化发展的主基调。

三、当前的基本状况及趋势

1. 以数字科技为代表的科技进步已经成为文化发展的重要引擎。"十三五"以来，数字科技在广度、高度、深度、跨度四个维度上实现了跨越性的进展，取得了较为丰硕的成效。文化科技发展处于新的起点。

2. 数字科技已成为支撑驱动文化发展的主要力量之一。"十三五"以来，适应人民需要的数字文化产品不断丰富，数字公共文化服务覆盖面持续扩大，数字文化产业整体实力显著增强，推动中华文化走向世界的文化开放格局进一步完善。以数字技术支撑的一批公共文化服务设施、渠道、装备和软件系统被广泛应用，形成一批面向需求的系统化集成解决方案和网络化运营服务平台，数字技术引领公共文化内容呈现形式、数字空间载体建设、互联共享的作用凸显。以技术创新、业态创新、内容创新和模式创新为主导的文化信息传输服务、文化创意和设计服务等新兴文化产业占比大、增长快，传统文化产业数字化和数字文化相关产品生产继续保持增长，数字科技引领高端文化专用装备制造的作用明显。文化产品和服务的生产、传播、消费的数字化与网络化蓬勃发展，与相关产业跨界融合发展呈常态，对外数字文化贸易的进出口结构得到进一步优化。数字技术在民族文化资源和特色文化资源的开发利用途径得到进一步拓展。

3. 数字科技在文化领域中的综合创新应用极为深刻地影响并改变着文化发展的环境、业态、格局。文化为体、科技为酶。近些年来，数字科技已经全面融入文化创作、生产、传播、服务、消费以及文化服务与模式创新、文化内容与形式创新、文化产业升级与业态创新、文化市场监管与服务创新等全链条中。

4. 数字文化已经成为当今社会文化的一种新文化存在形态。数字文化是以信息技术为基础、在网络空间形成的文化活动、文化方式、文化产品、文化观念的集合。数字文化是现实社会文化的延伸和多样化的呈现，同时也形成了其自身独特的文化行为特征、文化产品特色和价值观念和思维方式的特点。

5. 数字科技引领的新浪潮正在深刻地影响文化发展的路径。全球已经融入大数据、工业4.0、网络智能化三大潮流中，文化大数据、信息通信技术、虚拟现实与增强现实、人工智能、视听表达技术、云计算、数字孪生等为代表的数字技术，已经成为推动潮流发展的七大技术。这些技术为文化发展植入了创新基因，将对当今及未来的生产生活方式产生革命性影响，加速了文化生产方式及发展模式的变革，开始了文化传播传承方式的新革命，促进了文化消费与接受方式的新变革。以科技为核心竞争力的一大批新兴文化业态应运而生，革命性地改变了我们所处时代的日常文化存在形态，将全面促进文化服务运营和文化产业链整合的大繁荣。

6. 文化与科技融合呈现加速推进态势，正有力地驱动数字文化创新。文化与科技的深度融合，已经为文化创新奠定坚实的基础。文化发展不断提出更多的科技诉求，科技发展在文化领域寻找到广泛的应用空间。经过多年持续积累，我国以数字科技为代表的文化科技实力实现整体跃升，与发达国家差距明显缩小，呈现领跑、并跑、跟跑"三跑"并存格局。文化数字化、数字文化产业化、文化产业数字化正在成为共识，在文化管理、文化创意、文化生产、文化展示、文化传播、文化交流、公共文化服务、文化遗产保护等领域，将越来越发挥出解放文化生产力和改变文化发展方式的巨大作用。

7. 数字科技的引擎牵引功能正加速驱动文化创新向协同发展迈进。我国以数字科技为代表的文化科技的跨越式进步，正助推各级文化行政管理部门积极深化文化科技体制改革，加快实施创新驱动发展战略，加快转变政府职能，不断提高政府文化行政治理效率，推进文化制度运行和文化政策落实的长效化、规范化、精密化和可操作化。以科技创新和模式创新为核心竞争力的各类数字文化平台将大量涌现，使文化创意、文化生产、文化消费、文化传播、文化贸易获得强大的平台托举支撑，资金、技术、人才、信息、项目以及创意环境等关键性要素，将获得超过预期的协同效应、聚集效应、漫溢效应、提升效应以及优化配置效应。文化科技的引擎牵引功能将进一步放大，在协同创新的文化发展道路上充分显示其主动性、能动性、导向性和可持续性，以源源不断的牵引力量驱动中国文化建设的各个具体方面。

四、推动与促进文化与科技融合，须着重把握好六个维度

一是应坚持社会主义先进文化发展的本质属性；
二是应坚持推动文化发展方式创新的根本要求；
三是应坚持促进文化事业进步、文化产业融合创新、文化管理有序三大结构性平衡；
四是应以形成文化科技创新体系和文化科技技术支撑体系为总体目标；
五是应坚持提高科技对现代文化产业体系、现代文化市场体系建设、现代公共文化服务体系构建和文化开放水平提升的驱动支撑能力；
六是应坚持推动新时代社会主义先进文化的繁荣昌盛。

五、推动与促进文化与科技融合的总体指导思想

按照坚定文化自信和建设社会主义文化强国与增强国家文化软实力的总体要求，牢固树立以人民为中心的工作导向，发挥科技对文化创新的驱动作用，加强文化与科技融合，深化文化科技体制机制改革，促进创新资源的合理配置，培育创新主体，增强创新动力，优化创新环境，切实提高科技对现代文化产业体系、现代文化市场体系建设、现代公共文化服务体系构建和文化开放水平提升的驱动支撑能力，推动社会主义先进文化的繁荣昌盛。

六、新时代文化与科技融合的使命定位和目标愿景

1. 围绕文化数字化、数字文化产业化、文化产业数字化三大方面，布置数字文化基础性和制约性技术攻关、数字文化服务场景创新、文旅融合技术集成等任务，推进文化和科技深度融合，发展数字文化消费经济新动能，提升国家文化软实力。数字文化发展的基础性和制约技术问题得到系统解决，数字化、专业化、智能化、生态化程度得到大幅提升，数字文化的新形态和新业态得到丰富发展，文化和科技成为我国经济和社会高质量发展的双引擎。

2. 解放与发展文化领域的数字生产力，通过建立数字文化发展的技术集成体系，解决文化创作作坊化、传播广播化、表现刻板化、资源孤岛化和监管人工化等突出问题，大幅提升文化创作和文化资源利用效率、文化传播和表现能力、文化智慧管理水平，大力发展数字文化服务新经济业态，改造提升传统文化业态，推动数字创意与设计赋能实

体经济发展，实现文化和科技深度融合。

3. 加快推动技术创新和应用，激发数据资源要素潜力，突破数字文化发展基础性与制约性技术瓶颈，开展重要领域和关键环节核心技术攻关，建立支撑文化产业数字化转型和引领数字文化新经济发展的文化服务与智慧治理技术集成体系，在网络视听、文化展演、数字艺术、文旅融合、创意与设计、交互娱乐、公共文化服务、非物质文化遗产保护、文化与相关产业融合等重要文化场景开展技术集成创新与应用服务示范。

七、拟解决关键科技问题并设立主要应用场景

（一）发展数字文化资源新优势

支持数字文化资源在采集、加工、获取、整备、管理、保护、保存、应用、传播、表现等全过程链条中相关技术和装备的研发，构建文化资源相关技术支撑平台和基础研发平台，加速文化资源信息化、网络化进程。支持数字文化资源的数据化专用技术研发，加强现代人文艺术学科研究的基础数据支撑；支持实现民族文化素材的创建、描述、组织、检索、服务与长期保存的技术、标准和装备研发；鼓励记录、保存、展现中国传统生活文化的新方法、新手段、新模式的研究，促进传统文化生活方式在现代生活中的有效保存和二次创新；支持数字文化资源记录与保存介质材料的研发，鼓励传统文化介质的现代复原复现工艺研究；推动文化资源与信息产业有效对接的模式创新，加快技术层面的文化资源整合与互联互通，着力打通数字化文化资源访问的关键技术环节，实现文化价值与产业应用的有效结合。

（二）推动新型文化业态融合创新

充分运用数字技术、网络技术、智能技术、材料技术，加快文化产业重要装备、材料、工艺、系统、平台的开发和利用，加快传统文化企业的转型升级步伐；促进新兴科技企业向文化领域的渗透，实现传统文化产业领域的颠覆式创新；推动大数据、云计算、虚拟现实、互联网＋、人工智能等新兴战略科技在文化领域的创新试点工作，形成由点带面的示范性应用，强化文化产品（服务）的互动性和体验性，触发文化产业的深刻变革；加速网络空间文化阵地的建设，加快技术与内容相结合的有效网络文化治理步伐；促进社交聚合等互联网成熟商业模式向文化产业领域的渗透，推动文化产业的业务融合创新；支持文化与相关产业双向或多向融合发展。

（三）拓展公共文化服务新空间

加快公共文化服务的数字化建设步伐，结合智慧城市、智慧社区、宽带中国等国家

重大战略举措，建立起技术先进、覆盖广泛、方便快捷的数字化公共文化服务网络与载体；研究制定一批公共文化领域标准规范和服务模式；支持主流媒体、智慧广电、智慧图书馆、新型城乡公共文化服务体系、重要文化和自然遗产、非物质文化遗产系统性保护、文物古籍保护、国家文化公园建设等专用设备与装备的研发；鼓励符合我国核心价值观的公共文化内容供给的新呈现、新表现和新揭示的相关技术和标准研发；支持一站式文化服务相关技术、装备、系统与平台的研发；针对博物馆、美术馆、文化馆等重要公共文化设施，开展相应的虚拟化、数字化、智能化特种体验装备研究；鼓励公共文化服务手段创新和新兴公共文化服务业态创新。

（四）推动文化发展方式转变并发展文化艺术新形态

引导创新要素向文化建设与发展集聚，强调文化与科技创新中的协同融合与技术集成，助推文化发展方式转变。加快文化艺术创作的集约化、专业化步伐，鼓励创作手段创新，催生与发展文化艺术新形态；支持网络文化制作、影视编辑、特效生成处理等专业生产工具和系统的研发；支持舞美、布景、道具、灯光、音响、机械、视效、观演互动等领域的技术与系统研发，鼓励虚拟现实、人机交互、自动控制等先进技术在演艺舞台中的集成应用；支持艺术创作与观众情感间的定量化分析研究；鼓励舞蹈、音乐、美术等编排数字化专用工具和创作工具的研发。

（五）提升政府文化行政治理效率

支持文化施政管理过程中的数据采集、交汇、存储、处理和分析等相关技术与系统的研发；鼓励文化遗产鉴定相关标准规范、参数指标、标准物质、装置装备的研究；开展艺术品的量化估值方法研究，建设相应数据库；针对演出场所、娱乐场所、公共文化设施建设，制定相应规划、验收、评估、公共安全、运营维护等强制性技术标准；推进文化行业相关计量检测和检验技术的研究；展开文化市场监管、文化市场诚信评估、文化内容版权保护等文化管理共性技术研究；支持对文化工作统计制度、指标体系、调查方法的研究，展开文化科技领域的软科学研究。

八、相关建议

1. 建议加大舆论宣传力度。广泛开展文化科技深度融合知识普及工作，增强全社会对文化科技驱动文化创新价值认同感，动员更多的媒体和专家就文化科技驱动文化创新的发展趋势、基本规律和探索实践等进行全方位讨论，营造文化科技融合与文化创新的社会氛围，解放思想，更新观念，凝聚智慧，形成合力，以理论先导推进文化自觉，以文化自觉引领文化创新。

2. 建议改善制度设计。尤其要改善顶层制度设计，要在政府行政平台形成文化科技创新和旅游科技创新的合力，统筹相关职能部门事权会商处置机制，在科技发展与文化发展财政方案中进一步添列文化科技融合发展预算支持科目，使各级政府对文化科技融合与文化创新发展更具调控能力。要制订文化科技创新中长期规划，在与国家科技发展规划与文化发展规划目标一致和指标匹配基础上，确立发展的时间表、路线图、发展标杆。要把文化科技融合纳入各级政府议事日程，尤其要纳入各级政府文化行政部门和科技部门的重要工作安排，促使相关工作成为政府文化治理制度运行内容的重要组成部分。

3. 建议尽快出台相关配套政策，激励人才，撬动项目，引导更多文化科技企业实现研发升级，促进文化科技创新可持续稳步推进。要逐步出台具有明确针对性的文化科技创新导向政策，清晰定位，找准方向，加强引导，扩大支持范围并加强支持力度。要逐步出台具有明确针对性的经济政策，对文化科技企业资质审定、投资准入、融资渠道、税收优惠等给予政策倾斜，助推文化科技企业实现跨越式发展。要逐步出台具有明确针对性的文化科技复合人才政策，引导人才培养，激励人才成长，促进杰出人才参与国际竞争，为复合人才切实提供住房、户籍、子女入学、出国深造、科研环境等生活保障。

4. 建议着力打造文化科技发展平台，夯实基础，整合资源，形成文化科技战略优势。要优先发展国家级文化科技融合示范基地建设，在项目、资金，人才及相关领域加大支持力度，确立刚性指标，聚集能量，迅速形成具有国际竞争能力的研发团队、研发规模、研发优势，形成文化科技深度融合并驱动文化创新的强大竞争团队。要鼓励更多的文化事业单位积极投身基于文化科技融合的技术升级、装备升级、服务升级和文化建设升级，鼓励更多的文化企业努力实现文化科技融合所带来的转型效应、竞争力效应、市场拓展效应和可持续效益增长效应。要布局与建设区域文化科技重点实验室，为抢占文化科技融合高地组织起实力雄厚的战略科技力量。

5. 建议将已经实施的各类文化科技融合项目做大做强，增加支持力度，扩大支持范围，提高支持有效性。要进一步完善相关政府职能部门之间的联合会商制度，加强相关各方政策功能链接，实现文化科技融合进程中的信息资源共享，形成推进文化科技融合的行政合力。要按照适当的年度递增比例较大幅度扩大"重点研发计划专项资金"中涉及文化科技的资金规模并增强项目支持力度。

虚实融合放大演艺魅力*

刚刚过去的"五一"假期,在各地整合资源优势推出的丰盛文旅大餐中,精彩纷呈的文化演出尤为引人注目。不仅是剧场、音乐厅、戏台等文化观演空间好戏连台,高品质演出不断,一些文化演出还走出剧场,走向景区,走进形态各异的演出空间,大型实景演出、沉浸式演出、云演艺等以新颖的文化演出模式和视觉冲击力让观众大饱眼福。

舞台变化的背后,离不开数字技术的支撑。

近年来,随着数字技术的迅猛介入,围绕舞台艺术的创作、生产与传播消费,涌现出许多新的技术应用和实践探索。从典型的镜框式舞台空间,到虚实互动、打破时空的舞台空间;从传统的美术幕景,到LED屏幕、立体投影、全息投影带来的立体多元的视觉呈现;从单纯的你演我看、固定位置观看,到观众与舞台之间的界限被不断打破,出现行进式、交互式的观演模式,观众参与到文化演出中来……持续扩展的舞台空间,不断深化的观演关系,日渐丰富的演出形式,激活了文化演出的内容与形式创新,助推演艺行业的高质量发展。

总的来看,在科技与艺术融合的背景下,今天的文化演出朝着增强虚实融合的方向持续探索,通过数字技术应用,努力把真实的舞台表演与虚拟的舞美内容无缝整合在一起,使表演艺术、观演环境、视效呈现、声效呈现、运动呈现凝结成一门综合艺术,打造穿越时空、亦真亦假、如梦似幻的舞台效果。

以视效呈现为例,传统的虚实融合方式,往往是将舞美视频事先制作好,演员须配合舞美,演出内容严格按既定的排演时序进行,这不仅对实际演出活动是一种挑战,也需要演员反复排演,容错率极低。而现在,借助观演空间三维扫描与建模、观演空间声场与灯光仿真、多目标演员实时定位跟踪与动作识别、动态内容实时生成、演出排演与编辑控制等技术与系统,实时捕捉演员的空间定位和表演动作,进行相应的虚拟舞美内容调整和驱动生成,实时渲染出与演员当前位置和动作相匹配的投影内容,演员活动与虚拟舞美内容的"时序配合"将更加"宽松",这样不仅保证了虚实融合的整体效果和协调性,也大大提升了演员表演时的自由度,为文化演出的表现力、感染力与影响力提供了强大的技术支撑。

在2022年北京冬奥会开幕式的和平鸽展示环节,小朋友们手持白色的和平鸽模型,

---

* 本文原载于《人民日报》聚焦·文化数字化,2023年5月12日,收入本书时有改动。

在场内自由愉快地奔跑，与脚下的星星雪花嬉戏互动。这个表演场景是在人工智能动作捕捉技术的支持下实现的。世界上第一次在这么大的场景中对超过600人的演员集体实时捕捉互动。通过多个摄像头跟踪演员，运用计算机视觉算法计算出每个演员的位置，然后在服务器里实时生成渲染对应的画面，再将它叠加到地屏显示系统中去，呈现具有强烈冲击力的虚实融合效果。

如今，大型实景演出深受旅游景区青睐。这些演出的舞台幕景可能就是真实的山体、峭壁、树丛，传统演出的平面幕、弧形幕、球幕等规则幕投影不再适应，异形实体投影技术可支持在实际演出过程中进行虚拟内容实时动态生成、投影内容实时几何校正、实时色彩补偿，直至最终将虚拟舞美投射出来。在许多景区推出的夜间实景演出中，就通过异形实体投影实现丰富纹理变化的投影效果，在岩石、河谷、建筑物等景观之上投射缤纷的动态影像，给游客带来梦幻体验。依托剧情、表演、舞美，利用景区环境、后期道具、虚拟影像、观演互动等综合形式，提升舞台演出的内容丰富性和观赏性，形成崭新的故事化情境体验，激发观众的感官体验及情感共鸣。这已经成为数字时代舞台演艺的重要方向。

舞台是数字技术的重大应用场景。数字技术改变着舞台的形制面貌，增强着舞台的艺术感染力，也使观众的审美体验和欣赏习惯发生了巨大变化，催生和培育着新的演出形态。期待在科技和艺术融合发展的过程中，舞台技术不断迭代升级，绽放舞台演艺的更多魅力，以体现时代创造活力、契合当代审美旨趣的精彩演出，更好地满足人们的精神文化需求。

第二部分
视听技术

视听觉融合效应及其信息融合处理方法综论*

一、引言

众所周知，人们都有这样一种感受：当置身于或者观赏一处辽阔的场景（一幅平静的画面）时，比如优美的草原或者宁静的湖泊，人们会自然陶醉其中，耳边仿佛响起了一段舒缓优美的曲子；反之，当人们正在欣赏一段舒缓优美的曲子时，若向其播放一段展现惊涛骇浪的视频，人们会感到不适，甚至会对这种不和谐产生抵触。以上现象说明，人对于外界信息的感知过程并不都是独立存在的，人脑是一个优化的多感官信息融合系统，它能自动关联来自不同感官通道（眼、耳等）的不同模态信息（图像、声音等），并对外界事物进行统一感知、联想、表达和评价。这种现象广泛存在于人们的生产与生活中，具有普遍性。本文将这种视觉信息和听觉信息相互影响并共同作用于人的现象称为视听觉融合效应。显然，这种现象以人的心理过程为基本前提。

本文将视听觉融合效应中视觉信息与听觉信息的相互关系总结为以下四种：和谐、冲突、忽略以及博弈。由上文可知，优美的草原景色、宁静的湖泊风光与舒缓优美的曲子之间的关系为"和谐"；惊涛骇浪的视频与舒缓优美的曲子之间的关系为"冲突"。区别于"和谐"与"冲突"，"忽略"与"博弈"反映的是视觉信息与听觉信息的主次关系。例如，在与某人谈话时，人的注意力会集中在谈话之中而忽略背景中其他人以及他们的对话，这就是"鸡尾酒会效应"（cocktail party effect）。视觉信息与听觉信息之间同样会产生竞争机制，这种视觉信息与听觉信息相互竞争并有一方占据主导的关系即"忽略"；在日常的生产与生活中，更多见的是视觉信息与听觉信息的交织混合，若无法分清视觉信息与听觉信息的主次关系，即"博弈"。

---

* 本文原载于《中国传媒大学学报（自然科学版）》2019年第26卷，与王爽、蒋玉暕、刘京宇合作。收入本书时有改动。

二、相关领域研究现状与分析

在心理学领域，视觉与听觉感官之间的相互关系已得到论证。1976年，McGurk等人验证了人类对外界信息的认知是基于不同感官信息而形成的整体性理解，任何感官信息的缺乏或不准确，都将导致大脑对外界信息的理解产生偏差，这个现象被称为"McGurk现象"。2008年，Olivier等人用自我报告和对比反应时间的方法证明，在视听内容情绪一致的情况下，可提高图片情绪感受性，当不一致时，视听内容的表达将会产生相互抑制的效果。心理学家将人抽象化成信息加工系统，包括感觉输入的编码、贮存和提取的全过程。由于人内部心理过程的不可见性，受限于现有技术水平，研究者只能通过观察输入和输出的结果构建信息加工的大致轮廓，信息加工过程中如何对信息进行阶段性操作，每一阶段如何产生输出以及产生何种输出，各阶段如何进行协同工作等细节问题均未形成统一认识。

在艺术学领域，艺术家以音乐、舞蹈、电影、美术、摄影等多种艺术表现形式为切入点，探讨了视听觉融合多模态作用下的审美及情感体验并且进行了实践，取得了一定成果。例如，电影中的声画匹配理论，将声音与画面在呈现内容上相呼应，或是现实与心理相呼应，可表达出深刻内涵。再例如，中国作曲家谭盾也曾于2005年4月在上海沪申画廊举办谭盾音乐视觉展。谭盾说，视听艺术本来就是一家人，作曲家的作品虽然最后落实在乐谱上，但在创作过程中是非常形象的。但是，这些理论多以感性经验为基础，虽然逐步进行了一些定量化研究，其结果缺少实验数据支撑，并且未考虑个性化差异，为后期工程化应用带来不便。

在脑科学与神经科学领域，科学家们尝试从细胞生物学和分子生物学角度理解神经回路是如何感受周围世界并采取行动的，并且进一步研究了人类情感生活的生物学基础。但是，人脑由百亿级神经细胞组成，这些神经细胞通过树突和轴突组成一个庞大的神经网络，试图以分子、突触、神经元等为研究对象，从微观水平上揭开大脑与心灵之谜变得异常困难。人脑是一个极为复杂的系统，其整体行为具有非线性相关性和动态不确定性的特点。虽然脑成像技术和脑电波技术为脑科学研究打开了一条研究思路，试图从系统、全脑、行为等宏观水平上全面阐述人和动物在感知客体、形成表象、推理决策时信息加工过程及其神经机制，但是受限于现有技术水平，神经元的连接模式尚未被完全描绘清楚。

在信息科学领域，对视觉信息和听觉信息的研究最早始于视觉信号处理和听觉信号处理这两个独立领域。视觉方面已有许多研究成果，如图像检索、多媒体数据分类、运动跟踪、人脸识别、表情识别等。随着人工智能的兴起，在大数据背景下，研究者通过训练学习模型对图像进行识别，大大提高了识别准确率，并在自动驾驶等领域得到了广泛应用。听觉方面主要集中在对音乐、语音的研究，例如音乐检索、流派分类、语音识别、语音情绪检测等众多领域。其研究方法主要从三个角度展开：通过自我报告、行为表达、生理测量的主观评价方法；基于音频底层特征提取的语义分析方法；基于乐理（如旋律、节奏、曲式）的语义分析方法。近年来，跨模态研究逐渐成为研究热点，主要包括image-text研究、audio-text研究和image-audio研究。研究者们采用不同方法为不同模态数据建立跨模态映射模型，主要方法为：利用深度学习算法构建不同模态数据共享层或者将不同模态数据经过高度抽象后映射到一个公共表示空间，如典型关联分析（Canonical Correlation Analysis，CCA）技术，从而建立不同模态数据之间的关联。这类技术可以为研究视听觉融合效应提供技术支持。

综上所述，对视听觉融合效应的研究涉及多个学科，研究者需充分认识到其与各个学科的区别与联系，在充分学习和理解各个学科理论与方法的基础上，发展针对视听觉融合效应的、科学可行的研究思路与方法，避免产生研究误区。涉及的学科如表1所示：

表1 视听觉融合效应研究涉及学科分类

一级学科	二级学科
自然科学类	数学
	生物学
	心理学
	信息科学与系统科学
医药科学类	基础医学
工程与技术科学类	信息与系统科学相关工程与技术
	电子、通信与自动控制技术
	计算机科学技术
人文与社会科学类	艺术（美）学
	社会学
	民族学与文化学
	教育学

三、研究对象与基本概念

由于人内部心理过程的不可见性，本文将人脑视作"黑箱模型"（black box），即不考虑内部物理单元完整拓扑结构的情况下，通过研究模型输入与输出之间的关系建立视觉信息与听觉信息之间的关联。因此，本文将视听觉融合效应的研究对象转化为视觉信息和听觉信息的融合过程，即研究人在不同模态信息作用下，运用视觉、听觉意象的生成和融合规律以及信息技术手段，探索视觉信息和听觉信息的相互关系。其研究目的是使人进一步认知视觉信息与听觉信息的融合机制，建立视听觉关联模型，并将其应用在众多视听交互领域。

其中，"人"需要进一步明确其所属区域、民族、年龄等可能引起差异化结果的因素。"输入"指视觉信息与听觉信息的数据表征，包括底层特征、中层特征和高层特征。底层特征指物理特征，视觉特征如颜色、形状、纹理等，听觉特征如音高、音长、响度等；中层特征指感知特征，例如颜色的冷暖感、胀缩感、动静感等，构图中的平衡感、动态张力等，音色中的丰满度、粗糙度、协和度等；高层特征指语义特征，是人们对视听内容的抽象概念的反映，例如情感、和谐感与美感。视觉信息与听觉信息可实现高层语义特征的一致性。"输出"指视觉信息与听觉信息的四种融合关系：和谐、博弈、忽略以及博弈；"信息融合处理"指通过信息技术手段，以人的心理过程为基本前提，通过计算机智能模拟人脑对视觉信息与听觉信息的融合处理机制。

四、研究方法与技术路线

随着互联网的普及，网络上充斥着大量的多媒体数据，不同模态数据之间的检索与匹配需要通过机器学习的方法对跨模态数据进行关联映射。机器学习是关于理解与研究人类学习内在机制的学科，通过学习自动提高计算机程序自身水平。近年来，机器学习理论在诸多应用领域得到成功的应用与发展，已成为计算机科学的基础及热点之一。机器学习的研究是根据生理学、认知科学等对人类学习机理的了解，建立人类学习过程的计算模型或认识模型，其理论的发展与成熟为研究视听觉融合效应提供了可行的方法与路径。

主观评价实验是从人的主观角度出发，对实验对象进行描述或评价的实验。视听觉融合效应以人的心理过程为基本前提，心理学实验是其必要的研究方法。因此，需要设计科学有效的主观评价实验方法，根据特定场景需求，为以人的心理过程为基本前提的特征提取提供准确的针对性强的实验数据，再通过一系列统计分析方法进行特征量化。

综上所述，本文主要采取机器学习算法与主观评价实验相结合的方法进行研究，结合心理学、艺术学、脑科学与神经科学、信息科学等学科的现有理论成果挖掘中高层特征，寻找异构数据公共映射空间，建立视听关联模型，深入理解视觉信息与听觉信息之间的融合关系。本文给出以下三种研究思路：

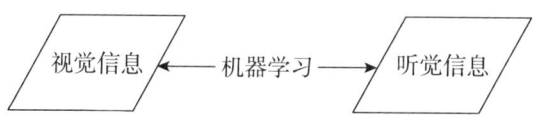

图 1　视觉信息与听觉信息的直接关联

如图 1 所示，思路一在建立大规模视听觉融合数据库的基础上，运用机器学习算法，对视觉信息与听觉信息进行直接匹配。输入特征为底层特征。该思路适用于有特定场景需求的应用型研究。

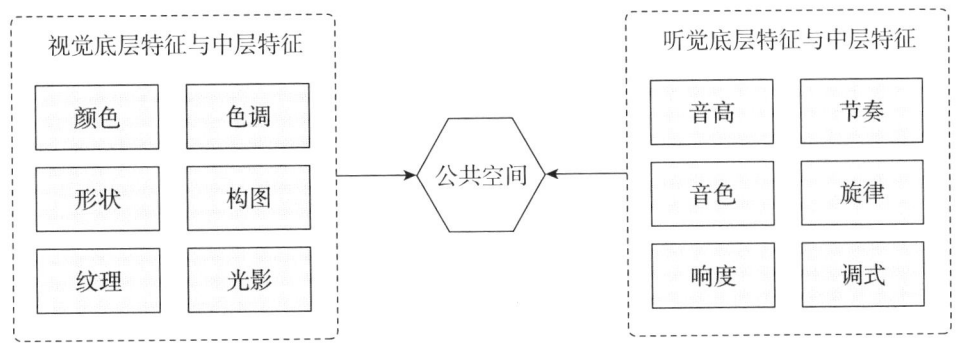

图 2　视觉信息与听觉信息通过公共空间关联

如图 2 所示，思路二通过将视觉特征与听觉特征映射到公共的高层特征空间来建立两者的关联模型，例如情感语义空间、美感语义空间、和谐性语义空间等。输入特征为底层特征或者中层特征。

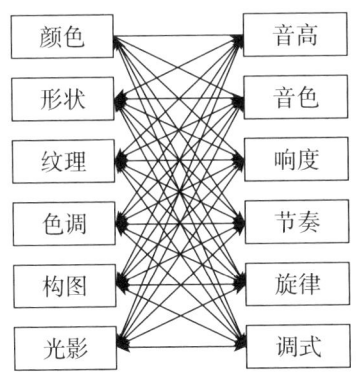

图 3　视觉信息与听觉信息通过中底层特征关联

如图 3 所示，思路三通过主观评价实验研究视听觉底层特征和中层特征之间的直接映射关系，从而建立各特征之间的关联模型。这种映射关系可以是一对一映射，也可以是一对多、多对一映射，并且可以跨越层级约束。该思路适用于针对视觉信息与听觉信息的融合处理机制的基础型研究，是具有开创性和延续性的研究思路。

五、研究重点与难点

（一）视听觉融合数据库的构建

目前已有较多单模态标准数据库，如国际情绪图片系统（IAPS）、国际情感数码声音系统（IADS）等。主要存在以下问题：（1）未说明建库过程及素材筛选原则；（2）未验证数据库中素材标注特征的完备性；（3）未建立基于视听觉融合素材的标准数据库；（4）由于时间、地域的不同，素材标注标签具有差异性，无法直接使用。因此，有必要建立一个基于视听觉融合素材的标准数据库，为后续研究提供数据支持。

该数据库内容力求完备，其中包含视觉、听觉两个单模态数据库以及一个视听觉融合的多模态数据库。视觉数据库包括图像、视频、文本等内容，听觉数据库包括环境声、语音、音乐、音效等内容，视听觉融合数据库包括影视、MV、广告等内容。

（二）视觉数据与听觉数据中高层特征的挖掘与提取

在信息科学领域，视觉信息与听觉信息隶属于不同模态，这里的不同模态指不同的多媒体数据，研究视听觉融合效应的过程即研究不同模态映射关系的过程。不同模态的数据表征不同，物理层特征也存在较大差异，且一般来说特征维数较高，存在"语义鸿沟"的问题。目前，这类研究往往选取物理层特征进行关联，其关联机制无法做进一步挖掘，关联效果也受到限制。另一方面，对于视听一致性的研究聚焦在心理物理特性方面。视听一致性应该遵循物理特性与心理过程的一致性。但是，目前的一些研究只针对物理特征分析上的主观感知的变化，当务之急是视觉信息与听觉信息融合内容的心理感受量化关系以及关联结构一致性的研究。

人可以通过简单的看和听就能深刻体会到视听觉融合信息所传递出的情感。例如，在观赏两部电影时，一个有配乐，一个没有配乐，人能明确感受到两个电影表达的情感区别；还有，人在欣赏音乐电影（Movie Video，MV）时也能比单独欣赏音乐获得更多的情感体验。以上现象表明，人的情感体验机制能很好地解决不同语义信息之间的"语义鸿沟"问题。需要注意的是，"和谐"与"冲突"对应不同信息刺激下情感反射的匹配情况，但"忽略"与"博弈"反映的是视觉信息与听觉信息的主次关系，其中不涉及或者只部分涉及情感反射。因此，以符合人的心理过程为前提条件，挖掘视觉信息与听觉信息在高层特征上的语义一致性是一条可行路径。本文将高层特征按作用过程分为直接作用特征和间接作用特征。直接作用特征指信息直接作用于人所产生的生理反射，如冷暖感、轻重感、明暗感、粗糙感等；间接作用特征指在信息作用于人产生生理反射的基础上，加入人的记忆与联想等所产生的心理反射，如情感。此外，可以结合艺术领域挖掘专业特征,如美学特征:构图、重心、张力等。如何挖掘中高层特征,并制订中高层特征的参数提取与量化方法,完善系统权重、行为初值及量化边界,使其符合视觉信息与听觉信息的作用规律是本问题的研究重点与难点。

(三)非直接观测数据的参数提取与量化评估

本文中的非直接观测数据指主观评价实验数据,例如人的情感特征为非直接观测数据。对于非直接观测数据,需要寻找可能的同态拟合关系,将非直接观测数据转化为可测量的数据、量化关系或不同支路系统的权重系数。人脑的视听觉情感融合过程具有典型的复杂系统特征。在这一过程中,对信息的传递和处理具有明显的非线性相关性和动态不确定性的特点,其并不是几种生理信号的简单叠加,各组成部分之间、不同层次的组成部分之间相互关联、相互制约,并有复杂的相互作用。此外,人的视听觉情感的产生也并不只是来自外部的信息刺激,同时还有记忆、联想等其他因素作用。并且,人针对同一刺激的情感反射随着时间的推移并不是一成不变的。因此,如何挖掘共性因素与差异化因素,将两者有机结合,并完备非直接观测数据模型,是研究的难点。

(四)异构数据公共空间的映射

由于视觉信息与听觉信息具有底层特征异构及高层语义相关的特点,可分别将底层特征映射至高层语义空间,例如情感语义空间,以此建立视听关联。或者针对底层空间特征异构性问题,利用跨模态学习方法挖掘跨媒体数据间的潜在关联,例如协同训练(Co-Training)方法、多核学习(Multiple Kernel Learning)方法和共享子空间学习(Subspace Learning)方法。

(五)匹配原则的确定

信息融合处理的最后环节是将量化特征数据与标注数据通过学习模型进行关联,并根据一定的匹配原则建立视觉信息与听觉信息的融合模型。匹配原则指视听觉融合效应中视觉信息与听觉信息之间关系的评判标准。由上文可知,"和谐"与"冲突"对应不同信息刺激下情感反射的匹配情况,但"忽略"与"博弈"反映的是视觉信息与听觉信息的主次关系,其中不涉及或者只部分涉及情感反射。因此,需要借助心理学现有的理论成果及实验方法,针对本文提出的视觉信息与听觉信息的四种关系,制订视觉信息与听觉信息的匹配原则。

六、研究展望

首先，对人视听觉融合效应形成机制的研究不仅能够促进计算机科学技术在人工智能领域的发展，还能产生实际的社会效益。例如，发掘人的行为倾向，行为倾向可反映分享者对某个事件、某个公众人物、某个产品、某个企业的态度，通过对这些媒介承载行为的分析，可获得重要的商情、舆情资料，并将其进一步应用在生产实践和舆论引导中。其次，研究视听觉融合机制还有助于科学的纵深发展，具有极强的现实意义。视听觉融合可广泛应用于影视、广告、剧场演出等方面，有利于推动商业、文化及科技产业的发展。最后，视听觉融合的研究还有助于推动人工智能技术在不同领域的应用和发展，尤其是机器人、医疗和教育等领域，并展望其能够提供更加和谐的人机交互能力，从而彻底改变人们的工作生活方式。

综上所述，研究视听觉融合效应的信息融合处理具有相当广阔的应用前景。在艺术领域中的主要应用有：影视配乐、造型设计、建筑设计、服装设计等；在工业工程领域中的主要应用有：声景设计、工程建筑中的室内照明设计等；在广告商业领域中的应用主要有：包装设计、研究文化消费行为倾向、设计营销手段等；在医疗领域的应用主要有：视觉障碍、听力损伤治疗与康复等；在教育领域的应用主要有：视听交互辅助教学等。

七、结语

本文将视觉信息和听觉信息相互影响并共同作用于人的现象称为视听觉融合效应，并且针对该效应提出了以信息融合处理为核心的研究思路、技术路线以及研究重点与难点，为该领域的研究提供了理论依据以及方法指导。

参考文献

[1] KOCH I, LAWO V. Switching in the cocktail party: exploring intentional control of auditory selective attention[J]. Journal of experimental psychology: human perception and performance, 2011, 37(4): 1140–1147.

[2] 阿姆海恩. 视觉思维 [M]. 成都：四川人民出版社，1998.

[3] 黄瑶. 浅谈视觉传达设计与心理学 [J]. 台声·新视角，2006，(1)：225–226.

[4] 黄镝. 异构数据库的跨库检索技术综述 [J]. 图书情报工作，2003，47(6)：94–97，109.

[5] 邵曦，刘君芳，季茜成. 基于情感的家庭音乐相册自动生成研究 [J]. 复旦学报（自然科学版），2017，56(2)：149–158.

[6] 杨钦淋. 音乐背景下跨视听通道的情绪冲突效应 [D]. 重庆：西南大学，2013.

[7] KUSUM G P. CHUA C-S. Image level fusion method for multimodal 2D + 3D face recognition[J]. Image analysis and recognition 5th international conference 2008：984-992.

[8] SHIN H, KIM S-D, CHOI H C. Generalized elastic graph matching for face recognition[J]. Pattern recognition letters, 2007, 28(9): 1077-1082.

[9] 王晓刚. 图像识别中的深度学习 [J]. 中国计算机学会通讯，2015，11(8)：15-21.

[10] 王艺帆. 自动驾驶汽车感知系统关键技术综述 [J]. 汽车电器，2016(12)：12-16.

[11] 孟子厚. 音质主观评价的实验心理学方法 [M]. 北京：国防工业出版社，2008.

[12] 唐孝威，杜继曾，陈学君. 脑科学导论 [M]. 杭州：浙江大学出版社，2006.

[13] 杨天亮，辛裴，雷旭. 人类大脑结构和功能的性别差异：来自脑成像研究的证据 [J]. 心理科学进展，2015，(4)：571–581.

[14] 张磊. 跨媒体语义共享子空间学习理论与方法研究 [D]. 北京：北京交通大学，2015.

[15] 张宪荣，陈麦，季华妹. 工业设计理念与方法 [M]. 北京：北京理工大学出版社，1996.

[16] 杉山将. 图解机器学习 [M]. 许永伟，译. 北京：人民邮电出版社，2015.

[17] 刘玮，魏龙生. 计算机视觉中的目标特征模型和视觉注意模型 [M]. 武汉：华中科技大学出版社，2016.

[18] 梁宁建. 当代认知心理学（修订版）[M]. 上海：上海教育出版社，2014.

[19] GAO X P, XIN J H. Investigation of human's emotional responses on colors[J]. Color research and application, 2006, 31(5): 411-417.

[20] 李莉婷. 色彩构成 [M]. 武汉：湖北美术出版社，2002.

[21] MCGURK H，MACDONALD J. Hearing lips and seeing voices[J]. Nature, 1976, 264(5584): 746-748.

[22] 倪祥龙，康建设，王广彦，等. 黑箱模型输出不确定性的敏感性分析 [J]. 计算机仿真，2014，31(4)：22–26.

[23] 曲庆云，赵晓梅，阮桂海，等. 统计分析方法——SAS 实例精选 [M]. 北京：清华大学出版社，2004.

[24] 朱滢. 实验心理学 [M]. 北京：北京大学出版社，2014.

[25] COLLIGNON O, GIRARD S, GOSSELIN F. Audio-visual integration of emotion expression[J]. Brain research, 2008, 1242(4): 126-135.

[26] 张华，蒋玉暕，蒋伟. 基于情感的视听关联问题 [J]. 中国传媒大学学报（自然科学版），2017，24(1)：35–40.

[27] 张菁，关玲. 影视视听语言 [M]. 北京：中国传媒大学出版社，2014.

[28] 姚以让. 声与色的交响 [M]. 北京：中央音乐学院出版社，2006.

[29] 黄祥林，沈玉荪. 基于内容的图像检索技术研究 [J]. 电子学报，2002，30(7): 1065–1071.

[30] 张磊，赵耀，朱振峰. 跨媒体语义共享子空间学习研究进展 [J]. 计算机学报，2017，40(6): 1394–1421.

A Study of Visual Attention Elements with Experiment Analysis Based on Composition *

1. INTRODUCTION

There is a certain interaction between human vision and hearing. The preliminary correlation based on the physical layer feature information of visual and auditory has been applied in many application scenarios, but the research on the matching processing of visual and auditory information based on human audio-visual perception is basically in a blank state. Therefore, visual and auditory fusion information processing and analysis based on human audio-visual perception becomes crucial. Visual and auditory fusion information processing and analysis refers to the acquisition of human sensory information through computer processing of visual and auditory information. Among them, the mining and extraction of visual features is a difficulty and emphasis of this study. Based on the related research results of art theory and aesthetic psychology, image composition features are mined and extracted, which belongs to the research category of visual middle-level perception feature mining and extraction.

Composition is the arrangement of visual elements in the image frame, which is an essential aspect in the creation of a large number of art works. Perceptual psychologists, art theorist Rudolf Arnehaim in the book *The Art and Visual Perception*, says, in a work of art, the distribution of all of its elements must achieve a state of balance. "If a work of art lacks balanced composition, it becomes difficult to understand the intended meaning conveyed by the piece. Visual balance refers to the reasonable arrangement of elements so that their visual weight in the whole picture achieves a state of balance. An important factor influencing composition balance is visual weight, which is precisely used to describe the degree to which elements in the picture attract people's visual attention. The elements that attract more visual attention in the picture have a larger visual weight, whereas elements

---

① The paper was originally published in *2019 IEEE/ACIS 18th International Conference on Computer and Information Science (ICIS)*, June 2021, and has since been revised with new information. It was co-authored by Wei Jiang, Yanan Su, and Shuang Wang.

that attract less attention have a smaller visual weight. Combined with the visual attention mechanism, the visual weight of significant elements in an image plays a crucial role in visual balance.

The research purpose of this paper includes two aspects: (1) to build a database to provide data basis for the extraction of visual perception features; (2) mining visual attention elements to provide technical support for quantifying balance features based on composition.

There are many research achievements in the field of visual attention at home and abroad. Most of the early visual attention models can be traced back to the feature integration theory proposed by Treisman and Gelade in 1980. Koch and Ullman first introduced the concept of salience map in topographic map form to express the degree of attention to each position in the scene, and proposed a visual attention model based on feed-forward network. Inspired by the typical structure of neurons, Itti et al. first proposed the idea of using center-periphery difference to calculate salience, that is, visual attention. In contrast, Ma and Zhang extract the regions of interest from the salience map based on local contrast using a fuzzy growth method that mimics human mental behavior. Harel et al. proposed a graph-based visual salience model and transformed the problem of visual attention modeling into finding the equilibrium distribution of Markov chains. Bruce and Tsotsos proposed an information-maximized attention model and used Shannon's self-information to calculate the salience. Gao and Vasconcelos proposed a method to calculate salience based on mutual information between features and class labels. This field has attracted a large number of scholars' enthusiasm in the past decade. But existing ideas often stem from psychological discoveries about the human visual system, or from computer calculations of common attributes of salient regions, with little attention paid to visual attention elements based on human visual perception. Visual attention element is the element in the image that can attract people's visual attention. Therefore, the main task of this paper is to screen out visual attention elements based on human visual perception.

This paper is divided into five chapters. Chapter one is the introduction. In the second chapter, a screenshot material library of film and television scenes based on composition is constructed, and PAD dimensional emotion model and harmony degree are marked. In the third chapter, based on the second chapter, the subjective evaluation experiment of visual attention element screening is carried out. Chapter four analyzes and discusses the experimental results. The fifth chapter summarizes the whole paper and looks forward to the next step.

2. MATERIAL LIBRARY CONSTRUCTION

At present, commonly used databases include cifar-10 and cifar-100 datasets, Caltech101 and Caltech 256, INRIA Holidays and so on. However, existing databases are all specific to specific research topics, which cannot guarantee that they are applicable to this experiment. For this reason, it is necessary to establish a material library for image composition.

2.1 Construction of Composition Material Library

In this paper, the process of building a screenshot material library for film and television scenes based on composition is shown in Fig. 1.

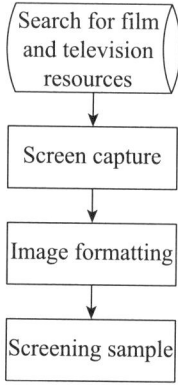

Fig. 1 Material library build process

Sources of film and television resources

The pictures used in this paper to build the composition material library are from the screenshots of film and television scenes, and some of them are from the screenshots of film and television scenes based on color. Through the screening of films and television with outstanding composition above 8.0 on Douban by film and television art professionals, 58 films and television covering different countries and different types were finally determined.

Material screenshot specification

Use PotPlayer to play according to the original proportion, and intercept the screen with obvious scene composition. Interception requirements include non-stretching; The content of the picture is clearly visible and cannot be too dark; Remove the semantic information with obvious emotional orientation; Avoid duplicate scenarios, etc.

Image processing

The common image processing software Photoshop was used to remove the black edges of the image uniformly, and the resolution was set to 1280×720ppi uniformly.

Feature selection

Summarize the existing composition rules, including rule of thirds, diagonal rule, golden section, depth of field, symmetry rule, etc. The processed images were screened repeatedly to ensure that all the composition rules could be covered. Finally, 120 images were determined to be used to build the image material library. Some images in the material library are shown in Fig. 2.

Fig. 2 Some pictures show material library

2.2 Quantitative Labeling Experiment of Three-Dimensional PAD Emotional Model

This experiment is to annotate the emotional dimension PAD model for the composition material base built in section 2.1. PAD 3d model is a dimensional observation model proposed by Mehrabian and Russell in 1974. PAD refers to the three dimensions of pleasure, arousal and dominance. Pleasure refers to the feeling of pleasure or unhappiness under the stimulus of signals. Arousal refers to the degree of stimulation in the signal feel excited or do not lift the spirit; Dominance refers to the feeling of being in a dominant or dominated position under the stimulus of signals. So far, there has not been a consistent international standard for dimensionally affective labeling, and artificial scoring system is generally adopted.

Subjects

In line with the principle of convenient sampling, 20 students from Communication University of China were selected as subjects to participate in the experiment, including 11 female students and 9 male students, aged between 20 and 25, in good health, with normal vision and without eye diseases.

Experimental Environment

The experiment was carried out in the laboratory A104, Comprehensive Building, Communication University of China. The display is a 75-inch SONY kd-75 x 9400D hd display. Before the beginning of the experiment, the experimental environment was arranged in advance, and a total of 10 seats were placed. The seats were arced in two rows with the display screen as the center, so as to make the viewing distance and viewing angle comfortable for each subject as far as possible, as shown in Fig. 3.

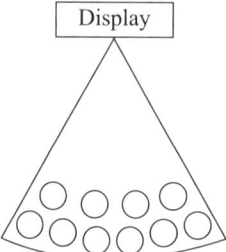

Fig. 3 Seating plan

Scoring Standard

In this experiment, five scales were used, such as the degree of pleasure. Then "-2" "-1" "0" "1" "2" respectively represented "very unhappy, unhappy, neutral, pleasant, very pleasant", and the degree of arousal and dominance were the same.

The Experimental Steps

In order to help the subjects better understand labeled emotional states and further improve the accuracy of labeled data, adjectives describing emotional states are combined with vivid cartoon characters in the scale proposed in literature, as shown in Fig. 4. Before the formal experiment, carefully explain the labeling experiment process to the subjects to ensure that each subject fully understands the concept of each dimension of PAD, and then the following experiment can be started.

Fig. 4 PAD cartoon (From top to bottom are pleasure, arousal and dominance)

The specific steps of the experiment are as follows:

Firstly, the subjects viewed the first picture for five seconds.

Secondly, the subjects were required to make a PAD 3d emotional score for the pictures they watched according to the 5-grade rating standard, and mark the score in the corresponding position of the experimental table for 15 seconds.

Finally, repeat the above procedure to evaluate the next picture until all images are evaluated.

Matters Needing Attention

The evaluation process of the subjects shall not exceed half an hour, so as to avoid the occurrence of physical discomfort, eye fatigue and other symptoms, leading to inaccurate scores. Therefore, in the middle of the experiment, the subjects were allowed to rest before the experiment.

2.3 The Harmony Degree was Quantified by Experiment

Harmony refers to the sense of symmetry, appropriateness and harmony when individuals see a certain picture. Harmony is a state of visual balance, which is used to further verify the validity of visual balance of images in the material library.

The labeling experiment of the harmony degree of the material base based on composition is consistent with the subjects, experimental environment, scoring standard and matters to be noted in the evaluation of 3d emotion model. The specific experimental steps are as follows:

Firstly, the subjects viewed the first picture for five seconds.

Secondly, the subjects were asked to rate the harmony of the pictures according to the 5-grade rating standard, and mark the score in the corresponding position in the experimental table for 5 seconds.

Finally, repeat the above procedure to evaluate the next picture until all images are evaluated.

2.4 The Material Distribution

As shown in Fig. 5, it can be seen from the PAD annotation of the statistical material library that the materials in this material library are evenly distributed on the emotional dimension of PAD, which reduces the error of the following experiment.

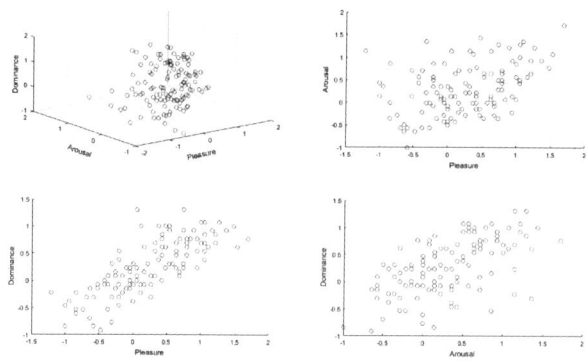

Fig. 5 PAD emotional distribution

3. VISUAL ATTENTION ELEMENT SCREENING EXPERIMENT

The task of this experiment is to find out the elements in the picture that attract visual attention, mark them, and rate the visual attention degree of the whole picture. This experiment is consistent with the experimental environment and subjects of the material library labeling experiment. This experiment was carried out in two times.

3.1 First Experiment

Grouping

On average, the images were randomly divided into 20 groups, each containing 6 images. Place each set of photos as thumbnails on a full-sized white background in two rows and three columns. That is, each group contains 7 pictures, 1 thumbnail and 6 thumbnail originals. The arrangement of each group of pictures is shown in Fig. 6. In order to make the subjects fully understand the experimental task, the experimental purpose, experimental steps, evaluation index definition and scoring standard were introduced in detail before the experiment.

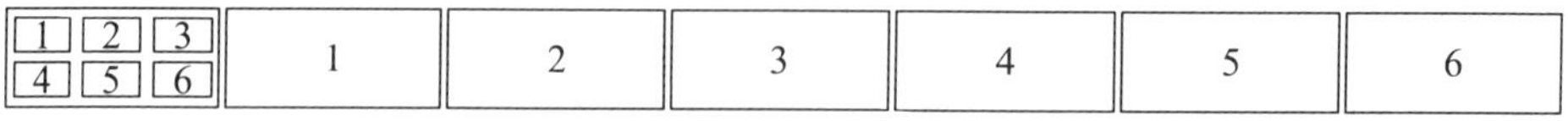

Fig. 6 Grouping diagram

The Experimental Steps

First, play the thumbnails of the first group of pictures. The subject needs to choose the picture that can attract the most visual attention, and fill in 100 points in the corresponding position of the form. Take this picture as the standard, and grade the remaining 5 pictures on the thumbnail, with the score ranging from 0 to 100.

Second, according to the sequence in figure 4, 6 original pictures in this group are played in turn. The subjects need to mark the elements that can attract visual attention on the pictures, ranging from 1 to 5.

Third, repeat the first two steps and play the next set of pictures until the end of the experiment.

Matters Needing Attention

Try to put aside your feelings and personal preferences.

The most visual attention is directed to the most visual attention rather than the first.

If there are multiple principals of a type, further distinctions can be made. For example, two people need to mark which one attracts more attention from you.

Ignore the habit of looking from left to right and wait until you've seen all the parts of the image before deciding on the most visually appealing ones.

In order to avoid causing visual fatigue or physical discomfort of the subjects, the score was not accurate. After 10 groups of evaluation, the subjects rested for 5 minutes.

3.2 Second Experiment

The Experiment Purpose

The purpose of this experiment is to prevent the first experiment's grouping from being affected by differences in score levels. Therefore, for each participant, 100 images were selected, with 20 images in the second grade, and the fractional weight was calculated. According to the scores from the second experiment, the images that scored over 100 points were grouped again. The raw scores of the other images were multiplied by the percentage of the rating scores, which were used as the final score.

Twenty 100-point images were randomly placed on a white background the size of the original image in four rows and five columns.

The Experiment Steps

The first step is to watch the thumbnail of the 100-point picture of the subject, select the picture that can attract the most visual attention, and fill in 100 points in the corresponding position of the form.

The second step is to take the selected pictures as the standard and score the remaining 19 pictures. More than 100 pictures can be selected as 100 points, with the score ranging from 60 to 100 (the default "pass" of the pictures rated as 100 points in the first experiment is 60 or greater).

4. RESEARCH RESULTS AND DISCUSSION

4.1 Reliability Analysis

IBM SPSS Statistics 24 was used to analyze the experimental data, and the consistency test results were shown in Table 1.

Table 1 Consistency test

Title	Pleasure	Arousal	Dominance	Harmony	Visual Attention
Cronbach's Alpha	0.939	0.950	0.850	0.964	0.939
Test–retest Reliability	0.886	0.886	0.870	0.886	–

Cronbach's Alpha is used to measure the internal consistency of a group of questions in the questionnaire, and the retest reliability refers to the repeated measurement of the same batch of subjects at different times, that is, the external consistency. As can be seen from Table 1, the internal reliability coefficient reaches more than 0.8, suggesting that the scale has a high internal consistency. The retest data reliability coefficient is greater than 0.8, indicating the strong correlation between the two data. Therefore, the experimental results are considered credible.

4.2 Visual Attention Element Statistics

Significant elements of the markers were counted and divided into six categories according to content similarity, as shown in Table 2. The first behavior is visual attention element type. The number immediately below each category corresponds to the marked visual attention element, and the number after each element represents the marked times. The more times it was tagged, the more visual attention it was thought to attract. The first category of the table is the color category, which belongs to the color category whether it is a single color contrast or multiple color combinations. Brightness can be regarded as a color with zero hue and saturation, so it is classified as a color. The second category is the texture category, which refers to those areas with similar repetitive individuals, with a granular sense, and a sharp contrast with the surrounding. The third category is shape category, which refers to the shape and appearance of objects or graphics. Common regular shapes include rectangle, triangle, circle and so on. The plane geometry is composed of lines, which can be classified into one category for quantification. The fourth category is spatial position, which is divided into absolute position and relative position. Relative position refers to the position relationship between objects, the distance from significant objects or the arrangement of repeated rules, all of which belong to relative position. The fifth category is depth of field, both foreground depth and posterior depth of field are part of depth of field. The sixth category is the perception category, which refers to objects that can be easily recognized, such as people or animals. Another part is the silhouette of significant objects, which can be recognized by human beings based on the contour to attract more attention. This article does not consider perceptive classes because they are of concern because of their content rather than object characteristics.

A Study of Visual Attention Elements with Experiment Analysis Based on Composition

By analyzing the first five categories in Table 2 and the histogram of classification statistics in Fig. 7, it is easy to see that color category is the category with the most marks, followed by shape category and spatial position category, which are significantly more than the remaining two categories. Therefore, it is considered that the color, shape and spatial position in a picture are more likely to attract visual attention. In the color category, large area of the same color area is a kind of element that has been marked the most times. Compared with other elements, large area of the same color area with high brightness and large contrast has been marked more times, indicating that people pay more attention to large area of the same color area and brightness in the color category.

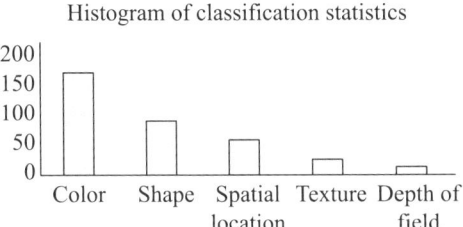

Fig. 7 Classification statistics

Table 2 Visual attention element

	Color class-172	Texture class-17	Shape class-86	Spatial location class-60	Depth of field class-9	*Perception class-109*
Salient elements	a large area of same color – 55	large texture complexity -17	salient line – 64	absolute position:	depth of filed – 6	*salient object -104*
	high brightness – 47		circular – 10	symmetry axis – 25	the scene ahead – 3	*concise – 5*
	high brightness contrast – 31		rectangle – 9	central location – 19		
	color contrast – 17		triangle – 3	power points – 10		
	colorful – 17			three point line – 1		
	color harmony – 5			the relative position:		
				repetitive regular arrangement – 3		
				with other salient object distance – 2		

For the shape class, the marked line is the most, and it is more than the sum of the marked times of other classes, indicating that continuous straight lines and curves are more attractive than specific shapes. In the spatial position class, symmetry axis and center position are marked more frequently, indicating that the elements at the symmetry axis and center position are more attractive to visual attention. In addition, the elements of the three points of strength can attract more visual attention. For depth-of-field elements, people are more aware of the clear elements in the depth-of-field composition.

4.3 Visual Attention-Harmony

The relationship between the visual attention degree and the harmony degree caused by a picture is shown in Fig. 8. When the picture is very harmonious, the visual attention is the most, which is much higher than other cases, indicating that people pay attention to and pursue the balance and harmony of the picture subconsciously. In this experiment, no one marked the very discordant database, so the degree of visual attention it attracted could not be determined. But in several other cases, the neutral ones were the ones that drew the least visual attention, in line with people's low interest in pictures without highlights in daily life.

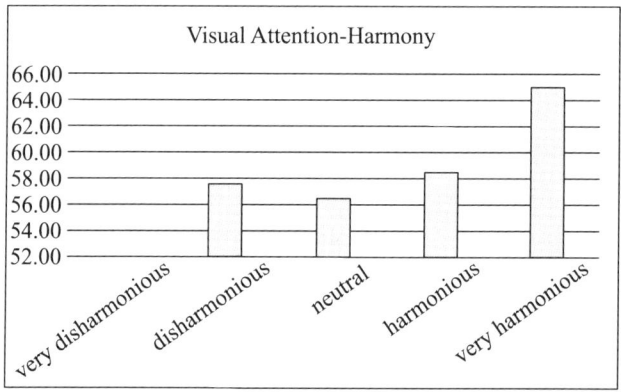

Fig. 8 Visual Attention-Harmony

4.4 PAD - Harmony

PAD emotional model scores with different degrees of harmony are shown in Fig. 9. One interesting finding: discordant images are often sensitive, unpleasant, and passive; For neutral pictures, people's emotional ups and downs are not obvious, indicating that people pay less attention to neutral pictures; When people saw the harmonious pictures, all the emotion scores were plus, which was a positive emotion. As the degree of harmony increases, people's feelings of pleasure become very strong, and the degree of arousal and dominance are higher than the general harmonious pictures, and tend to be more positive emotions. It can be thought that the more harmonious the picture, the more positive emotions can be aroused.

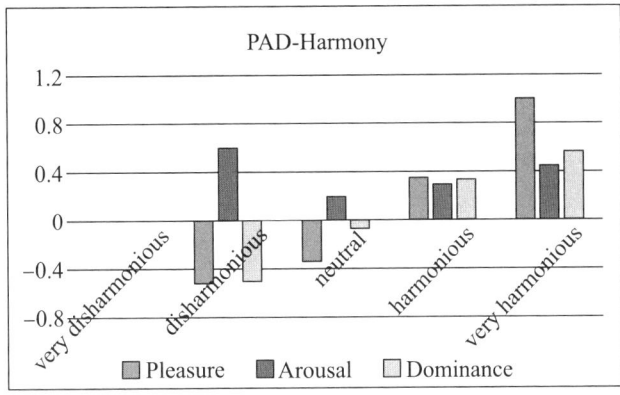

Fig. 9 PAD - Harmony

4.5 PAD - Visual Attention

The score of PAD emotional model with different visual attentions is shown in Fig. 10. With the increase of visual attentions caused by pictures, the degree of pleasure, arousal and dominance tends to be positive, indicating that pleasant, exciting and confident pictures can attract people's visual attention more.

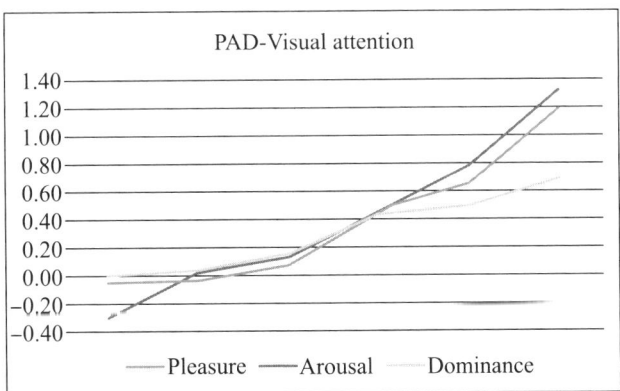

Fig. 10 PAD - Visual Attention

It can be seen from the above that the more harmonious the picture is, the more balanced the vision is, the more visual attention will be aroused, and the more positive the emotion will be. In art and visual perception, "why do people need balance? The answer is: 'because it makes people feel gratified and happy'", which is exactly consistent with our analysis.

5. CONCLUSION

In this paper, the subjective evaluation experiment of visual attention element screening was carried out by building a material base based on image composition features, and the elements causing visual attention were screened out and classified and summarized. The final visual attention elements can be divided into the following six categories: color, texture, spatial position, shape, depth of field and perception. The main conclusions are as follows: (1) color class, shape class and spatial position class element is the most can cause the visual attention of three kinds of elements; (2) in the color category caused more visual attention is the high brightness and large area of the same color region; (3) shape class in the prominent line can cause visual attention; (4) in the spatial position class is located in the axis of symmetry and the center position can cause the visual attention. Finally, the validity is verified by consistency test.

Visual attention element screening is an important step in the feature mining and extraction of image composition, which provides technical support for the quantification of visual balance in the next composition and promotes the research on the mining and extraction of visual perception features in the processing of audio-visual fusion information. At the same time, it has great reference value to the model building of visual attention domain.

ACKNOWLEDGMENT

This study was supported by Key Laboratory Research Funds of Ministry of Culture and Tourism.Title: Audio-visual Oriented Research on Visual Perceptual Feature Extraction.

REFERENCES

[1] Liu L, Chen R, Wolf L, et al. Optimizing photo composition [J]. Computer Graphics Forum, 2010, 29(2):469-478.

[2] Arnheim R. Art and visual perception [M]. 1st ed. Teng S, Zhu J, trans. Chengdu: People's Publishing House of Sichuan, 1998: 43-66.

[3] Treisman A M, Gelade G. A feature-integration theory of attention [J]. Cognitive psychology. 1980, 12:97-136.

[4] Koch C, Ullman S. Shifts in selective visual attention: towards the underlying neural circuitry [J]. Hum neurobiol, 1985, 4(2):219-227.

[5] Itti L, Koch C, Niebur E. A model of saliency-based visual attention for rapid scene analysis [J]. IEEE trans pattern anal mach intell. 1998, 20(11):1254-1259.

[6] Ma Y F, Zhang H J. Contrast-based image attention analysis by using fuzzy growing [C]. Proceedings of the Eleventh ACM International Conference on Multimedia. USA, 2003:

374-381.

[7] Harel J, Koch C, Perona P. Graph-based visual saliency [C]. Proc Adv Neural Inf Process Syst. Canada, 2006: 545–552.

[8] Bruce N, Tsotsos J. Saliency based on information maximization [C]. Proc Adv Neural Inf Process Syst. Canada, 2005: 155-162.

[9] Gao D, Vasconcelos N. Bottom-up saliency is a discriminant process [C]. Proceedings of the 11th International Conference on Computer Vision. Brazil, 2007: 185-190.

[10] Hou X, Zhang L. Saliency detection: a spectral residual approach [C]. Proceedings of IEEE Conference on Computer Vision and Pattern Recognition. USA, 2007: 1-8.

[11] Murray N, Vanrell M, Otazu X, et al. Saliency estimation using a non-parametric low-level vision model [C]. Proceedings of IEEE Conference on Computer Vision and Pattern Recognition. USA, 2011: 433-440.

[12] Seo H J, Milanfar P. Nonparametric bottom-up saliency detection by self-resemblance [C]. IEEE Conference on Computer Vision and Pattern Recognition Workshops. 2009: 45-52.

[13] Mehrabian A. Basic dimensions for a general psychological theory [J]. Moral Psychology, 1989.

[14] Zhang T. Research on emotional speech based on PAD three-dimensional emotional model [D]. Taiyuan: Taiyuan University of Technology, 2018.

The Association Between Timbre of Musical Sound and Texture*

1. INTRODUCTION

Music and pictures are two important media for people to understand the world. They can generate corresponding psychological feelings when acting on people alone. Not only that, music and pictures will influence each other when acting on people at the same time. For example, the reason why horror movies are so horrible is inseparable from the roll of weird incidental music. If accompanied by cheerful music, the feeling of horror will be greatly destroyed. Predecessors have done some research in the association of music and images. Taking synesthesia as the entry point, Zhou studied objects that can be expressed by music and concluded that music can express visual objects. That is to say, there is a certain association between music and visual images. Many researchers have also studied the association between music and color, one of the most important features of images. Palmer and others used the method of subjective evaluation experiment to prove the strong association between music and color, and believed that the association was mediated by emotion. Zhang also believes strong associations between music and color mediated by emotion. A large number of studies have shown that music and pictures are correlated, but timbre and texture as two elements of music and pictures respectively, are they correlated?

Langlois and others studied the relationship between music and texture, and believed there was a strong association between music and texture. Unlike the association between color and music, the association of music and texture is not only related to emotions, but also to other factors. All of the above studies on the association of music and images are qualitative studies that do not quantify this association. There is also no specific study of the association between the timbre features of music and the texture features of images. In order to further study the association between timbre and texture, this paper obtains timbre

---

① The paper was originally published in *2019 IEEE/ACIS 18th International Conference on Computer and Information Science (ICIS)*, June 2019, and has since been revised with new information. It was co-authored by Xiaoyi Zhang, Jingyu Liu, and Wei Jiang (corresponding author).

perception features and the matching relationship between timbre and texture by subjective evaluation experiment. Then Pearson correlation coefficient is used to verify whether there is an association between timbre and texture. If there is an association, Machine Learning is used to establish the association model.

This paper studies the association between texture and timbre, and they are two sub-features respectively of vision and auditory sense. Generally speaking, it belongs to the field of audio-visual fusion, which can provide basic data and technical support for the research of audio-visual fusion. The structure of this paper is as follows: the second part introduces the selection of texture materials used in the subjective evaluation experiment and the implementation process of the subjective evaluation experiment; The third part introduces the process of analyzing the timbre perception features and the matching data of texture and timbre obtained from the subjective evaluation experiment. In the fourth part, the data were input into Logistic, random forest and BP neural network. The prediction model of texture-timbre matching relationship was established, and the performance of each model was compared. The fifth part summarizes this paper and explains the next research plan.

2. SUBJECTIVE EVALUATION EXPERIMENT

Texture Feature Extraction

First of all, we need to select the texture pictures used in subjective evaluation experiments according to the features of each texture picture. Therefore, the following texture features are extracted with a total of 44 dimensions:

Gray level co-occurrence matrix: for an image, the gray value is i at the coordinates (x, y), and the distance between the coordinates (x, y) and $(x + \Delta x, y + \Delta y)$ in the θ direction is d. The probability of the gray value being j at the coordinate $(x + \Delta x, y + \Delta y)$ is $P(i, j, d, \theta)$, as in (1):

$$P(i,j,d,\theta) = \{[(x,y),(x+\Delta x, y+\Delta y)] / f(x,y) = i, f(x+\Delta x, y+\Delta y) = j\} \quad (1)$$

The theta generally takes 0°, 45°, 90°, 135°. Thus, a probability matrix is obtained, namely, the gray level co-occurrence matrix.

Fractal dimension: A grayscale image can be decomposed into a number of boxes of size $L \times L \times L'$, where L is the number of pixels, L' is the gray value, and N_L is the number of boxes in the image. Then, the fractal dimension is as in (2):

$$D = \lim \frac{\log N_L}{\log L^{-1}} \quad (2)$$

Gaussian Markov model: assuming that s is a point in the image where the gray value is y(s), the Gaussian Markov model can be expressed by formula (3):

$$y(s) = \sum_{r \in N_s} \theta_r \left[y(s+r) + y(s-r) \right] + e(s) \quad (3)$$

where $[y(s+r)+y(s-r)]$ is the neighborhood of point s, r is the neighborhood radius, θ_r is the coefficient, and $e(s)$ is the zero-mean Gaussian noise sequence.

Gabor filtering: extracting texture features with Gabor filtering can better simulate the visual perception characteristics of human visual system. Common Gabor filters are shown in formula (4):

$$\varphi_{(u,v)}(z) = \frac{\|k_{(u,v)}\|^2}{\sigma^2} e^{-\left(\frac{\|k_{(u,v)}\|^2 |z|^2}{2\sigma^2}\right)} \left[e^{jk_{u,v} \cdot z} - e^{-\frac{\sigma^2}{2}} \right] \tag{4}$$

where u is the direction and v is the scale factor. $Z = (x, y)$, $k_{u,v} = k_v e^{j\varphi_u}$, $k_v = k_{max} / f^v$, $\varphi_u = \pi u / 8$, k_{max} is the maximum frequency.

Wavelet feature: The separable variable method constructs a one-dimensional wavelet function and a scale function into a two-dimensional wavelet function for texture feature extraction.

Tamura features: in 1978, Tamura et al. proposed a texture feature extraction method based on human visual perception of texture, which is mainly composed of the following six features:

Coarseness (coarse or fine): the size or number of texture elements that make up the texture image.

Contrast (high contrast or low contrast): the dynamic range of gray levels in the image and the sharpness of the edges.

Directionality (directional or nondirectional): Whether the image has a clear direction or not.

Line-likeness (line-like or blob-like): Whether the shape of the texture element is line-shaped or blob-shaped.

Regularity (regular or irregular): Whether the elements that make up the texture are regular, and whether the position of the element is regular.

Roughness (rough or smooth): If you touch this texture, it feels rougher or smoother.

Texture Image Selection

The texture images used in this paper were selected from 111 texture images in the Brodatz texture library. The image selection process mainly includes the following steps:

In order to minimize the influence of the brightness of the picture on the experimental results, the brightness z-score of each texture images is calculated, and then the image with the z-score greater than 1.5 is removed. The images left after screening are screened again in the same way. There are 83 images remaining after this step.

In order to avoid the semantic information carried in the image from interfering with the judgment of the subject, the image with obvious semantic information in the library is removed. As shown in Fig. 1:

Fig. 1 Images with obvious semantic information

The extracted 44-dimensional texture features were used for System Clustering and Multi-dimensional Scaling (MDS).

System Clustering is also called hierarchical clustering. Each sample in the data is an initial cluster, and then the two closest samples are merged step by step. In this paper, the average distance is adopted to calculate the distance, as in (5) :

$$d_{avg}(C_i, C_j) = \frac{1}{|C_i||C_j|} \sum_{x \in C_i} \sum_{z \in C_j} dist(x, z) \tag{5}$$

Multidimensional scaling analysis is to place n samples in a relatively low-dimensional space, such as m-dimensional space, and keep the distance between any two samples in m-dimensional space the same as the original distance. This distance is generally calculated by Euclidean distance. Assuming that the coordinates of sample i and sample j in the m-dimensional space are $X_i = (x_{i1}, x_{i2}, \cdots, x_{im})$ and $X_j = (x_{j1}, x_{j2}, \cdots, x_{jm})$ respectively, the Euclidean distance d_{ij} between the two points is:

$$d_{ij} = \sqrt{\sum_{k=1}^{m}(x_{ik} - x_{jk})^2} = \| X_i - X_j \| \tag{6}$$

The obtained cluster pedigree map and MDS distribution map are respectively shown in Fig. 2 and Fig. 3, and the images are filtered according to the obtained results. Filter the images based on the results of the cluster analysis and the following criteria:

(1) Ensure that selected images cover all categories.
(2) Do not select texture images that carry obvious semantic information.
(3) In the subjective sense, the similarity between the images is small, and the texture features are comprehensive.
(4) Ensure that the pictures are more scattered on the multidimensional scale analysis map.

The last 18 texture images selected are shown in Fig. 4.

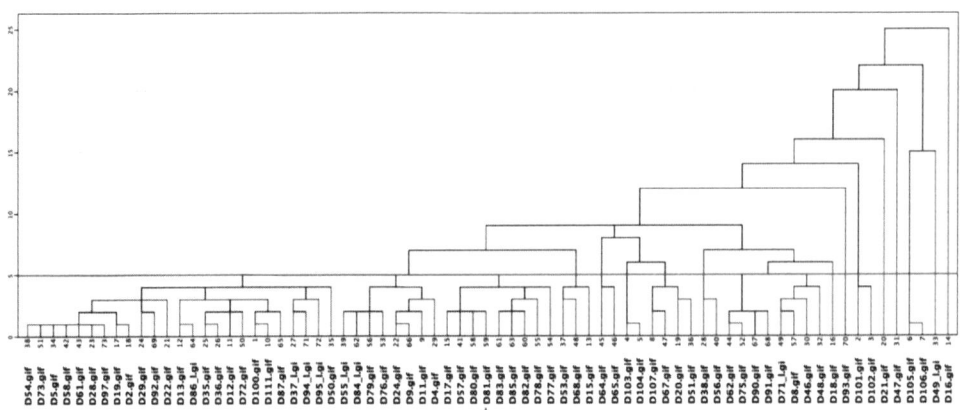

Fig. 2 Cluster pedigree map of texture images

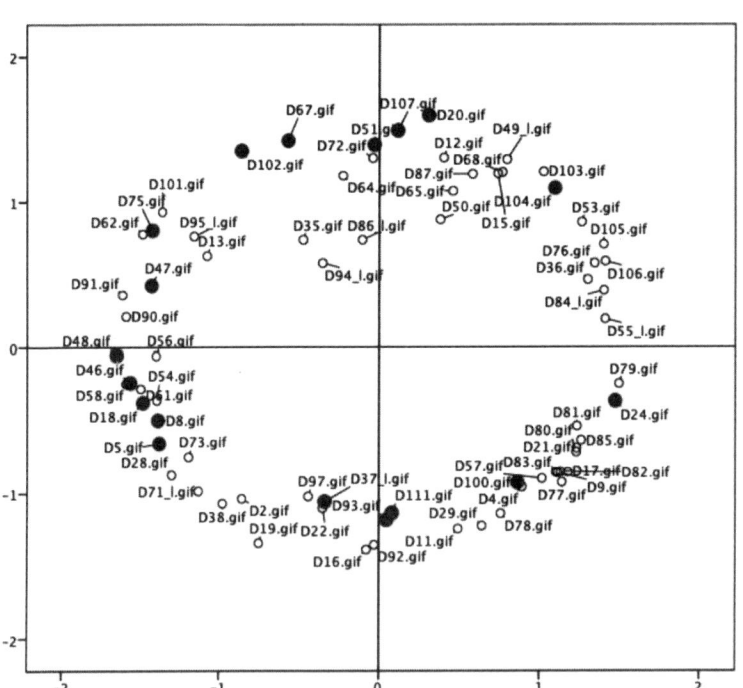

Fig. 3 Multi-dimensional scaling map of texture images

Scan the QR code to see colorful figures

Scan the QR code to see colorful figures

The Association Between Timbre of Musical Sound and Texture

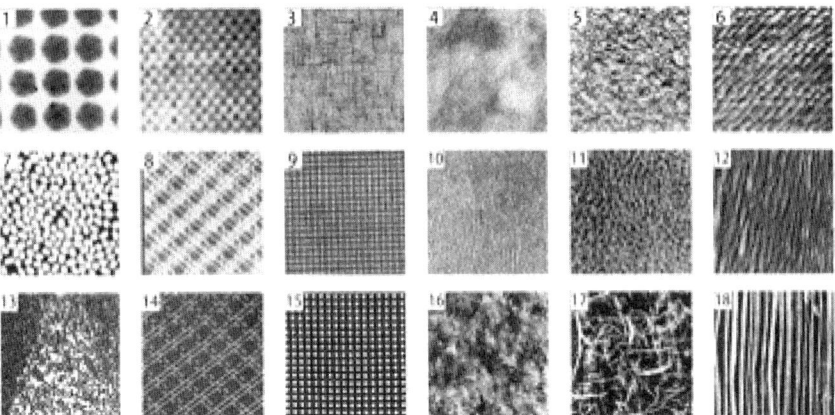

Fig. 4 Final elected texture image

In Figure 3, the red color is the distribution position of the selected texture image in the two-dimensional space. It can be seen that the selected image covers the whole space and can represent various types of texture images.

Subjective Evaluation Experiment

The subjective evaluation experiment mainly consists of two parts: the first part is the timbre perception feature annotation; the second part is the timbre and texture association.

Both experiments used 72 segments of audio recorded in the anechoic room. Each audio contained only one musical scale variation without a specific melody. The 72-segment audio includes 24 Western instruments (such as clarinet, harp, piano, etc.) and 48 national instruments (such as *erhu* fiddle, lute, *xun*, etc.). The two parts of the experimental subjects were the same, with a total of 32 students, including 11 male students and 21 female students. They are all students of Communication University of China, aged between 20 and 30, and have a certain listening experience.

For the experiment of the first part of the timbre perception feature annotation, the subjects evaluated on the 9-level scale for the five pairs of timbre perception features of the 72-segment audio. These five pairs of timbre features are derived from previous research, including: bright-dark, dry-soft, sharp-thick, rough-pure, hoarse-concord.

In the second part of the experiment of timbre and texture association, the subjects were asked to select 3 texture images that matched the timbre of the played audio and 3 texture images that did not match from the 18 texture images displayed on the screen while listening to 72 audio clips.

3. EXPERIMENTAL DATA ANALYSIS

Data Processing

In order to verify whether there is a correlation between timbre and texture, this paper will use the value of audio timbre features and corresponding texture features that matched (or mismatched) the audio for correlation analysis. The values of timbre perception features were obtained by subjective evaluation experiments of the timbre perception feature annotation. Considering that the timbre features used are perception features, the Tamura texture feature proposed by psychology, was used for correlation analysis.

The experimental data were processed according to formula (5). For the instrument audio m (m=1, 2, … ,72), the number of texture image t (t=1, 2, … ,18) selected to match the audio is $N_t^{m,y}$, and the Tamura feature i of texture image t is T_t^i (i =1, 2, … ,6), then the average value $TC^{m,y,i}$ (i =1, 2, … ,6) of the texture feature i that match the audio m is:

$$TC^{m,y,i} = \frac{1}{96} * \sum_{t=1}^{18}\left(N_t^{m,y} * T_t^i\right) \qquad (7)$$

Similarly, the average value $TC^{m,n,i}$ (i = 1, 2, … , 6) of the texture feature i that does not match the audio m are:

$$TC^{m,n,i} = \frac{1}{96} * \sum_{t=1}^{18}\left(N_t^{m,n} * T_t^i\right) \qquad (8)$$

The subject r (r = 1, 2, 32) evaluates the timbre perception feature x of the audio m as $e_r^{m,x}$, then the average evaluation value of 32 subjects is used as the value y of timbre perception feature x of the audio m, as in (9):

$$E_x^m = \frac{1}{32} * \sum_{r=1}^{32} e_r^{m,x} \qquad (9)$$

Pearson Correlation Analysis

Fig. 5, 6, 7, 8 are scatter plots of an average texture feature that match (mismatch) the audio changing with one timbre feature. The horizontal axis is a certain timbre feature of audio m, and the vertical axis is a certain texture feature:

The Association Between Timbre of Musical Sound and Texture

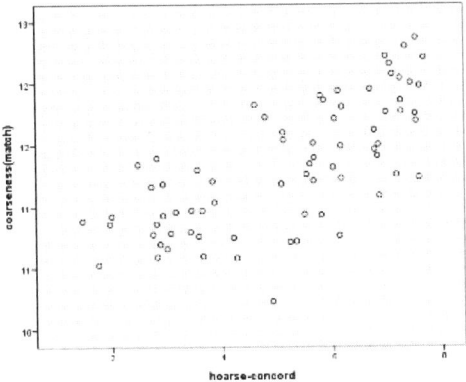

Fig. 5 An scatter plots of coarseness changing with hoarse-concord (match)

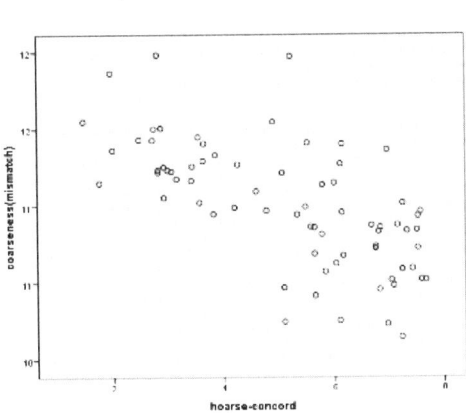

Fig. 6 An scatter plots of coarseness changing with hoarse-concord (mismatch)

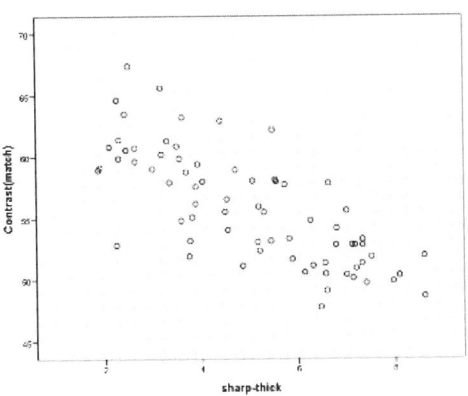

Fig. 7 An scatter plots of contrast changing with sharp-thick (match)

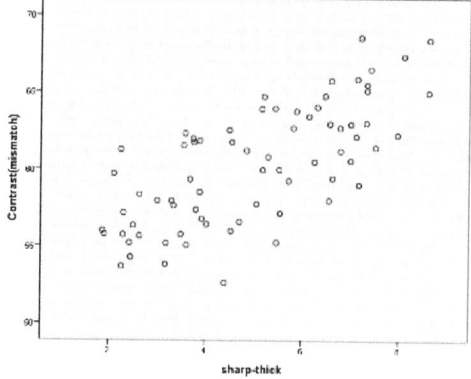

Fig. 8 An scatter plots of contrast changing with sharp-thick (mismatch)

It can be seen from these figures that there is an obvious correlation between some timbre features and texture features. And the trend of the feature value of the selected matched texture changing with the timbre feature is opposite to that of the mismatched texture changing with the timbre feature. For example, the texture thickness that matches the hoarse- concord increases with the increase of the degree of concord, while the texture thickness that does not match the hoarse-concord decreases with the increase of the degree of concord.

Furthermore, Pearson correlation coefficient is used to analyze the correlation between 5 pairs of timbre features and 6-dimensional texture average feature values that match (mismatch) the audio. The results are shown in Table 1:

Table 1 Pearson correlation coefficient between timbre features and texture features

	Bright-dark	Dry-soft	Sharp-thick	Rough-pure	Hoarse-concord
Coarseness (match)	−0.335	0.698	0.025	0.677	0.708
Contrast (match)	−0.659	0.066	−0.752	0.275	0.174
Directionality (match)	−0.188	−0.455	−0.449	−0.325	−0.387
Line-likeness (match)	0.244	−0.040	0.260	−0.125	−0.088
Regularity (match)	−0.024	−0.069	−0.083	−0.121	−0.123

Table 1 Continued

	Bright-dark	Dry-soft	Sharp-thick	Rough-pure	Hoarse-concord
Roughness (match)	−0.682	0.141	−0.734	0.343	0.248
Coarseness (mismatch)	0.278	−0.652	−0.034	−0.630	−0.655
Contrast (mismatch)	0.649	−0.140	0.716	−0.303	−0.212
Directionality (mismatch)	0.317	0.152	0.482	0.033	0.068
Line-likeness (mismatch)	−0.212	−0.078	−0.322	0.010	0.018
Regularity (mismatch)	0.048	0.014	−0.037	−0.032	−0.001
Roughness (mismatch)	0.654	−0.201	0.687	−0.356	−0.271

As can be seen from Table 1, some texture features are strongly correlated with timbre features, such as: coarseness with dry-soft, rough-pure and hoarse-concord; contrast and roughness with bright-dark and sharp-thick. The absolute value of the correlation coefficient peaked at 0.752. There is also an insignificant correlation between roughness and bright-dark, directionality and all kinds of features of timbre, line-likeness and sharp-thick, roughness and rough-pure.

On the whole, the softer, purer, concordant music selects a texture with a larger texture element size. And the darker, thicker sound selects a texture with a lower contrast and roughness. From the above data, it can be seen that there is a strong association between texture and timbre.

4. TIMBRE AND TEXTURE ASSOCIATED MODEL

The data obtained from the subjective evaluation experiment are sorted into a sample including 5-dimensional timbre features, corresponding 6-dimensional texture features and matching tags between them. If the match tag is 1, it means match, and 0 means mismatch. A total of 13398 pieces of sample data were input into the machine learning algorithm for modeling.

Logical regression, random forest and BP neural network algorithm were used for modeling.

Logistic regression actually transforms the predicted value z obtained by linear regression into h by using Sigmoid function, and the value h represents the probability estimation classified as positive examples. According to the determined decision boundary, it is generally 0.5. If $h \geqslant 0.5$, it is classified as a positive example; if $h \leqslant 0.5$, it is classified as a negative example. The Sigmoid function is as in (10):

$$h = \frac{1}{1+e^{-z}} \tag{10}$$

The random forest uses the Bootstrap to extract n data sets from the original data set. The number of samples in each data set is approximately 2/3 of the original data set. A tree is established for each data set. During the establishment process, a subset containing k attributes is randomly selected for each node, and then an optimal attribute is selected from the subset to branch.

BP neural network usually consists of input layer, hidden layer and output layer. When the algorithm runs, it will pass the input layer information forward layer by layer. The error is calculated after passing to the output layer, and then the error is propagated back to the hidden layer. The neural network used in this paper has a hidden layer with 6 nodes.

When modeling, 80% in the data set is used as the training set, and the remaining 20% is used as the test set. The evaluation indicators commonly used in binary classification are: Precision, Recall, and AUC (Area Under Curve). Precision refers to the proportion of correctly predicted data in the predicted matched data. Recall refers to the proportion of correctly predicted data in the data that is actually matched, and AUC (Area Under Curve) is the Area Under ROC Curve.

$$\text{Precision} = \frac{TP}{TP+FP} \tag{11}$$

$$\text{Recall} = \frac{TP}{TP+FN} \tag{12}$$

where TN is the number of data predicted to be mismatched and actually mismatched; FP is the number of data predicted to be matched and actually mismatched; FN is the number of data predicted to be mismatch and actually matched; TP is the number of data predicted to be matched and actually matched.

It can be seen that the precision rate and recall rate are negatively correlated. High precision rate means low recall rate. The AUC can measure the situation between the two. The higher the AUC, the better.

The modeling results of the three algorithms used in this paper are shown in Fig. 9:

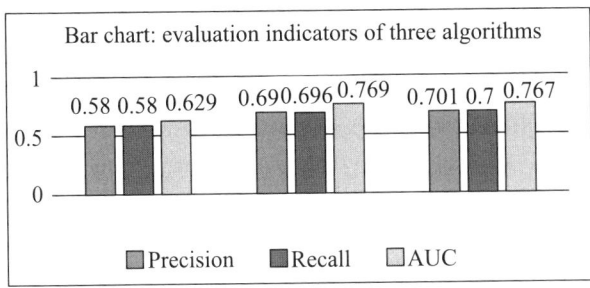

Fig. 9 Bar chart: evaluation indicators of three algorithms

It can be seen from Fig. 9 that the results of random forest and BP neural network are better than Logistic. The performance of the classification of random forest and BP neural network is similar. The precision and recall rate of BP neural network can reach 70%, which can realize the task of predicting the matching relationship between texture and timbre.

5. CONCLUSION

In this paper, the following conclusions can be drawn based on the Pearson correlation coefficient: some texture features are strongly correlated with timbre features, such as: coarseness with dry-soft, rough-pure and hoarse-concord; contrast and roughness with bright-dark and sharp-thick.

The prediction results of the matching relationship between texture and timbre features by Logistic, random forest and BP neural network show that the random forest and BP neural network have higher precision, and the precision of BP neural network reaches 70%, which further verifies the association between timbre and texture. Prediction of the matching relationship between timbre and texture can be achieved.

The following work will be carried out in the next step: supplement the data volume, try more machine learning algorithms, and analyze and screen more texture features to build more accurate, stable and generalized models.

REFERENCES

[1] Zhou H. Music and the world it represents [M]. Beijing: Central Conservatory of Music Press, 2004.

[2] Palmer S E, Schloss K B, Xu Z, et al. Music-color associations are mediated by emotion [J]. Proceedings of the national academy of sciences of the United States of America, 2013, 110(22): 8836-8841.

[3] Zhang C. The role of emotion between music and color association [D]. Shanghai: East China Normal University, 2014.

[4] Langlois T, Peterson J, Palmer S E. Visual texture, music, and emotion [J]. Journal of vision, 2014, 14(10): 437.

[5] Liao M, Chen G. Classification of remote sensing images based on gray level co-occurrence matrix [J]. Scientific and technological innovation, 2018(28): 20-21.

[6] Zhao Y, Hu J, Li M, et al. Fractal dimension of image texture feature representation [J]. Journal of Shanghai Dianji University, 2011, 14(1): 39-43.

[7] Wang Y, Wang H. Application of rank GMRF in textural description and recognition [J]. Computer engineering and applications, 2011, 47(25): 202-204.

[8] Meng B, Wang X, Li D. Color texture features extraction based on quaternion Gabor [J]. Computer engineering and science, 2018, 40(9): 1636-1645.

[9] Wang S, Yi X, Yan W. The extraction of texture features based on wavelet transform [J]. Sci-tech information development & economy, 2008, 18(11): 149-150.

[10] Tamura H, Mori S, Yamawaki T. Textural features corresponding to visual perception [J]. IEEE transactions on systems, man, and cybernetics, 1978, 8(6): 460-473.

[11] Brodatz P. Textures: a photographic album for artists and designers [M]. New York: Dover Publications, 1966.

[12] Zhou Z. Machine Learning [M]. Beijing: Tsinghua University Press, 2016.

[13] Shi X, Yin A, Chen X. RSSI and multidimensional scaling based indoor localization algorithm [J]. Chinese journal of scientific instrument, 2014, 35(2): 449-456.

[14] Wang J, Guo Z. Logistic regression model: method and application [M]. Beijing: Higher Education Press, 2001.

[15] Cutler A, Cutler D R, Stevens J R. Random forests [J]. Machine learning, 2001, 45(1): 157-176.

[16] Huang L. BP neural network algorithm improvement and application research [D]. Chongqing: Chongqing Normal University, 2008.

A Study of Color–Emotion Image Set Construction and Feature Analysis*

1. INTRODUCTION

Human perception towards outside world exists dependently. Human brain is an optimized multi-sensory information fusion system, which can correlate different modal information from different sensory channels automatically, and can uniformly perceive, associate, express and evaluate the outside world. Researchers refer to this phenomenon that visual information and auditory information interact with each other and act on people together as the audio-visual fusion effect. The method of information processing is widely used to study this effect, and the precondition for this research is to construct the visual material sets and auditory material sets.

The mechanism of human emotions can well solve the "gap" between visual information and auditory information. The National Institute of Mental Health (NIMH) has constructed the International Affective Picture System (IAPS) and the International Affective Digital Sound system (IADS) in 1998. These two systems are respectively labelled by Pleasure, Arousal and Dominance, which are the normalized emotional stimulation systems. Since their inception, IAPS and IADS are widely used in the field of audio-visual emotion. However, they ignore the relation between visual information and auditory information. In vision, color has rich visual perceptual features, including cool-warm, heavy-hard, swell-shrink, etc. The formation of these feelings both depends on human visual characteristics and physical properties of light. In addition, color can also cause strong emotional reflections of people.

First of all, this paper constructs the color-emotion image set and provides the guidance for the audio-visual fusion material set. Secondly, based on the construction scheme, this paper introduces each step in detail, including the collection and processing of materials, features extraction and the experiment to label materials. Thirdly, this paper analyzes the

---

① The paper was originally published in *2019 IEEE/ACIS 18th International Conference on Computer and Information Science (ICIS)*, June 2019, and has since been revised with new information. It was co-authored by Wei Jiang (corresponding author), Shuang Wang, Yanan Su, and Jingyu Liu.

features, which is the most important part. Finally, a conclusion is given.

2. IMAGE SET CONSTRUCTION SCHEME

Based on the construction of color-emotion image set, Fig. 1 gives the general scheme about constructing an image set to offer theory guidance, method suggestion and technical support for the future work.

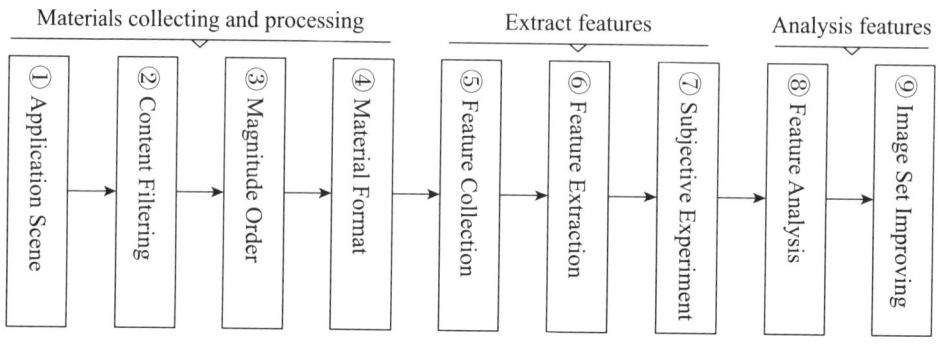

Fig. 1 Image set construction flow chart

Part one ranges from step 1 to step 4, including collecting and processing materials. Firstly, it is necessary to make sure the application scene and the classification method of this scene. Secondly, the content which may affect the results must be excluded. Thirdly, collect the materials according to the above requirements and magnitude order. Finally, process the material format unified.

Part two ranges from step 5 to step 7, including feature extraction and subjective experiment. Feature extraction contains subjective feature extraction and objective feature extraction. Subjective experiment refers to emotion labeling by subjects.

Part three ranges from step 8 to step 9, including feature analysis and image set improving. After feature extraction, analysis is needed including data reliability analysis, feature completeness test and correlation analysis among features. Then, the materials are supposed to be improved according to the analysis. Finally, it is a continuous process to improve materials according to the expansion of the detailed research, the change of application scene and the update of relevant technologies.

3. MATERIAL COLLECTING AND PROCESSING

3.1 Application Scene Determining

The application scene of audio-visual fusion is the research of audio-visual matching in films. The materials come from screenshots of the scene in films. Scene refers to a group of continuous shots at a single location, and the screenshot of a scene refers to one still picture in the scene, namely a single frame. A film set is needed to construct the image set. This paper crawls the data from popular movie webs, namely Douban, Mtime, Internet Movie Database (IMDB) and Apple Trailer. The classification standard is summarized into 23 types. They are dramatic film, romance film, comedy, science fiction film, action film, suspense film, crime, horror film, war film, literary film, film noir, biography, erotic film, music film, family film, thriller, adventure film, fantasy film, dance film, historical film, western film, costume film and swordsmen film. The number distribution of different film types is shown in Fig. 2.

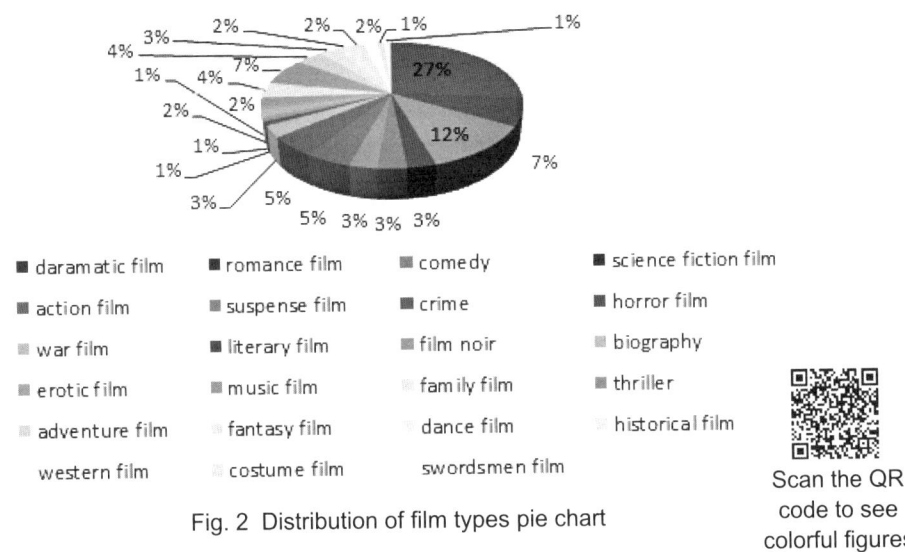

Fig. 2 Distribution of film types pie chart

Scan the QR code to see colorful figures

This paper plans to download 100 films. To reserve the distribution information, the numbers of different types are downloaded following the distribution. In addition, the rating and fever of a film are both taken into consideration. This paper puts the film which has the high rating from the popular films into the set.

3.2 Content Filtering

In this paper, the requirements of the contents of materials are as follows:

(a) The screenshots are in color, and do not contain virtual characters (except animals).

(b) The screenshots are clearly visible, and it is best to see all details clearly.

(c) The screenshots with obvious semantic information of emotional orientation are supposed to be deleted. e.g. characters with visible expression, something that have some symbolic significance such as the national flag, text information, including subtitles, billboards, newspapers, etc.

(d) Avoid repeated scenes.

(e) Try to choose screenshots that can stimulate the physical or psychological reactions of people.

3.3 Format and Magnitude Determining

The color-emotion image set contains a total of 120 screenshots, with the resolution of 1280*720dpi and the aspect ratio of 16:9. The screenshots do not contain black edges, and the format is unified as JPEG which can get a better image quality with the minimal disk space. It is supposed to be noted that the image processing should avoid stretching, and ensure that there is no obvious difference in the spatial position of the original object in the screenshot.

4. OBJECTIVE FEATURE EXTRACTION

The objective features of this paper are color features, namely hue feature and color tone feature. On one hand, based on the hue as the classification standard, this paper divides the Itten Twelve-color Phase Loop into six evenly-spaced uniform distribution as the basic colors. As shown in Fig. 3, this paper regards red (R:255, G:0, B:0), yellow (R:255, G:255, B:0), green (R:0, G:255, B:0), cyan (R:0, G:255, B:255), blue (R:0, G:0, B:255), magenta (R:255, G:0, B:255) as six basic attributes of hue feature. On the other hand, based on the color tone as the classification standard, this paper divides color tone into three basic attributes, including cool tone, warm tone and medium tone. Among them, cool tone gives people a cool feeling, warm tone gives people a warm feeling, and medium tone gives people a fuzzy feeling. The screenshots in the image set are labeled by these attributes respectively according to these two classification standards.

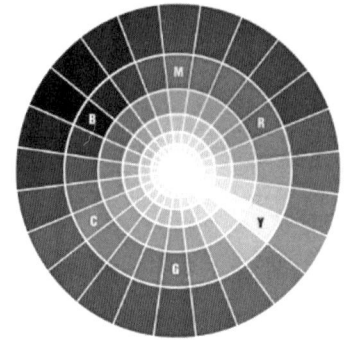

Fig. 3 Itten Twelve-color Phase Loop

Scan the QR code to see colorful figures

4.1 Dominant Color Extraction Algorithm (DCE)

Because of too many colors existing in a screenshot, this paper adopts a clustering algorithm to extract the dominate colors of the screenshot. Set $\{x^{(1)},...,x^{(2)}\}$ as the training samples, each $x^{(i)} \in R^n$, steps are as follows:

Step 1: Randomly select K clustering centroids $\mu_1, \mu_2, ..., \mu_k \in R^n$.

Step 2: For each sample i, calculate the class that it should belong to:

$$c^{(i)} := undersetj \arg\min \| x^{(i)} - \mu^{(i)} \|^2 \quad (1)$$

Among them, $c^{(i)}$ is the goal class which has the shortest Euclidean Distance between sample i and K clustering centroids.

Step 3: For each class j, recalculate the centroid of the class:

$$\mu_j := \frac{\sum_{i=1}^{m} 1\{c^{(i)} = j\} x^{(i)}}{\sum_{i=1}^{m} 1\{c^{(i)} = j\}} \quad (2)$$

Step 4: Repeat step 2 and step 3 until μ_j remains unchanged, and the iteration is finished.

When analyzing the color matching style of the scene, artists often use the color palette to present the dominate colors. In Fig. 4, a color palette is arranged from left to right in the form of equal area color blocks. A color palette can visually present the color matching style of the scene, and this paper designs the DCE Algorithm to present the color palette model. However, it also has some disadvantages of losing the spatial location information and energy distribution information of colors.

Scan the QR code to see colorful figures

Fig. 4 A screenshot of *Alice's Adventures in Wonderland 2* and its color palette

The following improvements has been made to the DCE Algorithm, which is called Weight Dominate Color Extraction Algorithm (WDCE). On the basis of the original clustering algorithm, the clustering center weight matrix *Tab* will be calculated, and the color palette matrix *sumR* which contains color weight information will be reconstructed. The flow chart of the WDCE Algorithm is shown in Fig. 5.

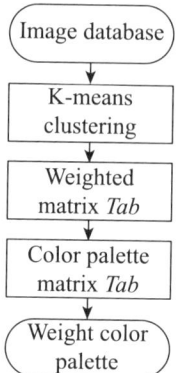

Fig. 5 The flow chart of WDCE Algorithm

Among them, the clustering center weight matrix *Tab=K*Tabulate* (*Value, Count, Percent*), *K* presents the number of clustering centers, and *Tabulate* matrix contains three basic parameters: *Value* presents the class identity, *Count* presents the number of samples in the class, *Percent* presents the class frequency. According to the weight of each cluster center of *Tab* matrix, the color palette matrix *sumR* can be reconstructed. Fig. 6 shows the comparison between the original screenshot and the weight color palette, where *K*=8.

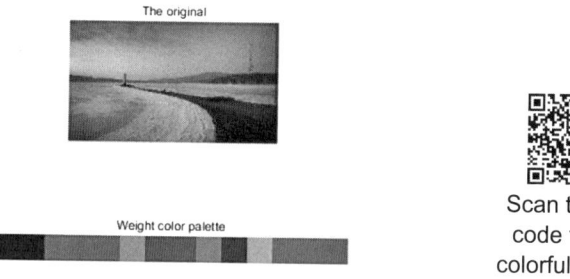

Fig. 6 The comparison between the original screenshot and the weight color palette

As shown in Fig. 6, the weight color palette retains the energy distribution information of colors and presents the color matching style of the film, which provides a better quantitative way to extract color features.

In this paper, the color with the highest energy distribution is selected as the classification basic. Compared to RGB color space, HSV color space is closer to human visual experience. Therefore, this paper uses HSV color space to quantify the color, and makes a choice among red, yellow, green, cyan, blue, magenta which has the shortest

Euclidian Distance with the quantified color as its hue attribute.

4.2 Cool-Warm Quantization Algorithm

In this paper, the membership function is improved on the basis of Wang's cool-warm quantization algorithm based on fuzzy mathematics, which takes red as the warm pole and cyan as the cool pole to make it more consistent with people's visual perception. Steps are as follows:

Step 1: Initialize the clustering center C: $c_1 = 0°$, $c_2 = 180°$.

Step 2: Initialize membership functions U:

$$u_{i,1} = \begin{cases} \cosh, & 0 \leqslant h < 90° \text{ or } 270° \leqslant h < 360° \\ 0, & \text{others} \end{cases} \quad (3)$$

$$u_{i,2} = \begin{cases} \cos(h-180°), & 90° \leqslant h < 270° \\ 0, & \text{others} \end{cases} \quad (4)$$

Among them, $u_{i,1}$ presents the membership function of warm attribute and $u_{i,2}$ presents the membership function of cool attribute.

Step 3: Update the clustering center C as follows:

$$c_j = \frac{\sum_{i=1}^{n} u_{ij} x_i}{\sum_{i=1}^{n} u_{ij}} \quad (5)$$

Step 4: Update the membership functions U as follows:

$$u_{i,j} = \frac{1}{\sum_{k=1}^{c} \left(\frac{\| x_j - c_i \|}{\| x_j - c_k \|} \right)^{\left(\frac{2}{m-1}\right)}} \quad (6)$$

Step 5: Repeat step 3 and step 4 until $u_{i,j}$ remains unchanged, and the iteration is finished.

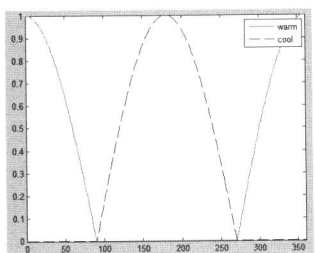

Scan the QR code to see colorful figures

Fig. 7 The improved initialization membership function

In this paper, the screenshot is labeled according to the membership function value of cool-warm attribute. As shown in Fig. 7, when warm>cool, warm tone is labeled. When warm<cool, cool tone is labeled. When warm=cool, medium tone is labeled.

4.3 Subjective Feature Extraction

Emotional labeling of screenshots is carried out through the subjective evaluation experiment. PAD emotion model is selected, and P presents pleasure, A presents arousal and D presents dominance.

Subjects: 10 college students. The male/female ratio was 3:7. There was no color blindness among subjects.

Materials: 120 screenshots and 6 repeated screenshots with a random order.

Conditions: The experiment was arranged in the underground sound insulation room, and the light environment was supposed to be consistent each time. A display was used to play materials with the aspect ratio of 16:9 so that materials would not be out of shape.

Procedures: Subjects were required to score P, A, D for each material at five scales.

5. EXPERIMENT RESULTS AND ANALYSIS

5.1 Reliability Analysis of Emotion Labeling Experiment

Table 1 Reliability analysis

	Pleasure	Arousal	Dominance
Cronbach's alpha	0.879	0.713	0.802
Test-retest	0.934	0.879	0.872

As shown in Tab. 1, the results of Cronbach's alpha and test-retest meet the requirements, so the experimental results are reliable.

5.2 Correlation Analysis Between Color and PAD

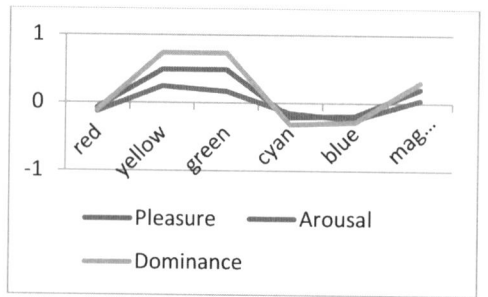

Scan the QR code to see colorful figures

Fig. 8 Mean distribution diagram between color and PAD

As shown in Fig. 8, the value of P, A and D show the consistent change trend in the clockwise direction from red to magenta: it gradually increases from red to yellow, reaches a peak between yellow and green, then gradually decreases from green to cyan, reaches a valley between cyan and blue, and finally rises again from blue to magenta, and circulates in turn. It can be seen that emotions corresponding to yellow and green are relatively positive, while emotions corresponding to cyan and blue are relatively negative. The value of P, A and D cross the zero point in the interval from green to cyan, indicating that the transition colors from green to cyan has no obvious emotional tendency.

5.3 Standard Deviation Analysis Between Color and PAD

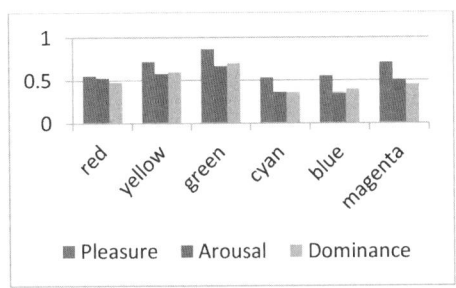

Scan the QR code to see colorful figures

Fig. 9 Standard deviation distribution diagram between color and PAD

As shown in Fig. 9, the standard deviation of P is the highest in each basic color class, and the difference between the standard deviations of A and D is not big in each class, indicating that the score difference of P in the same basic color class is higher than those of A and D, which may result from the weaker influence of color on P than those of A and D. The standard deviations of cyan to P, A and D are all the lowest compared with other basic colors, indicating that cyan has obvious emotional tendency. The standard deviations of green to P, A and D are all the highest compared with other basic colors, indicating that the emotional tendency of green is fuzzy.

5.4 Correlation Analysis Between Color and Film Type

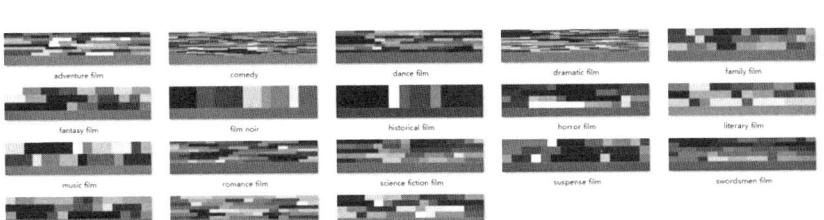

Scan the QR code to see colorful figures

Fig. 10 Weight color palette distribution diagram with different film type

As shown in Fig. 10, some typical film types are selected to present the correlation between color and film type. The top of the picture shows the superposition of all the weight color palettes with the same film type, and the bottom is the mean value of all the colors. There are some interesting findings:

(a) To increase a tension feeling, adventure films may have high contrast on brightness.
(b) To create a nostalgic style, the saturation of literary films may be lower.
(c) Because of the sense of science and technology, blue may be the dominate color of the science fiction films.
(d) The west is associated with the desert so that yellow is the dominate color of this film type.

5.5 Basic Information of the Image Set

This paper records the image set according to the following information: number, film name, film country, film type, intercepting time, hue, color tone, emotion. Other information is shown in Table 2 and Table 3.

Table 2 Basic information

Area	Number of Samples
Film	120
Associated Tasks	**Number of Features**
Regression	3

Table 3 Features and attributes information

Hue	*Red*	29	*Cyan*	19
	Yellow	40	*Blue*	12
	Green	9	*Magenta*	11
Color Tone	*Cool*	42		
	Warm	73		
	Medium	5		
Emotion	Pleasure			
	Arousal			
	Dominance			

6. CONCLUSION AND FUTURE WORK

Under the background of audio-visual fusion and audio-visual fusion information processing research, on the basic of specific application of audio-visual matching research, the principle contributions of this paper are:

(a) Establishing the color-emotion image set and proposing a construction scheme.
(b) Proposing a method to replace the screenshot with the color palette as the classification basis with the energy distribution information of color features.
(c) Improving the cool-warm quantization algorithm, which is more consistent with people's visual perception.
(d) Making an in-depth analysis between color, emotion and film type.
(e) Providing data support and technical support to the research on audio-visual fusion effect and audio-visual fusion information processing.

Next, the audio-visual fusion material set will be further expanded, including visual material associated with visual perception and the construction of auditory material set. Moreover, it actively seeks for more high-level semantic features of visual information and auditory information, and conducts in-depth research on audio-visual fusion on this basis.

ACKNOWLEDGMENT
This study was supported by Key Laboratory Funds of Ministry of Culture and Tourism. Title: Audio-visual Oriented Research on Visual Perceptual Feature Extraction.

REFERENCES

[1] Zhou H. Music and the world it represents [M]. Beijing: Central Conservatory of Music Press, 2004.
[2] Palmer S E, Schloss K B, Xu Z, et al. Music-color associations are mediated by emotion [J]. Proceedings of the national academy of sciences of the United States of America, 2013, 110(22): 8836-8841.
[3] Zhang C. The role of emotion between music and color association [D]. Shanghai: East China Normal University, 2014.
[4] Langlois T, Peterson J, Palmer S E. Visual texture, music, and emotion [J]. Journal of Vision, 2014, 14(10): 437.
[5] Liao M, Chen G. Classification of remote sensing images based on gray level co-occurrence matrix [J]. Scientific and technological innovation, 2018(28): 20-21.

[6] Zhao Y, Hu J, Li M, et al. Fractal dimension of image texture feature representation [J]. Journal of Shanghai Dianji University, 2011, 14(1): 39-43.

[7] Wang Y, Wang H. Application of rank GMRF in textural description and recognition [J]. Computer engineering and applications, 2011, 47(25): 202-204.

[8] Meng B, Wang X, Li D. Color texture features extraction based on quaternion Gabor [J]. Computer engineering and science, 2018, 40(9): 1636-1645.

[9] Wang S, Yi X, Yan W. The extraction of texture features based on wavelet transform [J]. Sci-Tech information development & economy, 2008, 18(11): 149-150.

[10] Tamura H, Mori S, Yamawaki T. Textural features corresponding to visual perception [J]. IEEE transactions on systems, man, and cybernetics, 1978, 8(6): 460-473.

[11] Brodatz P. Textures: a photographic album for artists and designers [M]. New York: Dover Publications, 1966.

[12] Zhou Z. Machine learning [M]. Beijing: Tsinghua University Press, 2016.

[13] Shi X, Yin A, Chen X. RSSI and multidimensional scaling based indoor localization algorithm [J]. Chinese journal of scientific instrument, 2014, 35(2): 449-456.

[14] Wang J, Guo Z. Logistic regression model: method and application [M]. Beijing: Higher Education Press, 2001.

[15] Cutler A, Cutler D R, Stevens J R. Random forests [J]. Machine learning, 2001, 45(1): 157-176.

[16] Huang L. BP neural network algorithm improvement and application research [D]. Chongqing: Chongqing Normal University, 2008.

Analysis and Modelling of Timbre Perception Features in Musical Sounds[*]

1. INTRODUCTION

The subjective perception of sound originates from three auditory attributes: loudness, pitch, and timbre. In recent years, researchers have established relatively mature evaluation models for loudness and pitch, but a quantitative calculation and assessment of timbre is far more complicated. Studies have shown that timbre is a critical acoustic cue for conveying musical emotion. It also provides an important basis for human recognition and classification of music, voice, and ambient sounds. Therefore, the quantitative analysis of timbre and the establishment of a parameterized model are of significant interest in the fields of audio-visual information processing, music retrieval, and emotion recognition. The subjective nature of timbre complicates the evaluation process, which typically relies on subjective evaluations, signal processing, and statistical analysis. The American National Standards Institute (ANSI) defines timbre as an attribute of auditory sensation in terms of which a listener can judge that two sounds similarly presented and having the same loudness and pitch are dissimilar, making it an important factor for distinguishing musical tones.

Timbre evaluation terms (i.e., timbre adjectives) are an important metric for describing timbre perception features. As such, a comprehensive and representative terminology system is critical for ensuring the reliability of experimental auditory perception data. Conventionally, timbre evaluation research has focused on the fields of music and language sound quality, traffic road noise control, automobile or aircraft engine noise evaluation, audio equipment sound quality design, and soundscape evaluation. Among these, research in English-speaking countries is relatively mature, as shown in Table 1. However, differences in nationality, cultural background, customs, language, and environment

---

① The paper was originally published in *Applied Sciences*, 2020, 10 (3), and has since been revised with new information. It was co–authored by Wei Jiang, Jingyu Liu, Xiaoyi Zhang, Shuang Wang, and Yujian Jiang.

inevitably affect the cognition of timbre evaluation terms. In addition, Chinese instruments differ significantly from Western instruments in terms of their structure, production material, and sound production mechanisms. The timbre of Chinese instruments is also more diverse than that of Western instruments and existing English timbre evaluation terms may not be sufficient for describing these nuances. As such, the construction of musical timbre evaluation terms is of great significance to the study of Chinese instruments.

Table 1 Previous studies on timbre evaluation terms

Author	Year	Objects of Evaluation	Evaluation Terms
Solomon	1958	20 different passive sonar sounds	50 pairs
von Bismarck	1974	35 voiced and unvoiced speech sounds, musical sounds	30 pairs
Pratt and Doak	1976	Orchestral instrument (including string, woodwind, and brass)	19
Namba, et al.	1991	4 performances of the Promenades in "Pictures at an Exhibition"	60
Ethington and Punch	1994	Sound generated by an electronic synthesizer	124
Faure, et al.	1996	12 synthetic Western traditional instrument sounds	23
Iwamiya and Zhan	1997	24 music excerpts from CDs on the market	18 pairs
Howard and Tyrrell	1997	Western orchestral instruments, tuning fork, organ, and softly sung sounds.	21
Shibuya, et al.	1999	"A" major scale playing on the violin (including 3 bow force, 3 bow speed, and 3 sounding point)	20
Kuwano, et al.	2000	48 systematically controlled synthetic auditory warning sounds	16 pairs
Disley and Howard	2003	4 recordings of different organs	7
Moravec and Štepánek	2003	Orchestra instrument (including bow, wind, and keyboard)	30
Collier	2004	170 sonar sounds (including 23 different generating source types, 9 man–made, and 14 biological)	148
Martens and Marui	2005	9 distorted guitar sound (including three nominal distortion types)	11 pairs
Disley, et al.	2006	12 instrument samples from the McGill University master samples (MUMS) library (including woodwind, brass, string, and percussion)	15

Table 1 Continued

Author	Year	Objects of Evaluation	Evaluation Terms
Stepánek	2006	Violin sounds of tones B3, #F4, C5, G5, and D6 played using the same technique	25
Katz and Katz	2007	Music recording work	27
Howard, et al.	2007	12 acoustic instrument samples from the MUMS library, 3 from each of the 4 categories (including string, brass, woodwind, and percussion).	15
Barbot, et al.	2008	14 aircraft sounds (including departure and arrival)	90
Pedersen	2008	Stimuli may be anything that evokes a response; such stimuli may stimulate one or many of the senses (e.g., hearing, vision, touch, olfaction, or taste)	631
Alluri and Toiviainen	2010	One hundred musical excerpts (each with a duration of 1.5s) of Indian popular music, including a wide range of genres such as pop, rock, disco, and electronic, containing various instrument combinations.	36 pairs
Fritz, et al.	2012	Violin sound	61
Altinsoy and Jekosch	2012	Sounds of 24 cars in 8 driving conditions from different brands with different motorization to the participants	36
Elliott, et al.	2013	42 recordings representing the variety of instruments and include muted and vibrato versions where possible (included sustained tones at E–flat in octave 4)	16 pairs
Zacharakis, et al.	2014	23 sounds drawn from commonly used acoustic instruments, electric instruments, and synthesizers, with fundamental frequencies varying across three octaves	30
Skovenborg	2016	70 recordings or mixes ranging from project–studio demos to commercial pre–masters, plus some live recordings, all from rhythmic music genres, such as pop and rock	30
Wallmark	2019	Orchestral instruments (including woodwind, brass, string, and percussion)	50

Timbre contains complex information concerning the source of a sound. Humans can perform a series of tasks to recognize objects by listening to these sounds. As such, the quantitative analysis and description of timbre perception characteristics has broad implications in military and civil fields, such as instrument recognition, music emotion recognition, singing quality evaluation, active sonar echo detection, and underwater target recognition. Developing a mathematical model of timbre perception features is vital to achieving a quantitative description of timbre. Two primary methods have conventionally been used to quantify timbre perception features. The first is the concept of psychoacoustic parameters. That is, by analyzing the auditory characteristics of the human ear, a mathematical model can be established to represent subjective feelings, such as sharpness, roughness, and fluctuation strength. Since most of the experimental stimulus signals in these experiments were noise, the calculated value for the musical signal differed from the subjective feeling, which is both limited and one-sided. Another technique combines subjective evaluation experiments with statistical analysis. In other words, the experiment is designed according to differences in perceived features from sound signals, from which objective parameters can be extracted. The correlation between objective parameters and perceived features is established through statistical analysis or machine learning, which is then used to develop a mathematical model of the perceived features. This approach has been widely used in the fields of timbre modeling, music information retrieval, instrument classification, instrument consonance evaluation, interior car sound evaluation, and underwater target recognition. However, the experimental materials in these studies were Western instruments or noise. Chinese instruments are unique in their mechanisms of sound production and playing techniques, producing a rich timbre variety. As such, it is necessary to use Chinese instruments as a stimulus to establish a more complete timbre perception model.

Timbre is an auditory attribute with multiple dimensions, which can be represented by a continuous timbre space. This structure is of great importance to the quantitative analysis and classification of sound properties. The semantic differential method was used in early timbre space research. Recently, multidimensional scaling (MDS) based on dissimilarity has been used to construct these spaces. For example, Grey used 16 Western instrument sound samples to create a three-dimensional (3D) timbre space. McAdams et al. studied the common dimensions of timbre spaces with synthetic sounds used as experimental materials, establishing a relationship between the dimensions of a space and the corresponding acoustic parameters. Martens et al. used guitar timbre to study the differences in timbre spaces constructed under different language backgrounds. Zacharakis and Pastiadis conducted a subjective evaluation and analysis using 16 Western musical instruments, proposing a luminance–texture–mass (LTM) model for semantic evaluation. In this process, six semantic scales were analyzed using principal component analysis (PCA) and multidimensional scaling (MDS) to produce two different timbre spaces. Simurra and Queiroz used a set of 33 orchestral music excerpts that were subjectively rated using quantitative scales based on 13 pairs of opposing verbal attributes. Factor analysis was included to identify major perceptual categories associated with tactile and visual properties, such as mass, brightness, color, and scattering. Multidimensional scaling requires the acquisition of a dissimilarity matrix between each sample. However, existing methods use a paired comparison technique for the subjective evaluation experiment. This approach not only involves a large experimental workload, it also imposes a higher professional requirement, making the evaluation scale difficult to control. This paper proposes a new indirect model for constructing timbre spaces based on the method of successive categories. In this system, the dissimilarity matrix is calculated based on experimental data from the method of successive categories. This reduces the workload and increases the stability and reliability of the data.

The remainder of this paper is organized as follows. Section 2 introduces the timbre library construction process and Section 3 develops the timbre evaluation terminology. Section 4 introduces the perception feature model, and the timbre space is constructed in Section 5. Section 6 concludes the paper. The research methodology for the study is presented in Fig. 1.

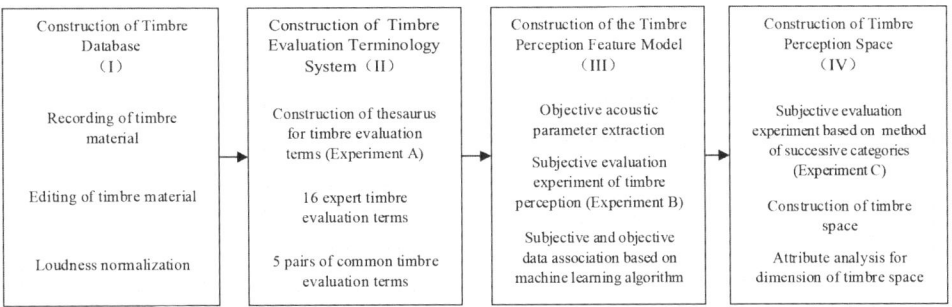

Fig. 1 The proposed methodology

2. TIMBRE DATABASE CONSTRUCTION

2.1 Timbre Material Collection

A high-quality database of timbre materials was constructed by recording all materials required for the experiment in a full anechoic chamber, with a background noise level of −2 dBA. The equipment included a BK 4190 free-field microphone and a BK LAN-XI3560 AD converter. The performers were teachers and graduate students from the College of

Music. Recordings consisted of musical scales and individual pieces of music. The Avid Pro Tools HD software was used to edit the audio material. The length of each clip was between 6–10s, the sampling rate was 44,100Hz, the quantization accuracy was 16 bits, and all audio was saved in the .wav format. Previous studies on timbre used Western instruments as stimulus materials. However, the variety of timbre samples needed to be as rich as possible to increase the accuracy of timbre perception features. The timbre variety was enriched by using a collection of 72 different musical instruments, including 36 Chinese orchestral instruments, 12 Chinese minority instruments, and 24 Western orchestral instruments. The names and categories of the 72 instruments are listed in Appendix A. A timbre library containing 72 audio files was constructed from the data.

2.2 Loudness Normalization

In accordance with the definition of timbre, the influence of pitch and loudness are often excluded from timbre studies. However, previous research has shown that timbre and pitch are not independent in certain cases. As such, timbre perception features presented in this paper include pitch as a factor. In order to eliminate the influence of loudness, a balance experiment was used to normalize the loudness of the timbre materials based on experimental results.

3. CONSTRUCTION OF THE TIMBRE SUBJECTIVE EVALUATION TERM SYSTEM

A timbre evaluation glossary including 32 evaluation terms was constructed and a subjective timbre evaluation experiment was conducted, based on a forced selection methodology (experiment A). Sixteen representative timbre evaluation terms were selected by combining the results of a clustering analysis. Finally, correlation analysis was used to calculate the correlation of these 16 evaluation terms. Six terms with a coefficient larger than 0.85 were removed. The remaining 10 terms were paired into five groups with opposite polarity (the absolute value of the correlation coefficient was greater than 0.81). These five pairs were used for timbre evaluation experiments based on the method of successive categories (experiment B), as well as the parametric modeling of timbre perception features.

3.1 Construction of the Thesaurus for Timbre Evaluation Terms

A thorough investigation of timbre evaluation terms was conducted under conditions of equivalent sound. A total of 329 terms were collected from the literature and a survey. Five people with a professional music background then deleted 155 of these terms (e.g., polysemy, ambiguous meaning, compound terms, etc.) that were, in their opinion, not suitable for a subjective experiment. A group of 21 music professionals listened to audio clips of the remaining 174 terms and judged whether they were suitable for describing the sound. The 32 most frequent evaluation terms were selected and a lexicon containing 32 timbre metrics was produced (Table 2). These terms completely describe all aspects of timbre dynamics, but they do include some redundant information, which needed to be assessed further using statistical analysis.

Table 2 A lexicon of 32 timbre evaluation terms in their original language (Chinese), with an accompanying English translation

暗淡 (dark)	饱满 (plump)	纯净 (pure)	粗糙 (coarse)
丰满 (full)	沙哑 (raspy)	干涩 (dry)	厚实 (thick)
尖锐 (sharp)	紧张 (intense)	空洞 (hollow)	明亮 (bright)
生硬 (rigid)	嘶哑 (hoarse)	透亮 (clear)	透明 (transparent)
粗涩 (rough)	单薄 (thin)	低沉 (deep)	丰厚 (rich)
厚重 (heavy)	浑厚 (vigorous)	混浊 (muddy)	尖厉 (shrill)
清脆 (silvery)	柔和 (mellow)	柔软 (soft)	刺耳 (raucous)
温暖 (warm)	纤细 (slim)	协和 (consonant)	圆润 (fruity)

3.2 Experiment A: A Subjective Evaluation Experiment Based on a Forced Selection Methodology

A subjective evaluation experiment was conducted in a standard listening room with a reverberation time of 0.3s, which conforms to listening standards. A total of 41 music professionals (21 males) participated in the experiment. Their ages ranged between 18 and 35 and they had no history of hearing loss. A forced selection methodology was employed in which audio clips from the material library were played in turn and subjects determined whether a given evaluation term was suitable for describing the audio clip. Clustering analysis and correlation analysis were then used to assess the experimental data (as discussed below), producing a music expert timbre evaluation term system (including 16 evaluation terms) and an ordinary timbre evaluation term system (including 5 pairs of evaluation terms with opposite polarity).

3.3 Data Analysis and Conclusion of Experiment A

A multidimensional scale was used to analyze the distance relationships for 32 evaluation terms in the two-dimensional space. The distance relationship between the 32 terms is shown in Fig. 2. It is evident from Fig. 2 that the distance between terms was small in some regions, indicating a high degree of correlation. In order to reduce the workload of subsequent timbre perception feature modeling, cluster analysis was used to further reduce the dimensionality of the evaluation terms. Fig. 3 shows a cluster pedigree diagram calculated using a system clustering method. Using this diagram and the selection frequency obtained previously, the 32 terms were combined to produce 16 timbre evaluation terms (see Table 3). These 16 terms constituted the music expert timbre evaluation system used in the modeling of timbre spaces (Experiment C).

Table 3 A musical expert timbre evaluation term system, including 16 timbre evaluation terms in their original language (Chinese) and the corresponding English translations

暗淡 (dark)	尖锐 (sharp)	协和 (consonant)	纯净 (pure)
粗糙 (coarse)	清脆 (silvery)	纤细 (slim)	单薄 (thin)
丰满 (full)	混浊 (muddy)	柔和 (mellow)	沙哑 (raspy)
厚实 (thick)	明亮 (bright)	嘶哑 (hoarse)	浑厚 (vigorous)

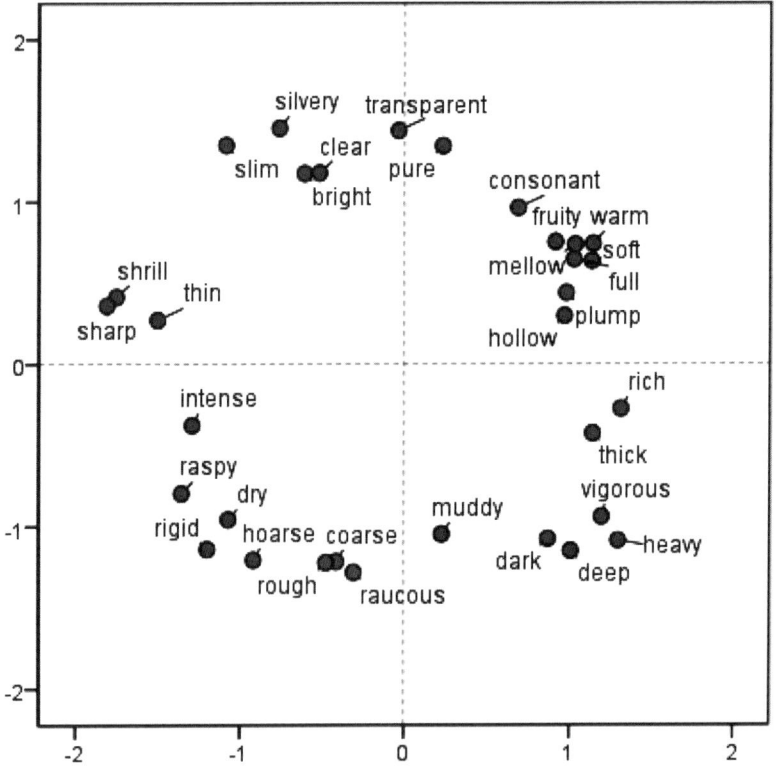

Fig. 2 The distance relationship between the 32 evaluation terms.

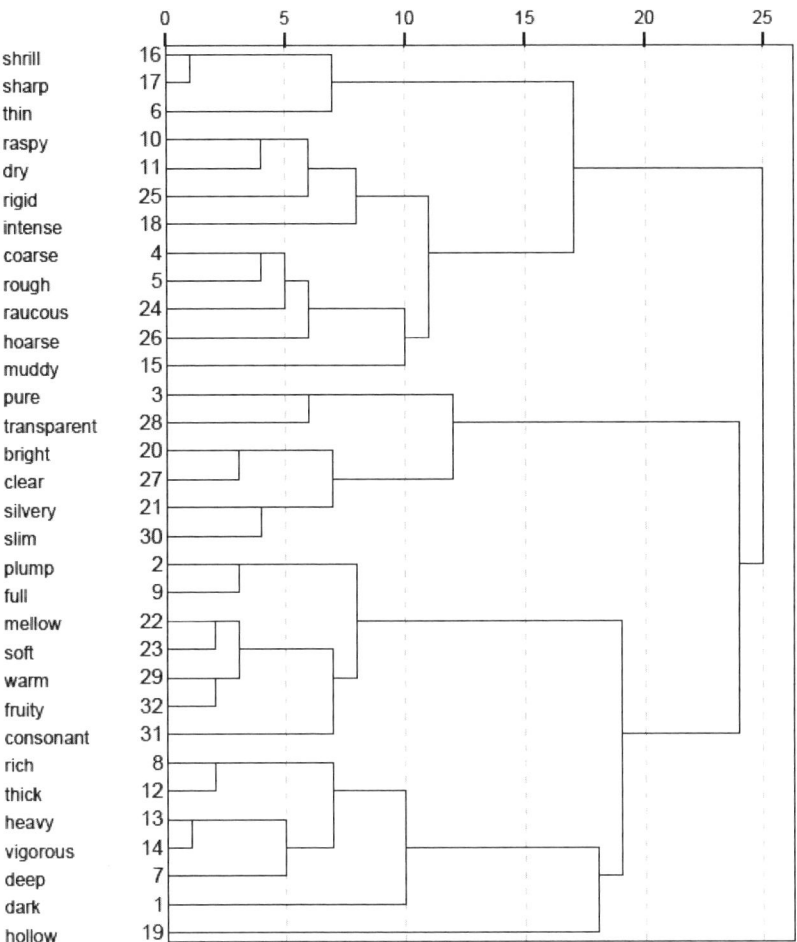

Fig. 3 A cluster diagram of 32 timbre evaluation terms.

A common timbre evaluation terminology system was then developed by calculating the Pearson correlation coefficient (PCC) for these 16 terms. The 6 terms with the highest correlation (PCC > 0.85) were excluded, resulting in a correlation matrix for the remaining 10 terms (Table 4). Terms with negative PCCs or large absolute values were selected from this matrix to form evaluation pairs with opposite meanings. These 10 terms were then combined to form five pairs (Table 5), constituting an ordinary timbre evaluation system. These pairs were used for the timbre evaluation experiment based on the method of successive categories (Experiment B) and the parametric modeling of timbre perception features.

Table 4 A correlation matrix for 10 timbre evaluation terms

	bright	dark	sharp	vigorous	raspy	coarse	hoarse	consonant	mellow	pure
bright	1.00	−0.99	0.90	−0.93	0.24	−0.48	−0.31	0.13	−0.27	0.47
dark	−0.99	1.00	−0.89	0.93	−0.20	0.49	0.33	−0.17	0.26	−0.48
sharp	0.90	−0.89	1.00	−0.93	0.58	−0.14	0.06	−0.24	−0.57	0.17
vigorous	−0.93	0.93	−0.93	1.00	−0.43	0.31	0.09	0.06	0.37	−0.28
raspy	0.24	−0.20	0.58	−0.43	1.00	0.61	0.74	−0.83	−0.82	−0.51
coarse	−0.48	0.49	−0.14	0.31	0.61	1.00	0.89	−0.82	−0.55	−0.92
hoarse	−0.31	0.33	0.06	0.09	0.74	0.89	1.00	−0.86	−0.62	−0.83
consonant	0.13	−0.17	−0.24	0.06	−0.83	−0.82	−0.86	1.00	0.79	0.75
mellow	−0.27	0.26	−0.57	0.37	−0.82	−0.55	−0.62	0.79	1.00	0.51
pure	0.47	−0.48	0.17	−0.28	−0.51	−0.92	−0.83	0.75	0.51	1.00

Table 5 An ordinary timbre evaluation term system including five pairs of evaluation terms in their original language (Chinese) and the associated English translations

Name	Correlation Coefficient
明亮 – 暗淡 (bright–dark)	−0.99
沙哑 – 柔和 (raspy–mellow)	−0.82
尖锐 – 浑厚 (sharp–vigorous)	−0.93
粗糙 – 纯净 (coarse–pure)	−0.92
嘶哑 – 协和 (hoarse–consonant)	−0.86

4. CONSTRUCTION OF A TIMBRE PERCEPTION FEATURE MODEL

Objective acoustic parameters were extracted from audio samples in 166 dimensions. The method of successive categories was then used to conduct a timbre perception evaluation experiment (Experiment B), as well as reliability and validity analysis for the resulting data. Linear regression, support vector regression, a neural network, and a random forest algorithm were used to construct a timbre perception feature model. The accuracy of this model was then evaluated and it was used to predict timbre perception features for new audio materials.

4.1 Construction of the Objective Acoustic Parameter Set

Timbre is a multidimensional perception attribute that is closely related to the time-domain waveform and spectral structure of sound. In order to establish a timbre perception feature model, an objective acoustic parameter set was constructed using 54 parameters extracted from the timbre database. Objective acoustic parameters refer to any values acquired using a mathematical model representing a normal sound signal in the time and frequency domains. These 54 parameters can be divided into 6 categories:

(1) Temporal shape features: calculated from the waveform or the signal energy envelope (e.g., attack-time, temporal increase or decrease, and effective duration).
(2) Temporal features: auto-correlation coefficients with a zero-crossing rate.
(3) Energy features: referring to various energy content in the signal (i.e., global energy, harmonic energy, or noise energy).
(4) Spectral shape features: calculated from the short-time Fourier transform (STFT) of the signal (e.g., centroid, spread, skewness, kurtosis, slope, roll-off frequency, or Mel-frequency cepstral coefficients).
(5) Harmonic features: calculated using sinusoidal harmonic modeling of the signal (e.g., harmonic/noise ratio, odd-to-even and tristimulus harmonic energy ratio, and harmonic deviation).
(6) Perceptual features: calculated using a model of human hearing (i.e., relative specific loudness, sharpness, and spread).

4.2 Calculation Method

The acoustic parameters were calculated as follows. The spectral centroid for the magnitude spectrum of the STFT is given by:

$$C_t = \frac{\sum_{n=1}^{N} M_t[n] \times n}{\sum_{n=1}^{N} M_t[n]} \qquad (1)$$

where $M_t[n]$ is the magnitude of the Fourier transform at frame t and frequency n. This centroid is a measure of the spectral shape, where higher centroid values indicate "brighter" sounds. Spectral slope was calculated using a linear regression over spectral amplitude values. It should be noted that spectral slope is linearly dependent on the spectral centroid as follows:

$$slope(t_m) = \frac{1}{\sum_{k=1}^{K} a_k(t_m)} \times \frac{K \sum_{k=1}^{K} f_k \cdot a_k(t_m) - \sum_{k=1}^{K} f_k \cdot \sum_{k=1}^{K} a_k(t_m)}{K \sum_{k=1}^{K} f_k^2 - \left(\sum_{k=1}^{K} f_k\right)^2} \qquad (2)$$

where $slope(t_m)$ is the spectral slope at time t_m, a_k is the spectral amplitude at k, and f_k is the frequency at k. Tristimulus values were introduced by Pollard and Jansson as a timbral equivalent to color attributes in vision. The tristimulus comprises three different energy ratios, providing a description of the first harmonics in a spectrum:

$$T1(t_m) = \frac{a_1(t_m)}{\sum_{h=1}^{H} a_h(t_m)},$$

$$T2(t_m) = \frac{a_2(t_m) + a_3(t_m) + a_4(t_m)}{\sum_{h=1}^{H} a_h(t_m)}, \quad (3)$$

$$T3(t_m) = \frac{\sum_{h=5}^{H} a_h(t_m)}{\sum_{h=1}^{H} a_h(t_m)},$$

where H is the total number of partials and a_h is the amplitude of partial h.

Spectral flux is a time-varying descriptor calculated using STFT magnitudes. It represents the degree of variation in a spectrum over time, defined as unity minus the normalized correlation between successive a_k terms:

$$\text{spectral flux} = 1 - \frac{\sum_{k=1}^{K} a_k(t_{m-1}) a_k(t_m)}{\sqrt{\sum_{k=1}^{K} a_k(t_{m-1})^2} \sqrt{\sum_{k=1}^{K} a_k(t_m)^2}}. \quad (4)$$

Inharmonicity measures the departure of partial frequencies f_h from purely harmonic frequencies hf_0. It is calculated as a weighted sum of deviations from harmonicity for each individual partial:

$$\text{inharmo}(t_m) = \frac{2}{f_0(t_m)} \frac{\sum_{h=1}^{H} (f_h(t_m) - hf_0(t_m)) a_h^2(t_m)}{\sum_{h=1}^{H} a_h^2(t_m)}, \quad (5)$$

where f_0 is the fundamental frequency and f_h is the frequency of partial h.

Spectral roll-off was proposed by Scheirer and Slaney. It is defined as the frequency $f_c(t_m)$ below which 95% of the signal energy is contained:

$$\sum_{f=0}^{f_c(t_m)} a_f^2(t_m) = 0.95 \sum_{f=0}^{sr/2} a_f^2(t_m), \quad (6)$$

where $sr/2$ is the Nyquist frequency and a_f is the spectral amplitude at frequency f. In the case of harmonic sounds, it can be shown experimentally that spectral roll-off is related to the harmonic or noise cutoff frequency. The spectral roll-off also reveals an aspect of spectral shape as it is related to the brightness of a sound.

The odd-to-even harmonic energy ratio distinguishes sounds with a predominant energy at odd harmonics (such as the Guan) from other sounds with smoother spectral envelopes (such as the Suona). It is defined as:

$$OER(t_m) = \frac{\sum_{h=1}^{H/2} a_{2h-1}^2(t_m)}{\sum_{h=1}^{H/2} a_{2h}^2(t_m)}. \quad (7)$$

Twelve time-varying statistics were calculated for the 54 parameters, including the maximum, minimum, mean, variance, standard deviation, interquartile range, skewness coefficient, and kurtosis coefficient, producing an objective acoustic parameter set containing 166 dimensions (see Table 6). In this paper, Timbre Toolbox and MIRtoolbox were used for feature extraction. The corresponding acoustic parameters were extracted from materials in the timbre database and the acquired data were used to construct a timbre perception feature model.

Table 6   Acoustic parameters

Feature Name	Quantity	Feature Name	Quantity
Temporal Features		***Harmonic Spectral Shape***	
Log Attack Time	1	Harmonic Spectral Centroid	6
Temporal Increase	1	Harmonic Spectral Spread	6
Temporal Decrease	1	Harmonic Spectral Skewness	6
Temporal Centroid	1	Harmonic Spectral Kurtosis	6
Effective Duration	1	Harmonic Spectral Slope	6
Signal Auto-Correlation Function	12	Harmonic Spectral Decrease	1
Zero-Crossing Rate	1	Harmonic Spectral Roll–off	1
Energy Features		Harmonic Spectral Variation	3
Total Energy	1	***Perceptual Features***	
Total Energy Modulation	2	Loudness	1
Total Harmonic Energy	1	Relative Specific Loudness	24
Total Noise Energy	1	Sharpness	1
Spectral Features		Spread	1

Table 6 Continued

Feature Name	Quantity	Feature Name	Quantity
Spectral Centroid	6	***Perceptual Spectral Envelope Shape***	
Spectral Spread	6	Perceptual Spectral Centroid	6
Spectral Skewness	6	Perceptual Spectral Spread	6
Spectral Kurtosis	6	Perceptual Spectral Skewness	6
Spectral Slope	6	Perceptual Spectral Kurtosis	6
Spectral Decrease	1	Perceptual Spectral Slope	6
Spectral Roll–Off	1	Perceptual Spectral Decrease	1
Spectral Variation	3	Perceptual Spectral Roll–Off	1
MFCC	12	Perceptual Spectral Variation	3
Delta MFCC	12	Odd–to–Even Band Ratio	3
Delta Delta MFCC	12	Band Spectral Deviation	3
Harmonic Features		Band Tristimulus	9
Fundamental Frequency	1	***Various Features***	
Fundamental Frequency Modulation	2	Spectral Flatness	4
Noisiness	1	Spectral Crest	4
Inharmonicity	1	***Total Number of Features***	166
Harmonic Spectral Deviation	3		
Odd–to–Even Harmonic Ratio	3		
Harmonic Tristimulus	9		

4.3 Experiment B: A Timbre Evaluation Experiment Based on the Method of Successive Categories

A subjective evaluation experiment was conducted in a standard listening room with a reverberation time of 0.3s, which conforms to listening standards. A total of 34 subjects (16 males) with a professional music background participated in the experiment. Their ages ranged from 18 to 35 and they had no history of hearing loss. The experimental subjective evaluation process was conducted as follows. Material fragments were played, and the subjects judged the psychological scale of the piece for each timbre perception feature (evaluation term) in sequence, scoring it on a nine-level scale. All experimental materials were played prior to the formal experiment to familiarize subjects with the samples in advance. This was done to assist each subject in mastering the evaluation criteria and scoring scale, reducing the discretization of evaluation data for the same sample. Each piece was played twice with an interval of 5s and a sample length of 6–10s. Each evaluation term was tested for 10min, with a 15-min break every half hour.

The validity and reliability of data from these 34 samples were analyzed to calculate a correlation coefficient between the scores for each subject. The Euclidean distance between the evaluation terms was calculated using cluster analysis to identify the two subjects with the largest difference in each group. Some subjects may not have had a sufficient understanding of the purpose of the experiment. Data from these subjects were excluded and not used for subsequent timbre perception feature modeling. The method of successive categories was used to conduct a statistical analysis of the experimental data. The theoretical basis for this approach assumes the psychological scale to be a random variable, subject to a normal distribution. The boundary of each category was not a predetermined value, but a random variable identified from the experimental data. The Thurstone scale was then used to process the data and produce a psychological scale for all timbre materials and each perception feature for modeling purposes. Figure 4 shows the resulting scale for 72 musical instruments in 5 timbre evaluation dimensions. In each image, the dotted line represents the average value of each instrument in the corresponding dimension.

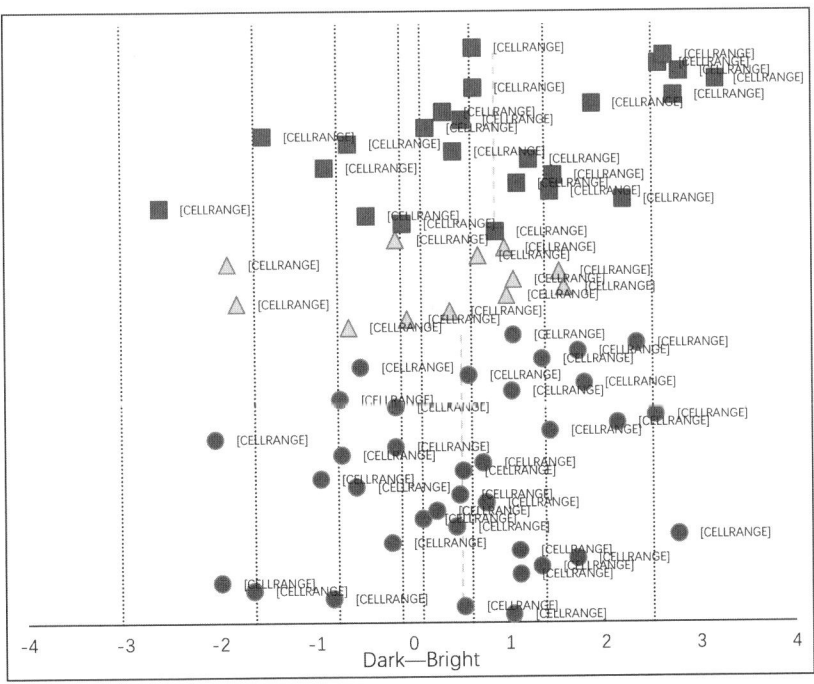

(a)

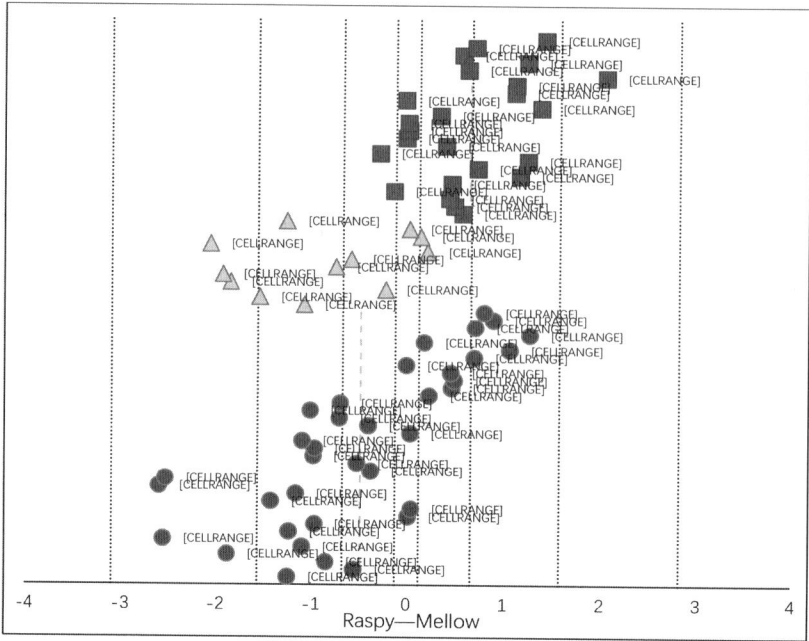

(b)

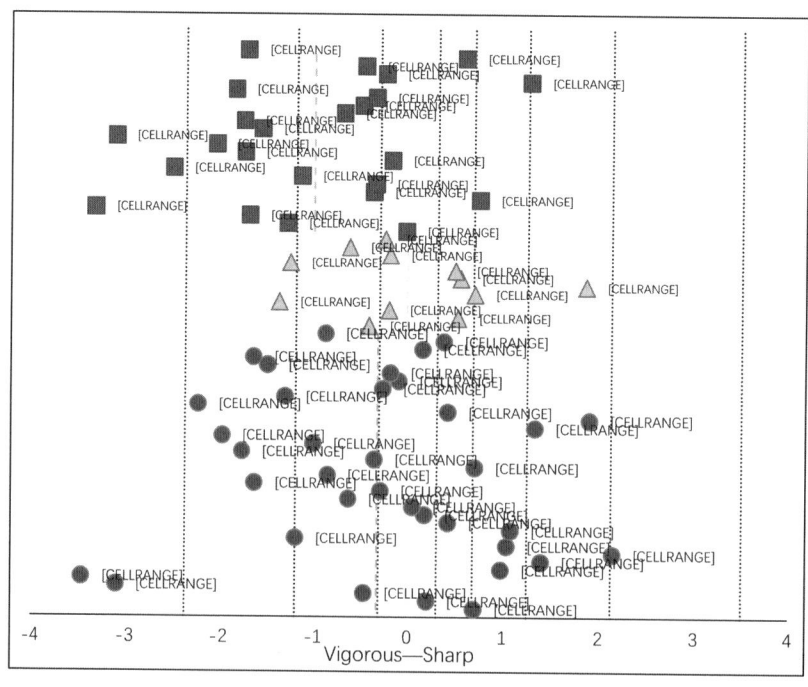

(c)

Analysis and Modelling of Timbre Perception Features in Musical Sounds

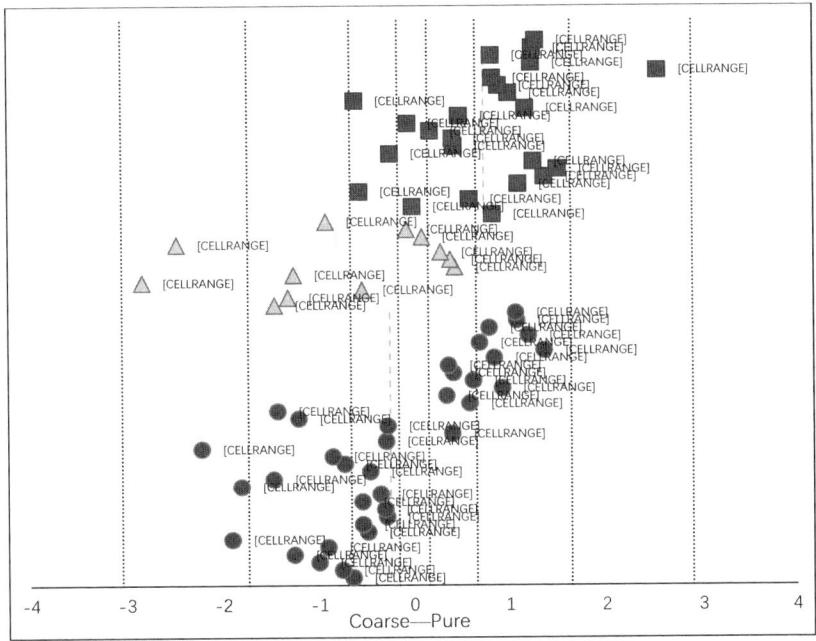

(d)

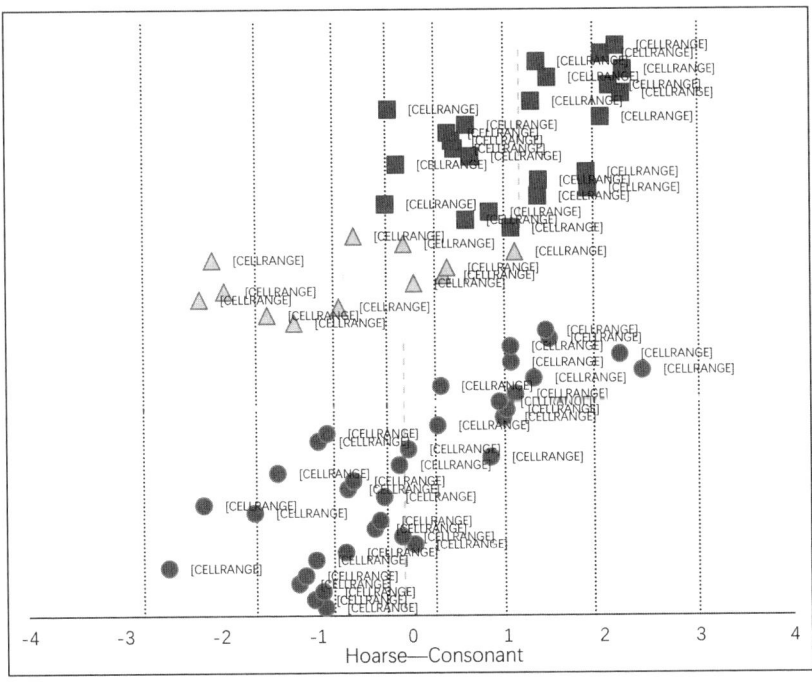

(e)

Fig. 4. A psychological scale of 72 musical instruments, including (a) bright/dark, (b) raspy/mellow, (c) sharp/vigorous, (d) coarse/pure, and (e) hoarse/consonant. The blue squares represent Western orchestral instruments, the yellow triangles represent Chinese minority instruments, and the red circles represent Chinese orchestral instruments. The dotted blue line represents the mean value of the Western orchestral instruments, the dotted yellow line represents the mean value of the Chinese minority instruments, and the dotted red line represents the mean value of the Chinese orchestral instruments.

It is evident from Fig. 4 that the distribution of timbre values for Chinese instruments differed significantly from Western instruments. For example, raspy/mellow and hoarse/consonant exhibited drastically different scales. This suggested the timbre database containing Chinese instruments had a richer variety of timbre types than a conventional Western instrument database. In addition, the distribution of timbre samples in the five timbre evaluation scale pairs was relatively balanced. This suggested the proposed evaluation terminology was representative of multiple timbre types and could better distinguish the attributes of different instruments. These factors could help to improve the accuracy of timbre perception feature models.

4.4 Construction of a Prediction Model

In this study, multiple linear regression, support vector regression, a neural network, and a random forest algorithm were used to correlate objective parameters and subjective evaluation experimental data to construct a mathematical model of timbre perception features. Stepwise techniques were used for variable entry and removal in the multiple linear regression algorithm, and radial basis functions were selected as kernels for support vector regression. A multi-layer perceptron was adopted in the neural network, which included a hidden layer. Random forest is a common ensemble model consisting of multiple CART-like trees, each of which grows on a bootstrap object acquired by sampling the original data cases with replacements.

Before modeling, feature selection was conducted for the target attribute to be predicted. This process consisted of three steps:

(1) Screening: removes unimportant or problematic predictors and cases.
(2) Ranking: sorts remaining predictors and assigns ranks; this step considers one predictor at a time to determine how well it predicts the target variable.
(3) Selecting: identifies the important subset of features to use in subsequent models.

During the modeling phase, 80% of the data were used for training and the remaining 20% were used for validation. The input to the model was a 166-dimensional objective parameter set and the output was the value of the five perception dimensions (bright/dark, raspy/mellow, sharp/vigorous, coarse/pure, and hoarse/consonant). Correlation coefficients were used to evaluate the accuracy of the model and represented the results of the correlation analysis between the model prediction data and subjective evaluation data, with higher coefficients representing a more accurate model.

The accuracy of prediction results for the four algorithms across the five perception dimensions are shown in Table 7. Fig. 5 provides a histogram of the prediction accuracy in different dimensions. These experimental results suggested that the proposed technique provided valid predictions in each of the five dimensions. The algorithm exhibiting the best performance exceeded 0.9 for bright/dark, sharp/vigorous, coarse/pure, and hoarse/consonant sound types. The averaged results indicated that the neural network (0.915) and random forest (0.864) outperformed multiple linear regression (0.665) and support vector regression (0.670). The neural network was particularly accurate in its predictions of the five perception dimensions.

Table 7 A comparison of the accuracies achieved by four algorithms

	Multiple Linear Regression	Support Vector Regression	Neural Network	Random Forest
Bright/Dark	0.706	0.696	0.913	0.856
Raspy/Mellow	0.573	0.571	0.858	0.813
Sharp/Vigorous	0.859	0.852	0.952	0.945
Coarse/Pure	0.481	0.518	0.928	0.827
Hoarse/Consonant	0.705	0.711	0.922	0.877
Average	0.665	0.670	0.915	0.864

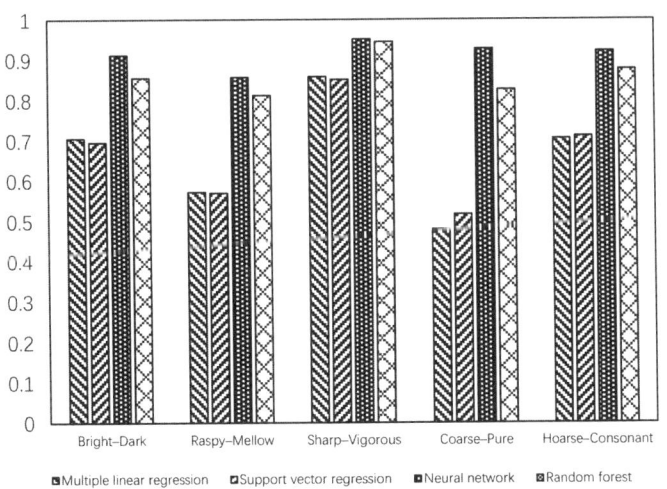

Fig. 5 A prediction accuracy histogram for the five perception attributes.

5. THE CONSTRUCTION OF TIMBRE SPACE

Multidimensional scaling (MDS) was used to construct a 3D timbre perception space to represent the distribution of 37 Chinese instruments more intuitively. Unlike many common analysis methods, MDS is heuristic and does not require assumptions about spatial dimensionality. It also offers the advantages of visualization and helps to identify potential factors affecting the similarity between terms. The construction of a timbre space includes three steps:

(1) Subjective evaluation experiment based on sample dissimilarity: where a dissimilarity matrix between samples was obtained using a subjective evaluation experiment. Existing research has conventionally paired up samples in the material database to score the dissimilarity. The process was simplified in this study, which reduced the workload.
(2) Dimension reduction of distance matrix based on MDS: where the MDS algorithm was used to calculate the dissimilarity matrix such that sample distances in high-dimensional spaces can be represented in low-dimensional spaces (usually two or three dimensions).
(3) Attribute interpretation of each dimension of timbre space: where the correlation between each dimension and the timbre perception features was analyzed using a statistical method. Interpretable attributes for each dimension were then acquired from this space.

The performance of multidimensional scaling algorithms depends on the sample dissimilarity matrix. In previous studies, this matrix was acquired using a subjective evaluation experiment that compared and scored the dissimilarity of any two samples. A total of $n^2/2$ experiments must be conducted for n samples. This quadratic relationship significantly increases the computational complexity and runtime, which makes quantifying the dissimilarity more difficult. This paper presents an improved methodology in which a set of evaluation indicators were selected (as complete as possible) and all samples were successively scored with each indicator. These results constituted the feature vector for the sample and the distance to each vector was calculated to obtain the dissimilarity of all samples. The 16 timbre evaluation terms shown in Table 3 were used to assess the attributes of each dimension during the analysis phase.

The method of successive categories was then used to conduct a subjective evaluation experiment on timbre materials for 37 Chinese instruments (Experiment C). Grade 9 was performed on 16 perception dimensions in Table 3 and the reliability and validity of the experimental data were analyzed. The Euclidean distance of the feature vectors was calculated, producing a dissimilarity matrix for 37 Chinese instruments. The MDS algorithm was used to process the timbre dissimilarity matrix and construct a 3D timbre perception space.

5.1 Experiment C: Subjective Evaluation Experiment Based on Sample Dissimilarity

Three factors were considered during sample selection to prepare the sound data needed in the subjective evaluation experiment:

(1) The appropriate number of samples: The number of samples must be sufficiently large to ensure the accuracy of the MDS algorithm and impose sufficient constraints on the model. In practice, however, it is difficult to establish precise rules for determining these data. However, empirical solutions do exist. In most MDS-based timbre studies, at least 10 sound samples are required for two-dimensional spaces and at least 15 sound samples are needed for three-dimensional spaces. In this paper, 37 kinds of Chinese instruments were used as experimental materials, which ensured that sufficient constraints were provided to the MDS model.

(2) The range of timbre variation: The range of timbre varies depending on the subject of the study, with larger instrumental variety (i.e., orchestral music) providing better data. Models constructed in this way can be applied more broadly to new timbre samples. In this study, 37 kinds of Chinese instruments were selected. As can be seen from Figure 4, compared with Western instruments, Chinese instruments had a wider distribution range in terms of their timbre evaluation scale. As such, the Chinese instrument samples selected in this paper ensured a diverse range of timbre samples.

(3) The uniformity of timbre sample distributions: The distribution of sound samples in each timbre perception attribute should be as uniform as possible. Timbre spaces are continuous perceptual spaces and a uniform distribution sample set is beneficial to the construction of continuous timbre spaces. Non-uniform sample distributions can degrade solutions to the MDS equations, preventing the structures between classes from being fully displayed. As seen in Figure 4, the samples selected in this study covered a broad range of timbre attributes and they were distributed at varying psychological scales, providing a uniform distribution.

Subjective evaluation of the experimental environment and the subjects was conducted as in Experiment B. The process was as follows: while playing each experimental sample, the subjects judged the psychological scale of the sample on 16 timbre perception features (timbre evaluation terms) in turn, scoring each on a 9-point scale.

5.2 The Construction of the 3D Timbre Space Using MDS

The reliability and validity processing method applied to the experimental data was the same as in Experiment B. The processed data were averaged and the mean score for all subjects on each evaluation term was calculated for each sample. These data were then used to calculate the timbre dissimilarity, expressed in the form of a distance matrix. The MDS algorithm was adopted in this paper, which considers individual differences between subjects and assigns a corresponding weight to each score. This approach considers terms in every dimension and more fully utilizes the experimental data. Multidimensional scaling is based on dissimilarity analysis for two samples in a timbre attribute space, which can be expressed using a distance matrix as follows:

$$d_{jk}^{i} = \sqrt{\sum_{r=1}^{R} w_{ir} \cdot (x_{jr} - x_{kr})^2}, \tag{8}$$

where d_{jk}^{i} represents the dissimilarity evaluation score for subject i assessing sounds j and k, w_{ir} represents the weight of subject i in the rth dimension, and x_{kr} represents the coordinates of sample k in the rth dimension.

Equation (8) was used to calculate the distance for 37 timbre feature vectors and the dissimilarity distance matrix for 37 samples (see Supplementary Materials). This matrix was used as input into the MDS algorithm. The number of timbre space dimensions was determined by referring to previous research results. The timbre space dimension was determined in three dimensions using Kruskal's stress function. The coordinates of each sound sample in 3D timbre space were acquired by using MDS to reduce the dimensionality of the dissimilarity distance matrix (Fig. 6).

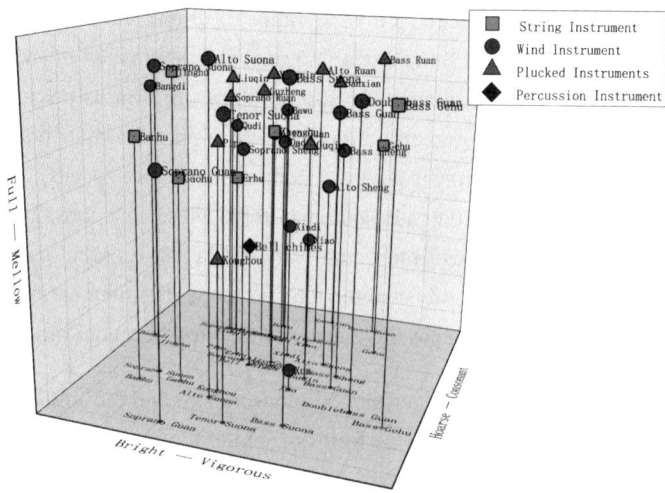

Fig. 6 A 3D timbre space for 37 Chinese instruments.

5.3 Perception Attribute Analysis of the Timbre Space Dimension

The correlation between 16 timbre perception attributes was calculated to analyze the auditory attributes of each dimension in the timbre space. The coordinates of the samples were projected into three dimensions to obtain the spatial distribution of the data. Pearson correlation coefficients were calculated between each dimension and the 16 timbre perception attributes (Table 8). Further analysis suggested dimension 1 was positively correlated with the "bright" perception attribute and negatively correlated with "vigorous." As such, dimension 1 could be defined as "bright/vigorous." Dimension 2 was positively correlated with "hoarse" and negatively correlated with "consonant." However, the correlation of dimension 3 was not as obvious, as it was only slightly correlated with "full/mellow." Figure 6 suggests that different types of instruments were distributed at different positions in the timbre space, which could be used to categorize individual timbres.

Table 8 The results of correlation analysis in 3D timbre space

Attribute	Dimension 1	Dimension 2	Dimension 3
纤细 (Slim)	0.97	−0.13	−0.11
明亮 (Bright)	0.97	−0.17	0.15
暗淡 (Dark)	−0.96	0.19	−0.14
尖锐 (Sharp)	0.95	0.23	0.14
浑厚 (Vigorous)	−0.99	−0.05	0.11
单薄 (Thin)	0.94	0.26	−0.10
厚实 (Thick)	−0.97	0.00	0.22
清脆 (Silvery)	0.96	−0.22	0.04
沙哑 (Raspy)	0.39	0.87	0.02
丰满 (Full)	−0.83	−0.38	0.33
粗糙 (Coarse)	−0.35	0.89	−0.06
纯净 (Pure)	0.34	−0.82	0.11
嘶哑 (Hoarse)	−0.15	0.93	−0.13
协和 (Consonant)	−0.02	−0.96	0.00
柔和 (Mellow)	−0.38	−0.80	−0.37
混浊 (Muddy)	−0.91	0.26	−0.16

6. Conclusions

This study presented a novel methodology for the analysis and modeling of timbre perception features in musical sounds. The primary contributions can be summarized as follows:

(1) A novel method was proposed for constructing two sets of timbre evaluation terminology systems in a Chinese context. Experimental results from a subjective evaluation showed that these terms could successfully distinguish timbre from different instruments.

(2) A timbre material library containing 72 musical instruments was constructed according to relevant standards. A subjective evaluation experiment was conducted using the method of successive categories. The psychological scales of the subjects were acquired using five pairs of perceptual dimensions. A mathematical model of timbre perception features was then developed using multiple linear regression, support vector regression, a neural network, and the random forest algorithm. Experimental results showed that this constructed model could predict perceptual features for new samples.

(3) An improved method for constructing 3D timbre space was proposed and demonstrated using the MDS algorithm applied to 37 Chinese instruments. Auditory perceptual attributes were determined by analyzing the correlation between the 3 dimensions of the timbre space and 16 perceptual attributes.

In future research, we will focus on the following three aspects of this study. First, supplemental sample materials will be acquired based on the existing timbre database. We will attempt to expand the variety and quantity of the data to improve the consistency and robustness of the model. Second, a subjective evaluation experiment, statistical analysis, and other techniques will be used to select timbre evaluation terms that accurately reflect the essential attributes of timbre to provide support for the construction of simple and effective timbre spaces. Third, the machine learning algorithm will be improved by including more subjective evaluation data. Additional correlation algorithms will also be tested to improve the accuracy of the model predictions. Finally, mathematical modeling will be implemented for each dimension in the timbre space. The distribution of other (i.e., Western) instruments will be compared to that of Chinese instruments to identify common patterns.

Author Contributions: Investigation, conceptualization, methodology, data curation, and writing (original draft, review, and editing): J.L.; project administration and supervision: W.J., Y.J., and S.W.; software, experimental process, and data processing: J.L. and X.Z. All authors have read and agreed to the published version of the manuscript.

Funding: This study was supported by the Key Laboratory Research Funds of Ministry of Culture and Tourism (WHB1801).

Conflicts of Interest: The authors declare no conflict of interest.

APPENDIX A

The timbre materials mentioned in Section 2.1 contains 72 instruments, including 37 Chinese orchestral instruments, 11 Chinese minority instruments, and 24 Western orchestral instruments (Table A1). The names of the Chinese orchestral instruments and Chinese minority instruments are given in their original languages (Chinese), with an accompanying English translation.

Table A1 Instrument list

Category	Type	Name of the Instrument			
Chinese Orchestral Instruments (37)	Bowed Instruments (7)	高胡 (Gaohu)	二胡 (Erhu)	中胡 (Zhonghu)	革胡 (Gehu)
		低音革胡 (Bass Gehu)	京胡 (Jinghu)	板胡 (Banhu)	
	Wind Instruments (17)	梆笛 (Bangdi)	曲笛 (Qudi)	新笛 (Xindi)	
		高音笙 (Soprano Sheng)	中音笙 (Tenor Sheng)	低音笙 (Bass Sheng)	
		高音唢呐 (Soprano Suona)	中音唢呐 (Alto Suona)	次中音唢呐 (Tenor Suona)	低音唢呐 (Bass Suona)
		高音管 (Soprano Guan)	中音管 (Alto Guan)	低音管 (Bass Guan)	倍低音管 (Doublebass Guan)
		埙 (Xun)	箫 (Xiao)	巴乌 (Bawu)	
	Plucked Instruments (10)	小阮 (Soprano Ruan)	中阮 (Alto Ruan)	大阮 (Bass Ruan)	
		柳琴 (Liuqin)	琵琶 (Pipa)	扬琴 (Yangqin)	古筝 (Guzheng)
		古琴 (Guqin)	箜篌 (Konghou)	三弦 (Sanxian)	
	Percussion Instruments (3)	编钟 (Bell chimes)	编磬 (Bianqing)	云锣 (Yunluo)	
Chinese Minority Instruments (11)	Bowed Instruments (4)	艾捷克 (Gijak)	四胡 (Sihu)	马头琴 (Matouqin)	潮尔 (Chaoer)
	Wind Instruments (4)	朝鲜唢呐 (Chaoxian Suona)	葫芦笙 (Hulusheng)	葫芦丝 (Hulusi)	大岑 (Dacen)
	Plucked Instruments (3)	热瓦普 (Rewap)	都塔尔 (Dutar)	伽倻琴 (Gayageum)	

Table A1 Continued

Category	Type	Name of the Instrument			
Western Orchestral Instruments (24)	Bowed Instruments (4)	Violin	Viola	Cello	Double bass
	Woodwind Instruments (6)	Piccolo	Flute	Oboe	Clarinet
		Bassoon	Saxophone		
	Brass Instruments (4)	Trumpet	Trombone	French horn	Tuba
	Keyboard Instruments (4)	Piano	Harpsichord	Organ	Accordion
	Plucked Instruments (1)	Harp			
	Percussion Instruments (5)	Celesta	Vibraphone Chimes	Xylophone	Marimba

REFERENCES

[1] Chen X. Sound and hearing perception [M]. Beijing: China Broadcasting and Television Press, 2006.

[2] Moore B C, Glasberg B R, Baer T. A model for the prediction of thresholds, loudness, and partial loudness [J]. J. Audio Eng. Soc., 1997, 45: 224-240.

[3] Meddis R, O'Mard L. A unitary model of pitch perception [J]. J. Acoust. Soc. Am., 1997, 102: 1811-1820.

[4] Patel A D. Music, language, and the brain [M]. Oxford: Oxford University Press, 2010.

[5] ANSI S1.1-1994. American National Standard Acoustical Terminology [S]. New York: Acoustical Society of America, 1994.

[6] Zwicker E, Fastl H. Psychoacoustics: facts and models [M]. Berlin, Heidelberg: Springer Science & Business Media, 2013.

[7] Cermak G W, Cornillon P C. Multidimensional analyses of judgments about traffic noise [J]. J. Acoust. Soc. Am., 1976, 59: 1412-1420.

[8] Kuwano S, Namba S, Fastl H, et al. Evaluation of the impression of danger signals-comparison between Japanese and German subjects [C]. Schick A, Klatte M, eds.

Contributions to Psychological Acoustics. Oldenburg: BIS, 1997: 115-128.

[9] Iwamiya S, Zhan M. A comparison between Japanese and Chinese adjectives which express auditory impressions [J]. J. Acoust. Soc. Jpn. (E), 1997, 18: 319-323.

[10] Stepanek J. Relations between perceptual space and verbal description in violin timbre [C]. acústica 2004 Guimarães. Guimarães: 2004: 077.

[11] Kim S, Bakker R, Ikeda M. Timbre preferences of four listener groups and the influence of their cultural backgrounds [C]. Audio Engineering Society Convention 140; 2016.

[12] Solomon L N. Semantic approach to the perception of complex sounds [J]. J. Acoust. Soc. Am., 1958, 30: 421-425.

[13] von Bismarck G. Timbre of steady sounds: a factorial investigation of its verbal attributes [J]. Acta Acust. United Acust., 1974, 30: 146-159.

[14] Pratt R L, Doak P E. A subjective rating scale for timbre [J]. J. Sound Vibrat., 1976, 45: 317-328.

[15] Namba S, Kuwano S, Hatoh T, et al. Assessment of musical performance by using the method of continuous judgment by selected description [J]. Music Percept., 1991, 8: 251-275.

[16] Ethington R, Punch B. SeaWave: a system for musical timbre description [J]. Comput. music J., 1994, 18: 30-39.

[17] Faure A, McAdams S, Nosulenko V. Verbal correlates of perceptual dimensions of timbre [C]. 4th International Conference on Music Perception and Cognition. Montréal, Canada, 1996.

[18] Howard D M, Tyrrell A M. Psychoacoustically informed spectrography and timbre [J]. Organised sound, 1997, 2: 65-76.

[19] Shibuya K, Koyama T, Sugano S. The relationship between KANSEI and bowing parameters in the scale playing on the violin [C]. IEEE SMC'99 Conference Proceedings. 1999 IEEE International Conference on Systems, Man, and Cybernetics (Cat. No.99CH37028); IEEE: Tokyo, Japan, 1999; Vol. 4: 305-310.

[20] Kuwano S, Namba S, Schick A, et al. The timbre and annoyance of auditory warning signals in different countries [C]. Proc. INTERNOISE 2000. Nice, France, 2000.

[21] Disley A C, Howard D M. Timbral semantics and the pipe organ [C]. Proceedings of the Stockholm Music Acoustic Conference 2003. Stockholm, Sweden, 2003: 607-610.

[22] Moravec O, Štepánek J. Verbal description of musical sound timbre in Czech language [C]. Proceedings of the Stockholm Music Acoustic Conference 2003. Stockholm, Sweden, 2003: SMAC–1–SMAC–4.

[23] Collier G L. A comparison of novices and experts in the identification of sonar signals [J]. Speech Commun., 2004, 43: 297-310.

[24] Martens W L, Marui A. Constructing individual and group timbre spaces for sharpness-matched distorted guitar timbres [C]. Audio Engineering Society Convention 119. 2005.

[25] Disley A C, Howard D M, Hunt A D. Timbral description of musical instruments [C]. International Conference on Music Perception and Cognition. Bologna, Italy, 2006: 61-68.

[26] Štepánek J. Musical sound timbre: verbal description and dimensions [C]. Proceedings of the 9th International Conference on Digital Audio Effects (DAFx-06). Citeseer: Montreal,

Canada, 2006: 121-126.

[27] Katz B, Katz R A. Mastering audio: the art and the science [M]. 2nd ed. Oxford: Focal Press, 2007.

[28] Howard D, Disley A, Hunt A. Towards a music synthesizer controlled by timbral adjectives [C]. Proceedings of 14th International Congress on Sound & Vibration. Cairns, Australia, 2007.

[29] Barbot B, Lavandier C, Cheminée P. Perceptual representation of aircraft sounds [J]. Appl. Acoust., 2008, 69: 1003-1016.

[30] Pedersen T H. The semantic space of sounds [M]. El Dorado: Delta, 2008.

[31] Alluri V, Toiviainen P. Exploring perceptual and acoustical correlates of polyphonic timbre [J]. Music Percept., 2010, 27: 223-242.

[32] Fritz C, Blackwell A F, Cross I, et al. Exploring violin sound quality: investigating English timbre descriptors and correlating resynthesized acoustical modifications with perceptual properties [J]. J. Acoust. Soc. Am., 2012, 131: 783-794.

[33] Altinsoy M E, Jekosch U. The semantic space of vehicle sounds: developing a semantic differential with regard to customer perception [J]. J. Audio Eng. Soc., 2012, 60: 13-20.

[34] Elliott T M, Hamilton L S, Theunissen F E. Acoustic structure of the five perceptual dimensions of timbre in orchestral instrument tones [J]. J. Acoust. Soc. Am., 2013, 133: 389-404.

[35] Zacharakis A, Pastiadis K. An interlanguage study of musical timbre semantic dimensions and their acoustic correlates [J]. Music Percept., 2014, 31: 339-358.

[36] Skovenborg E. Development of semantic scales for music mastering [C]. Audio Engineering Society Convention 141. 2016.

[37] Wallmark Z. A corpus analysis of timbre semantics in orchestration treatises [J]. Psychol. Music, 2019, 47: 585-605.

[38] Chen K A, Wang N, Wang J C. Investigation on human ear's capability for identifying non-speech objects [J]. Acta Phys. Sin., 2009, 58: 5075-5082.

[39] Herrera-Boyer P, Peeters G, Dubnov S. Automatic classification of musical instrument sounds [J]. J. new music Res., 2003, 32: 3-21.

[40] Bowman C, Yamauchi T. Perceiving categorical emotion in sound: the role of timbre [J]. Psychomusicology: music, mind, and brain, 2016, 26: 15-25.

[41] Gupta C, Li H, Wang Y. Perceptual evaluation of singing quality [C]. 2017 Asia-Pacific Signal and Information Processing Association Annual Summit and Conference (APSIPA ASC); IEEE: Kuala Lumpur, Malaysia, 2017: 577-586.

[42] Allen N, Hines P C, Young V W. Performances of human listeners and an automatic aural classifier in discriminating between sonar target echoes and clutter [J]. J. Acoust. Soc. Am., 2011, 130: 1287-1298.

[43] Wang N, Chen K A. Regression model of timbre attribute for underwater noise and its application to target recognition [J]. Acta Phys. Sin., 2010, 59: 2873-2881.

[44] Blauert J. Communication acoustics [M]. Berlin, Heidelberg: Springer, 2005.

[45] Jensen K. Timbre models of musical sounds [D]. Copenhagen: University of Copenhagen, 1999.

[46] Desainte-Catherine M, Marchand S. Structured additive synthesis: towards a model of sound timbre and electroacoustic music forms [C]. International Computer Music Conference (ICMC99). China, 1999: 260-263.

[47] Aucouturier J J, Pachet F, Sandler M. The way it sounds: Timbre models for analysis and retrieval of music signals [J]. IEEE Trans. multimedia, 2005, 7: 1028-1035.

[48] Burred J, Röbel A, Rodet X. An accurate timbre model for musical instruments and its application to classification [C]. Learning the Semantics of Audio Signals, Proceedings of the First International Workshop, LSAS 2006; Cano P, Nürnberger A, Stober S, Tzanetakis G, eds. Athens, Greece, 2006: 22-32.

[49] Wang X, Meng Z. The consonance evaluation method of Chinese plucking instruments [J]. Acta Acust., 2013, 38: 486-492.

[50] Sciabica J F, Bezat M C, Roussarie V, et al. Towards the timbre modeling of interior car sound [C]. Proceedings of the 15th International Conference on Auditory Display. Copenhagen, Denmark, 2009.

[51] Grey J M. Multidimensional perceptual scaling of musical timbres [J]. J. Acoust. Soc. Am., 1977, 61: 1270-1277.

[52] McAdams S, Winsberg S, Donnadieu S, et al. Perceptual scaling of synthesized musical timbres: common dimensions, specificities, and latent subject classes [J]. Psychol. Res., 1995, 58: 177-192.

[53] Martens W L, Giragama C N. Relating multilingual semantic scales to a common timbre space [C]. Audio Engineering Society Convention 113. 2002.

[54] Martens W L, Giragama C N, Herath S, et al. Relating multilingual semantic scales to a common timbre space-Part II [C]. Audio Engineering Society Convention 115. 2003.

[55] Zacharakis A, Pastiadis K. Revisiting the luminance-texture-mass model for musical timbre semantics: a confirmatory approach and perspectives of extension [J]. J. Audio Eng. Soc., 2016, 64: 636-645.

[56] Simurra Sr I, Queiroz M. Pilot experiment on verbal attributes classification of orchestral timbres [C]. Audio Engineering Society Convention 143. 2017.

[57] Melara R D, Marks L E. Interaction among auditory dimensions: Timbre, pitch, and loudness [J]. Percept. Psychophys., 1990, 48: 169-178.

[58] Zhu J, Liu J, Li Z. Research on loudness balance of Chinese national orchestra instrumental sound [C]. Proceedings of the 2018 national acoustical congress of physiological acoustics, psychoacoustics, music acoustics. Beijing, China, 2018: 34-35.

[59] EBU – TECH 3253. Sound Quality Assessment Material Recordings for Subjective Tests. Users' handbook for the EBU SQAM CD [S]. Geneva: EBU, 2008.

[60] Alías F, Socoró J, Sevillano X. A review of physical and perceptual feature extraction techniques for speech, music and environmental sounds [J]. Appl. Sci., 2016, 6: 143.

[61] Peeters G. A large set of audio features for sound description (similarity and classification) [R]. CUIDADO IST Project Report 2004, 54: 1-25.

[62] Peeters G, Giordano B L, Susini P, et al. The timbre toolbox: extracting audio descriptors from musical signals [J]. J. Acoust. Soc. Am., 2011, 130: 2902-2916.

[63] Pollard H F, Jansson E V. A tristimulus method for the specification of musical timbre [J].

Acta Acust. United Acust., 1982, 51: 162-171.

[64] Krimphoff J, McAdams S, Winsberg S. Caractérisation du timbre des sons complexes. II. Analyses acoustiques et quantification psychophysique [J]. J. Phys. IV, 1994, 4: C5–625–C625–628.

[65] Scheirer E, Slaney M. Construction and evaluation of a robust multifeature speech/music discriminator [C]. In: 1997 IEEE International Conference on Acoustics, Speech, and Signal Processing. Munich, Germany: IEEE Comput. Soc. Press 1997.

[66] Lartillot O. MIRtoolbox 1.7.2 user's manual [R]. Norway: RITMO Centre for Interdisciplinary Studies in Rhythm, Time and Motion, University of Oslo, 2019.

[67] Meng Z. Experimental psychological method for subjective evaluation of sound quality [M]. Beijing: National Defence of Industry Press, 2008.

[68] Hodeghatta U R, Nayak U. Multiple linear regression [M]. Berkeley, CA: Apress, 2017: 207-231.

[69] Yeh C Y, Huang C W, Lee S J. A multiple-kernel support vector regression approach for stock market price forecasting [J]. Expert Syst. Appl., 2011, 38: 2177-2186.

[70] Haykin S S. Neural networks and learning machines [M]. 3rd ed. Upper Saddle River: Pearson Education, 2009.

[71] Witten I H, Frank E, Hall M A, et al. Data mining: practical machine learning tools and techniques [M]. San Francisco, CA, USA: Morgan Kaufmann Publishers, Inc., 2016.

[72] Borg I, Groenen P J, Mair P. Applied multidimensional scaling [M]. Berlin, Heidelberg: Springer Science & Business Media, 2012.

[73] Chen K A. Auditory Perception and automatic recognition of environmental sounds [M]. Beijing: Science Press, 2014.

[74] Susini P, McAdams S, Winsberg S, et al. Characterizing the sound quality of air-conditioning noise [J]. Appl. Acoust., 2004, 65: 763-790.

[75] Tucker S. An ecological approach to the classification of transient underwater acoustic events: perceptual experiments and auditory models [D]. Sheffield: University of Sheffield, 2003.

[76] Shepard R N. Representation of structure in similarity data: problems and prospects [J]. Psychometrika, 1974, 39: 373-421.

[77] Borg I, Groenen P J F, Mair P. Variants of different MDS models [M]. Berlin, Heidelberg: Springer, 2013: 37-47.

[78] Borg I, Groenen P. Modern multidimensional scaling: theory and applications [J]. J. Educ. Meas., 2003, 40: 277-280.

Human Perceptual Responses to Multiple Colors: A Study of Multicolor Perceptual Features Modelling[*]

1. INTRODUCTION

Studies have shown that the chromatic stimuli can lead to direct psychological experiences, such as red, which makes people feel warm, and blue, which makes people feel cold. This phenomenon is also called color perception. Compared to color emotion, color perception belongs to direct psychological effects which refer to the psychological experience directly caused by the physical stimulus, with strong commonality, e.g., "cold/warm". Differently, color emotion belongs to indirect psychological effects which do not only stay in the shallow stage of feeling or perception, but also evoke other more complex psychological feelings, e.g., "happy/sad". Compared with color perception and color emotion, the former is objective and universal, while the latter is subjective and individual. Therefore, the quantitative analysis of color perception and the establishment of mathematical models are more feasible which are of great importance and have substantial application value in the fields of visual communication design, image information retrieval and emotion recognition.

Since color perception belongs to subjective feelings of human beings, the traditional methods mainly focus on basic attribute analysis and simple regression analysis based on subjective evaluation experiments. Sivik et al. studied semantic differences between colors through words such as "good/bad" and "comfortable/uncomfortable". Xin et al. studied descriptive dimensions through the words "warm/cold" "light/dark", and "heavy/light". With the semantic differential (SD) method, Osgood et al. carried out a quantitative study of color semantic space, and three independent factors, namely, evaluation, activity, and potency factor, were extracted. Gao et al. described color emotions by two orthogonal factors (the activity index and potency index) and one correlative factor (the definition

---

① The paper was originally published in *Color Research and Application*, 2020, 45, and has since been revised with new information. It was co-authored by Shuang Wang, Wei Jiang (corresponding author), Yanan Su, Jingyu Liu.

index). In addition, Gao et al. further studied the detailed relationship between color emotion indexes and hue, lightness and saturation. With the development of machine learning methods, some researchers have attempted to establish an accurate mathematical model for color perception. Wang et al. identified an orthogonal three-dimensional emotional factor and designed three novel image features to predict each emotional factor by using the support vector regression (SVR) algorithm for image retrieval. However, Wang et al. ignored the difference between emotion and perception, the image samples were paintings, and the interference of other semantic information on the evaluation results was not excluded.

Multiple colors are often present in applications, and different perceptual effects will be produced under the combination of multiple colors. However, most studies have focused on only perceptual features of single color. Therefore, on the basis of the above studies, this paper studied human perceptual responses to multiple colors and emphasized the modeling of multicolor perceptual features. To achieve this aim, multicolor samples smoothed by a circular average filter were used, and descriptive variables were adopted to evaluate the multicolor perceptual features. Then, by establishing the relationship between the multicolor objective features and the multicolor perceptual features, a mathematical model was established to realize the quantitative description of multicolor perception.

2. RESEARCH FRAMEWORK

The research framework is shown in Fig. 1. In step I, construct a multicolor image set as the source of samples, and smooth the samples by a circular average filter so that the interference from the edge information can be excluded (see Section 3). In step II, design and quantify the multicolor objective features (see Section 4). In step III, conduct a subjective evaluation experiment for the perceptual descriptive variables based on the SD method (see Sections 5.1-5.3). In step IV, establish the mathematical model from the multicolor objective features to the multicolor perceptual features with nine descriptive variables by the SVR algorithm (see Section 5.4).

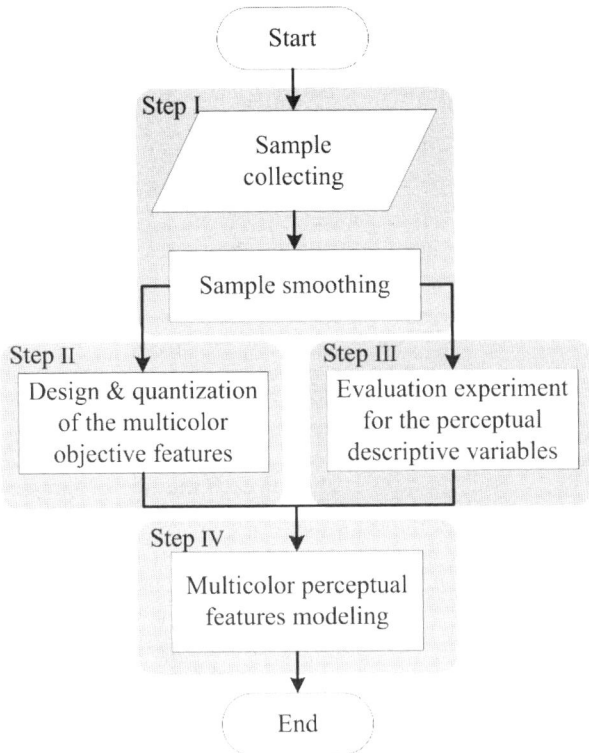

Fig. 1 Research framework for modeling multicolor perceptual features

3. MULTICOLOR IMAGE SET CONSTRUCTION

3.1 Samples Collecting

How to obtain multicolor samples is the first problem to be solved. The samples should conform to multicolor relationships in real life, and the matching types are supposed to be as rich as possible. Therefore, this paper selected the screenshots of film and television scenes which are based on real life as the samples, so that the samples have the characteristics of richness and authenticity compared with the synthetic samples. The selection criteria are as follows: (1) in color; (2) get rid of the virtual scenes; (3) exclude the screenshots which have other obvious semantic information, e.g., characters with clear expression; (4) the richer the multicolor matching types are, the better.

As a result, the samples are screenshots of film and television scenes, including a total of 164 multicolor images from 18 classic film types, and the resolution is 1280×720 dpi. The samples are labeled as one of the six basic colors that are reasonably distributed in the Itten twelve-part color wheel. The distribution of six basic colors of multicolor samples is shown in Table 1.

TABLE 1 The distribution of six basic colors of multicolor samples. Red (R: 255, G: 0, B:0), yellow (R: 255, G: 255, B: 0), green (R: 0, G:255, B:0), cyan (R: 0, G: 255, B: 255), blue (R: 0, G: 0, B: 255), and magenta (R: 255, G: 0, B: 255) are the basic colors uniformly distributed at equal intervals in the Itten Twelve-color Phase Loop.

Table 1　Distribution of six basic colors of multicolor samples

Basic color			
Red	29	Cyan	19
Yellow	30	Blue	30
Green	28	Magenta	28

As shown in Fig. 2, the saturation value of each multicolor sample is represented by the average value, so does the brightness value.

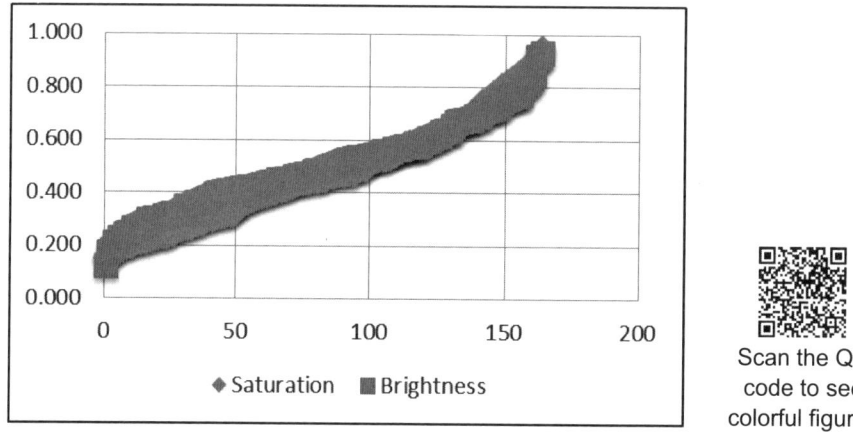

Scan the QR code to see colorful figures

Fig. 2　The distribution of multicolor samples in saturation and brightness attributes

3.2 Samples Smoothing

The multicolor samples contain not only color information but also edge information. People can recognize objects through edge information so that more semantic information, such as expression, can be processed, which may affect the evaluation of multicolor perception.

Therefore, this paper adopted a circular average filter to smooth the edge information. The main idea of the average filter is to replace the gray value of a pixel with the average value in its neighborhood. For the pixel (i, j) with the gray value $g(i, j)$, calculate the average value $\sqrt{\sum_{(x, y) \in \Omega} g(x, y)}$ of all the pixels in a circle template Ω with (i, j) as the center and n as the radius. Then, replace the original gray value $g(i, j)$ with the average value $\sqrt{\sum_{(x, y) \in \Omega} g(x, y)}$.

A subjective evaluation experiment was carried out to determine the smoothing degree. Six subjects participated in the experiment. As shown in Fig. 3, two images with abundant edge information were collected from each basic color category as the evaluation samples, and the samples were smoothed by 10 circular average filters respectively with the radius of the circle template from 10 pixels to 100 pixels (at interval of 10 pixels). The subjects were asked to evaluate the minimum smoothing radius that cannot see the edge information for each group of samples.

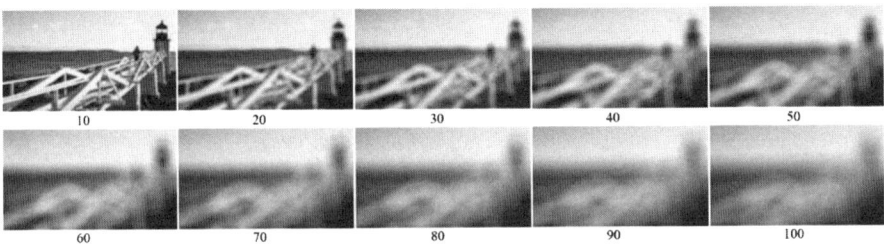

Fig. 3 One group of samples. The number below each image represents the radius of the circle template of each filter, and the unit is pixel

Table 2 shows the statistical data of each group of samples. According to the experiment result, $n = 50$ was adopted as the radius of the circle template to smooth each sample.

Scan the QR code to see colorful figures

Table 2 The statistical data of each group of samples

Group number	Mean	Standard deviation	Mode	Mode frequency
1	41.67	6.87	40	0.50
2	43.33	9.43	40	0.50
3	38.33	6.87	40	0.50
4	45.00	5.00	40	0.50
5	51.67	12.13	40	0.50
6	35.00	7.64	40	0.67
7	43.33	7.45	50	0.50
8	36.67	7.45	30	0.50
9	43.33	4.71	40	0.67
10	40.00	0.00	40	0.83
11	41.67	6.87	40	0.50
12	46.67	9.43	50	0.50

Fig. 4 shows the differences between the original sample and the smoothed sample. Figure 4-1(a) is the original sample, and Figure 4-1(b) is the smoothed sample. The scene information in the original sample, such as lanterns and railings, is blurred. Similarly, Figure 4-2(a) is the original sample, and Figure 4-2(b) is the smoothed sample. The expression information of the character in the original image is blurred.

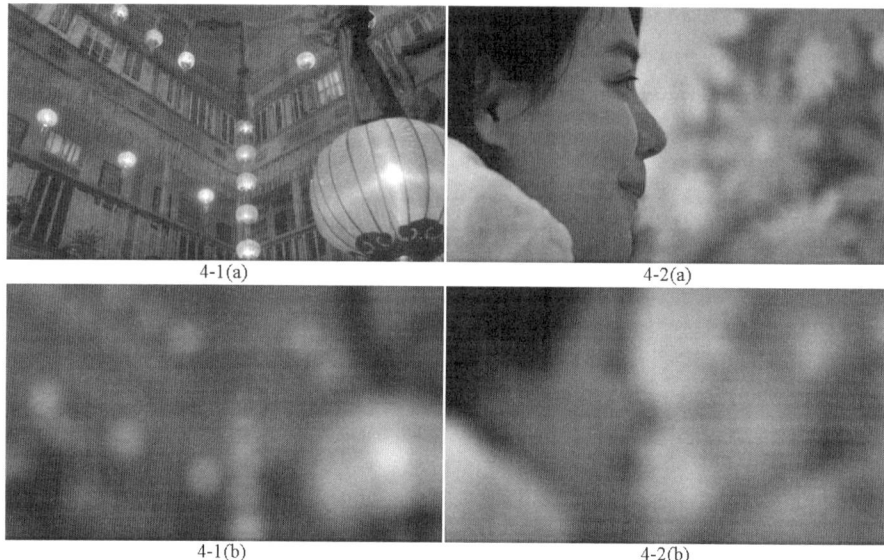

4-1(a)   4-2(a)

4-1(b)   4-2(b)

Fig. 4 The differences between the original sample and the smoothed one. Figure 4-1(a) is the original sample, and Figure 4-1(b) is the smoothed one. Figure 4-2(a) is the original sample, and Figure 4-2(b) is the smoothed one

Scan the QR code to see colorful figures

This paper experimentally confirmed that, on the premise of excluding the interference of edge information, the multicolor perception is not necessarily sensitive to the difference between different smoothing degrees (see Section 6.5).

3.3 Sample Preprocessing

K-means clustering was adopted to extract the dominant colors of each image, which were applied to multicolor perceptual feature extraction. Set $\{x^{(1)}, ..., x^{(m)}\}$ as the input value of m pixels from an image, where $x^{(i)}$ is the pixel value in RGB channels. The steps are as follows:

Step 1: Randomly select j clustering centroids $\{\mu_1, ..., \mu_j\}$, where j represents the number of clustering centroids and μ_j represents the pixel values of each clustering centroid.

Step 2: For each input value $x^{(i)}$, calculate the class that $x^{(i)}$ should belong to:

$$c^{(i)} := \arg\min_j \| x^{(i)} - \mu_j \|^2 \tag{3-1}$$

where $c^{(i)}$ is the target class with the shortest Euclidean Distance between $x^{(i)}$ and the j clustering centroids.

Step 3: For each class $c^{(i)}$, calculate the average value of $x^{(i)}$, which belongs to this class as the new clustering centroid μ_j.

Step 4: Repeat steps 2 and 3 until μ_j remains unchanged. n_j represents the number of $x^{(i)}$ that belongs to $c^{(i)}$.

This paper generated a color palette to represent dominant colors. As shown in Figure 5, μ_j represents the color, and n_j represents the length of each color on the color palette.

Scan the QR code to see colorful figures

Fig. 5 Color palette of a multicolor image generated by K-means clustering algorithm. μ_j represents the color and n_j represents the length of each color on the color palette. j is set to be 8

4. MULTICOLOR OBJECTIVE FEATURE SET CONSTRUCTION

To establish the multicolor perceptual feature models, a multicolor objective feature set was constructed, and the values of these features were extracted from the smoothed multicolor samples. This paper divided the multicolor objective features into two categories containing the color statistical features and the multicolor contrast features. The color statistical features are the features obtained through the statistics for different attributes of each color in the sample. The multicolor contrast features refer to the features obtained through the contrast relationships between multiple colors in the sample. As shown in Table 3, the 60-dimensional, binary, multicolor objective feature set was designed and quantified.

Table 3   The multicolor objective features. From left to right, the first column represents different feature categories. The second and third columns represent the multicolor objective features that belong to each category. The fourth column represents the number of dimensions of each feature

Feature category	Multicolor objective feature	Description	Dimension
Color statistical feature	H	Hue	45
	S	Saturation	
	B	Brightness	
	$f_1, f_2, f_3, f_4, f_5, f_6$	Color moment	6
	f_7	Color richness	1
	f_8, f_9	Space density	2
Multicolor contrast feature	f_{10}	Color tone contrast	1
	f_{11}	Cool/warm contrast	1
	f_{12}	Saturation contrast	1
	f_{13}	Brightness contrast	1
	f_{14}, f_{15}	Space contrast	2

4.1 Color Statistical Feature Quantization

Hue, saturation, brightness

According to Section 3.3, the color palette of each sample was obtained, and the resolution of each color palette was 15×1 dpi. H, S, and brightness (B) (HSB) color space is closely related to the method that people perceive color and brightness, so it is suitable for the study of human perceptual responses to multiple colors. Therefore, based on the HSB color space, this paper calculated the H, S, and B of each pixel from the color palette as a 45-dimensional feature vector.

Color moment

The color moment can represent the multicolor distribution of samples. Based on the HSB color space, the second-order moment and the third-order moment of the H, S and B of all pixels in each sample were adopted to construct a 6-dimensional feature vector:

$$f_1 = \left[\frac{1}{N-1}\sum_{i=1}^{N}(H-\bar{H})^2\right]^{1/2} \quad (4\text{-}1)$$

$$f_2 = \left[\frac{1}{N-1}\sum_{i=1}^{N}(S-\bar{S})^2\right]^{1/2} \quad (4\text{-}2)$$

$$f_3 = \left[\frac{1}{N-1}\sum_{i=1}^{N}(B-\bar{B})^2\right]^{1/2} \quad (4\text{-}3)$$

$$f_4 = \left[\frac{1}{N-1}\sum_{i=1}^{N}(H-\bar{H})^3\right]^{1/3} \tag{4-4}$$

$$f_5 = \left[\frac{1}{N-1}\sum_{i=1}^{N}(S-\bar{S})^3\right]^{1/3} \tag{4-5}$$

$$f_6 = \left[\frac{1}{N-1}\sum_{i=1}^{N}(B-\bar{B})^3\right]^{1/3} \tag{4-6}$$

where H, S, and B respectively represent the three channels (H, S, and B) in HSB color space and N represents the number of pixels in each sample.

Color richness

Information entropy can represent the confusion degree of information; that is, the higher the information entropy is, the less uniform and richer the color is. In this paper, calculate the information entropy of the grayscale image of each sample to construct a 1-dimensional feature vector:

$$f_7 = -\sum_{i=0}^{255}\sum_{i=0}^{255}P(i)\cdot log_2 P(i) \tag{4-7}$$

where $P(i)$ represents the proportion of pixels that have a grayscale value of i, $i \in [0, 255]$, namely, unitary grayscale entropy.

Space density

This paper segmented the color regions by the method of the watershed segmentation algorithm which measures the similarity (or difference) between the pixels in an image. Then, calculate the number of regions f_8 and the standard deviation of the numbers of different regions of f_9 to measure the space density of an image.

4.2 Multicolor Contrast Feature Quantization

Color tone contrast

Since color tones contain information on the hue and saturation, this paper quantified this feature on the basis of the International Commission on Illumination L*a*b (CIELAB) color space. L represents the brightness information, a represents the red and green information and b represents the yellow and blue information:

$$f_{10} = \left[\frac{1}{N-1}\sum_{1}^{N}(a_i^* - \overline{a^*})^2 + (b_i^* - \overline{b^*})^2\right]^{1/2} \tag{4-8}$$

where a_i^* and b_i^* represent a and b, respectively, in the CIELAB color space; $\overline{a^*}$ and $\overline{b^*}$ represent the average values of a and b, respectively, for each sample; N represents the number of pixels in each sample.

Cool/warm contrast

Because of the strong correlation between cool/warm and multicolor perception, this paper defined the cool/warm contrast referring to the early study performed by Ou and Sato. Based on the HSB color space, let the H of each pixel (i,j) of one sample be the input. The steps are as follows:

Step 1: Calculate the warm function $u_{(i,j),1}$ and the cool function $u_{(i,j),2}$:

$$u_{(i,j),1} = \begin{cases} \cos\ h, & 0 \leqslant h < 90° \text{ or } 270° \leqslant h < 360° \\ 0, & \text{otherwise} \end{cases} \quad (4\text{-}9)$$

$$u_{(i,j),2} = \begin{cases} \cos\ (h-180°), & 90° \leqslant h < 270° \\ 0, & \text{otherwise} \end{cases} \quad (4\text{-}10)$$

Step 2: Calculate the sum of $u_{(i,j),1}$ and $u_{(i,j),2}$ to represent the cool/warm degree:

$$u(i,j) = u_{(i,j),1} + u_{(i,j),2} \quad (4\text{-}11)$$

Step 3: Calculate the cool/warm contrast based on the $u(i,j)$:

$$f_{11} = \frac{\sum_{(i,j)} \sum_{(x,y) \in \Omega} |u(i,j) - u(x,y)|^2}{N} \quad (4\text{-}12)$$

where the pixel (x, y) represents the pixel within the block Ω of 8 neighborhood centers on the pixel (i, j), as shown in Fig. 6; N represents the number of pixels different from the pixel (i, j).

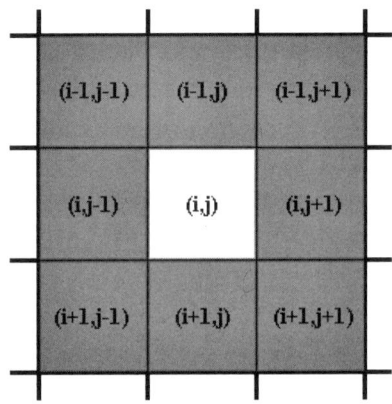

Fig. 6 The image block Ω of 8 neighborhood center on the pixel (i, j). $(x, y) \in \Omega$

Saturation contrast

Base on the HSB color space, let the S of each pixel (i, j) of one sample be the input:

$$f_{12} = \frac{\sum_{(i,j)}\sum_{(x,y)\in\Omega}|S(i,j)-S(x,y)|^2}{N} \qquad (4\text{-}13)$$

where the pixel (x, y) represents the pixel within the block Ω of 8 neighborhood center on the pixel (i, j); N represents the number of pixels different from the pixel (i, j).

Brightness contrast

Base on the HSB color space, let the B of each pixel (i, j) of one sample be the input:

$$f_{13} = \frac{\sum_{(i,j)}\sum_{(x,y)\in\Omega}|B(i,j)-B(x,y)|^2}{N} \qquad (4\text{-}14)$$

where the pixel (x, y) represents the pixel within the block Ω of 8 neighborhood center on the pixel (i, j); N represents the number of pixels different from the pixel (i, j).

Space contrast

This paper adopted the Itti visual attention model to segment the regions of interest (ROI) in the sample. The Itti visual attention model is a classic method for calculating the saliency based on the center-surround structure of the biological visual system, which focuses on hue, brightness and orientation as the salient features. The ROI is taken as the foreground, and the remaining area is taken as the background. The spatial features are extracted by comparing the differences between the foreground and background:

$$f_{14} = N_{front} / N_{background} \qquad (4\text{-}15)$$

where N represents the number of pixels in the foreground and background.

$$f_{15} = \overline{V}_{front} / \overline{V}_{background} \qquad (4\text{-}16)$$

where $\overline{V}$ represents the average brightness values of the foreground and background.

5. MULTICOLOR PERCEPTUAL FEATURE MODELLING

This section first introduces the selection of multicolor perceptual features. Then, the SD method was adopted to evaluate the multicolor perception of the smoothed multicolor samples, and the reliability of the experimental data was analyzed. Finally, a mathematical model from the multicolor objective features to the multicolor perceptual features was established by the SVR algorithm, which can predict the values of multicolor perceptual features of new samples.

5.1 Perceptual Descriptive Variable Collecting

In total, 260 perceptual description words were collected from the literature, questionnaires, and dictionaries. Then, the description words were reduced to a set of 148 according to the following principles: (1) remove the words with indirect psychological effect, e.g., "happy/sad"; (2) merge the words with similar semantics; (3) remove the words with unclear explanations. A preliminary experiment of selecting words from images was carried out, and the selected frequency of each word was recorded. Finally, the description words were organized into nine pairs to be as the descriptive variables according to the experimental results, as shown in Table 4.

Table 4 The perceptual description words. This paper carried out the experiment through Chinese words, and the corresponding English translations are offered below

No	Chinese word	English translation	Description
1	动－静	Dynamic–static, DS	Dynamic: change the original position or statement; Static: keep the original position or statement.
2	华丽－朴素	Gaudy–plain, GP	Gaudy: beautiful and glorious; Plain: (color, style, etc.) not rich or gaudy.
3	冷－暖	Cool–warm, CW	Cool: (feel) lower temperature; Warm: (feel) higher temperature.
4	明－暗	Light–dark, LD	Light: bright and full of light; Dark: lack of light as opposed to light.
5	轻－重	Light–heavy, LH	Light: low in weight and specific gravity; Heavy: high in weight and specific gravity.
6	软－硬	Soft–hard, SH	Soft: loose internal structure, easy to deform; Hard: tight internal structure, difficult to deform.
7	透明－浑浊	Transparent–turbid, TT	Transparent: (an object) can penetrate light; Turbid: contain impurities.
8	远－近	Far–near, FN	Far: long space distance; Near: short space distance.
9	胀－缩	Swell–shrink, SS	Swell: from small to large, or from short to long; Shrink: from large to small, or from long to short.

5.2 Subjective Evaluation Experiment for the Multicolor Perceptual Features

Subjects

Thirty subjects participated in the experiment. All of them were college students aged between 20 and 30 years old. No subjects were majoring in vision science. The male to female ratio was close to 1:1. Each subject was asked to take the Ishihara Color Blindness

Test to ensure their color vision was normal.

Experimental conditions

Fig. 7 shows the experiment settings. To avoid the interference of noise on the perceptual evaluation, the subjective evaluation experiment was carried out in a 5.37 m×6 m standard listening room where the background noise was kept below 30 dB(A). According to the Methodology for the Subjective Assessment of the Quality of Television Pictures (ITU-R BT.500-12), the ambient illumination of the monitor (i.e., the incident light formed by the surrounding environment on the monitor, measured in the vertical direction of the monitor) was kept at 200 lux (an illumination unit, representing the luminous flux received on the monitor per unit area).

Fig. 7 The operation interface of E-prime experimental platform. The red box shows the sample to be assessed, and the yellow box shows the perceptual descriptive variables displayed in a random order. Before entering this monitor, the sample to be tested will be displayed in full screen without transformation

Scan the QR code to see colorful figures

An E-prime experimental platform (2.0; PSYCHOLOGY SOFTWARE TOOLS, INC., Pittsburgh, USA) was used to present the stimuli and collect the data, and the operation interface on the BenQ XL2720-B color liquid crystal monitor carrying Windows Operating System (7; Microsoft Corporation, Redmond, USA) is shown in Figure 7. The aspect ratio of the monitor is 16:9, the same as the samples, to avoid sample transformations. The monitor was calibrated by Display Color Calibration Function from Windows Operating System before the experiment.

Experimental procedure

The subjects were asked to score all the samples on a 7-level scale of nine perceptual descriptive variables. Compared with the 5-level scale, the 7-level scale can obtain data with higher variability. It is easier to distinguish among samples compared with a 9-level scale. Take the descriptive variable "cold/warm" as an example: -3 means "very cold", -2 means "cold", -1 means "a little cold", 0 means "no cool/warm feeling", 1 means "a little warm", 2 means "warm", and 3 means "very warm". The 164 samples were divided into two parts, and each part contained 82 samples. Each subject spent 90 minutes on the experiment, including a 10-minute break after evaluating one part. There was only one subject participant in the experiment at a time. It took a total of three days to complete the experiments of all the 30 subjects.

5.3 Reliability Analysis

In this paper, Cronbach's alpha $\alpha = \dfrac{K}{K-1}\left(1 - \dfrac{\sum_{i=1}^{K}\sigma_{Y_i}^2}{\sigma_X^2}\right)$ was adopted to calculate the reliability. K represents the number of samples, σ_X^2 represents the population variance of the samples, and $\sigma_{Y_i}^2$ represents the variance of the samples to be tested. As shown in Table 5, the reliability coefficients are all greater than 0.8 after removing the experimental data whose correlation coefficient with the average value is less than 0.5, which meets the reliability requirements, so that the experimental data are reliable. The effectiveness of the experimental data of nine perceptual features is shown in Fig. 8.

Table 5 The results of reliability analysis

No	Descriptive variable	Cronbach's alpha
1	Dynamic-static, DS	0.876
2	Gaudy-plain, GP	0.948
3	Cool-warm, CW	0.952
4	Light-dark, LD	0.948
5	Light-heavy, LH	0.890
6	Soft-hard, SH	0.912
7	Transparent-turbid, TT	0.852
8	Far-near, FN	0.868
9	Swell-shrink, SS	0.928

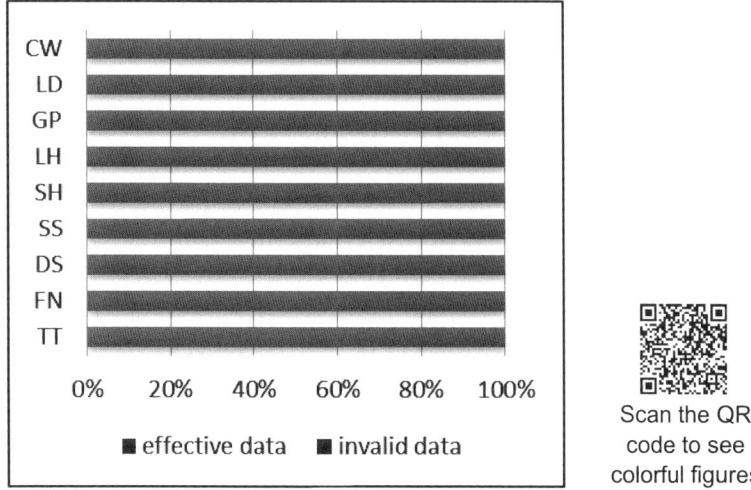

Fig. 8 The effectiveness of the experimental data of nine perceptual features

5.4 Multicolor Perceptual Feature Modelling

Machine learning can establish the relationship between multicolor objective features and multicolor perceptual features. The samples in this paper have the following characteristics: (1) small number of training set; (2) large number of features; (3) closely proximate among some feature values; (4) uniformly distribution of dominant color, saturation, and brightness features. Therefore, this paper adopted the SVR algorithm which is suitable for "small number of samples, large number of features". The basic idea of the SVR algorithm is to find a function that approximates the training points well by minimizing the prediction error. Let $D = \{(X, y_1), (X, y_2), \ldots, (X, y_m)\}$ be the training set, where X is the multicolor objective feature vector containing 60 dimensions, and y_i is the perceptual descriptive variables. The steps are as follows:

Step 1: To eliminate the influence of the difference in dimensions among different data, normalization was implemented in the first step:

$$x_i = \frac{x_i - \min\{x\}}{\max\{x\} - \min\{x\}} \quad (5\text{-}1)$$

$$y_i = \frac{y_i - \min\{y\}}{\max\{y\} - \min\{y\}} \quad (5\text{-}2)$$

Step 2: Because different multicolor perceptual features may be closely related to different multicolor objective features, the principal component analysis (PCA) algorithm was performed to reduce the dimensions of X. In this paper, the cumulative variance contribution rate of the principal components is not less than 95%.

Step 3: Find a mathematical model to make $|f(X)-y_i|$ as close as possible to ε, which represents the nine multicolor perceptual features. For SVR:

$$f(X)=\omega^T \Phi(X)+b \tag{5-3}$$

where ω and b are the parameters of the mathematical model; Φ is the nonlinear mapping which maps the X with finite dimensions to a high dimensional feature space so that the training set is linearly separable; $\Phi(X)$ represents the feature vector after mapping the X.

Step 4: When $|f(X)-y_i| \leqslant \varepsilon$, the loss is zero. Therefore, convert Equation (5-3) as follows:

$$\min_{\omega,b,\xi_i,\widehat{\xi}_i} \frac{1}{2}\|\omega\|^2 + C\sum_{i=1}^{m}(\xi_i+\widehat{\xi}_i) \tag{5-4}$$

$$\text{s.t.} f(X)-y_i \leqslant \varepsilon+\xi_i,$$

$$y_i - f(X) \leqslant \varepsilon+\widehat{\xi}_i,$$

$$\xi_i \geqslant 0, \widehat{\xi}_i \geqslant 0, i=1,2,\cdots,m. \tag{5-5}$$

where C represents the regularization constant; ξ_i represents the slack varaible. The minimum value of the ω can be calculated by the sequential minimal optimization (SMO) algorithm.

The 164 samples were divided into a training set and a testing set: 75% of the samples were in the training set, and 25% of the samples were in testing set. Here, the radial basis function (RBF) with the parameters g and c was adopted as the kernel function $K(x_i,x_j)$ to replace the $\Phi(x_i)^T\Phi(x_j)$. The g parameter can be seen as the inverse of the influence radius of the samples selected by the model as support vectors, which defines how far the influence of a single training example reaches, with low values meaning "far" and high values meaning "near". The c parameter represents the regularization constant. The parameter settings of each mathematical model are shown in Table 6.

Table 6 The parameter settings of each mathematical model

No	Multicolor perceptual feature	SVR Parameters	
		g	c
1	Dynamic–static, DS	0.09	0.50
2	Gaudy–plain, GP	0.13	4.00
3	Cool–warm, CW	0.09	2.00
4	Light–dark, LD	0.09	4.00
5	Light–heavy, LH	0.09	0.50
6	Soft–hard, SH	0.15	4.77
7	Transparent–turbid, TT	0.13	2.00
8	Far–near, FN	0.09	0.71
9	Swell–shrink, SS	0.13	1.00

6. EXPERIMENTAL EVALUATION AND ANALYSIS

This section evaluated the accuracy of the mathematical model of the nine multicolor perceptual features in Section 6.1. Here, the performance comparison of the SVR algorithm with other three typical machine learning algorithms was shown in Section 6.2. In Section 6.3, this paper evaluated the effectiveness of the multicolor objective features to different multicolor perceptual features. Then, the results of the factor analysis of multicolor perceptual features were shown in Section 6.4. Finally, the sensitivity of the multicolor perception to the difference between different smoothing degrees was also analyzed (see Section 6. 5).

6.1 Evaluation of the Mathematical Model

The correlation coefficient can reflect the relationship between the mathematical model and the experimental data of the subjective evaluation. The larger the coefficient is, the more accurate the model is. As shown in Table 7, for the whole set, the correlation coefficients between the nine multicolor perceptual features of the SVR outputs and those analyzed in Section 5 by subjective evaluation results are all more than 0.8, which shows the accuracy of the mathematical model. For the testing set, the correlation coefficients of "gaudy/plain" "cool/warm" "light/dark", and "swell/shrink" are all more than 0.85, which demonstrates the good prediction performance of the mathematical model. It is worth noting that the correlation coefficient of "far/near" is 0.505, which proves that "far/near" is related to multicolor perception, but it also proves that "far/near" may be caused by more than just multiple colors. In general, the mathematical model can make a good prediction for multicolor perception.

Table 7 The results of SVR training. RS is the training set, TS is the testing set, and WS is the whole set

No	Multicolor perceptual feature	Coefficient correlations		
		RS	TS	WS
1	Dynamic–static, DS	0.857	0.780	0.864
2	Gaudy–plain, GP	0.957	0.874	0.956
3	Cool–warm, CW	0.954	0.902	0.954
4	Light–dark, LD	0.956	0.880	0.957
5	Light–heavy, LH	0.948	0.716	0.943
6	Soft–hard, SH	0.957	0.830	0.952
7	Transparent–turbid, TT	0.941	0.593	0.917
8	Far–near, FN	0.730	0.505	0.839
9	Swell–shrink, SS	0.952	0.918	0.945

6.2 Evaluation of the Machine Learning Algorithm

For the testing set, this paper compared the prediction performance of the SVR algorithm with other three typical machine learning algorithms, namely the random forest algorithm, the linear regression algorithm, and the multilayer perception algorithm. First of all, the average values of the correlation coefficients of ***SVR***, ***RandomForest***, ***LinearRegression***, and ***MultilayerPerception*** are 0.778, 0.773, 0.621, and 0.572 respectively, which proves that the SVR algorithm has the best prediction performance. Then, as shown in Fig. 9, for the mathematical model of "dynamic/static" "gaudy/plain" "cool/warm" "light/dark" "soft/hard", and "swell/shrink", the SVR algorithm also has the best prediction performance. At the same time, the random forest algorithm plays better than the SVR algorithm in predicting "light/heavy" "transparent/turbid", and "far/near", whose correlation coefficients of "light/heavy" "transparent/turbid", and "far/near" are 0.764, 0.705, and 0.589.

Human Perceptual Responses to Multiple Colors: A Study of Multicolor Perceptual Features Modelling

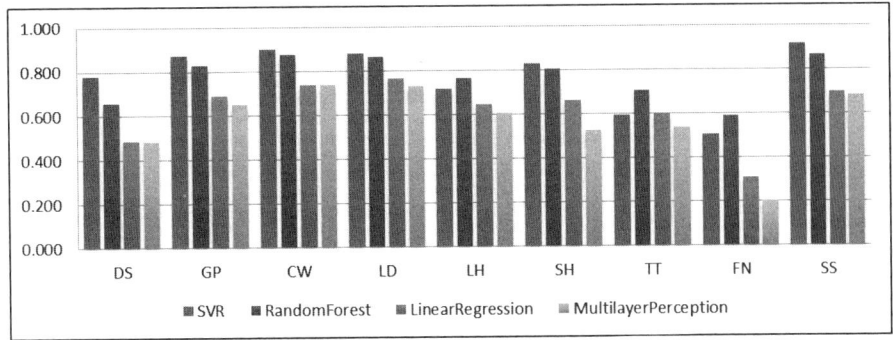

Fig. 9 The prediction performance of the SVR algorithm with other three typical machine learning algorithms

Scan the QR code to see colorful figures

6.3 Evaluation the Effectiveness of Multicolor Objective Features

This paper further analyzed the effectiveness of all the multicolor objective features. In this paper, the evaluation index is given by:

$$\delta = \left| \frac{\sum_{i=1}^{m}\left(x_i - \bar{x}\right)\left(y_i - \bar{y}\right)}{\sqrt{\sum_{i=1}^{m}\left(x_i - \bar{x}\right)^2}\sqrt{\sum_{i=1}^{m}\left(y_i - \bar{y}\right)^2}} \right| \tag{6-1}$$

where x_i represents the value of each multicolor objective feature; y_i represents the value of each multicolor perceptual feature. For each multicolor perceptual feature, the higher the δ is, the more effective the multicolor objective feature is.

There are some interesting findings. As shown in Table 8, for "dynamic/static", ***color tone contrast*** has the highest effectiveness. The higher the ***color tone contrast*** between multiple colors is, the more dynamic people feel. For "gaudy/plain", ***color tone contrast*** has the highest effectiveness. In addition, ***color moment*** (the second-order moment hue) also has a high effectiveness to "gaudy/plain", which proves that the greater the differences in hue, the gaudier people feel. For "cool/warm", ***color moment*** (the third-order moment hue) has the highest effectiveness. In addition, ***hue*** and ***color tone contrast*** also play well in evaluating the effectiveness of "cool/warm". For "light/dark" "light/heavy" "soft/hard", and "transparent/turbid", ***brightness*** has the highest effectiveness. The higher the brightness is, the lighter people feel. The higher the brightness is, the softer people feel. The higher the brightness is, the more transparent people feel. For "far/near", ***space density*** has the highest effectiveness. The denser the space is, the more the regions of multiple colors are, the far people feel. For "swell/shrink", ***color moment*** (the third-order moment hue) has the highest effectiveness, which illustrates the skewness of hue.

Table 8 Effectiveness evaluations for the multicolor perceptual features. The red background represents the maximum value for each column, and the blue background represents the minimum value for each column. The red box represents the maximum value for each row, and the blue box represents the minimum value e for each row

	DS	GP	CW	LD	LH	SH	TT	FN	SS
H	0.202	0.187	0.360	0.193	0.163	0.272	0.042	0.169	0.348
S	0.043	0.147	0.074	0.176	0.186	0.036	0.257	0.194	0.074
B	0.307	0.221	0.268	0.561	0.517	0.408	0.463	0.055	0.357
f_1	0.314	0.450	0.416	0.117	0.031	0.267	0.071	0.155	0.333
f_2	0.078	0.155	0.103	0.023	0.010	0.093	0.105	0.128	0.051
f_3	0.030	0.128	0.167	0.006	0.132	0.078	0.094	0.051	0.120
f_4	0.382	0.528	0.553	0.093	0.052	0.319	0.189	0.293	0.449
f_5	0.035	0.033	0.052	0.002	0.047	0.006	0.160	0.011	0.078
f_6	0.155	0.064	0.085	0.378	0.421	0.218	0.407	0.064	0.157
f_7	0.188	0.151	0.201	0.357	0.231	0.212	0.235	0.007	0.209
f_8	0.268	0.269	0.134	0.094	0.026	0.024	0.164	0.473	0.109
f_9	0.227	0.209	0.170	0.207	0.100	0.113	0.027	0.283	0.165
f_{10}	0.398	0.557	0.438	0.200	0.070	0.368	0.065	0.340	0.404
f_{11}	0.153	0.152	0.185	0.220	0.240	0.232	0.096	0.162	0.267
f_{12}	0.105	0.004	0.023	0.411	0.316	0.176	0.344	0.065	0.133
f_{13}	0.380	0.429	0.272	0.182	0.017	0.161	0.042	0.322	0.261
f_{14}	0.049	0.053	0.044	0.029	0.009	0.022	0.035	0.028	0.015
f_{15}	0.003	0.059	0.010	0.100	0.154	0.062	0.140	0.239	0.007

For other multicolor objective features, *saturation* is most relevant to "transparent/turbid", which proves that the lower the saturation is, the more turbid people feel. It is a little surprising that *color richness* is most relevant to "light/dark", which possibly results from the higher sensitiveness of color discrimination of the cones under the brighter environment. *Saturation contrast* is most relevant to "light/dark", and *brightness contrast* is most

Scan the QR code to see colorful figures

relevant to "gaudy/plain". ***Space contrast*** is most relevant to "far/near" with the low correlation with other multicolor perceptual features.

6.4 Factor Analysis

The correlation coefficients between any two multicolor perceptual features are given in Table 9. Many of the multicolor perceptual features are highly correlated with one another. Therefore, the PCA algorithm was performed to extract the underlying factors in the data.

Table 9 The correlation coefficients between any two multicolor perceptual features. The absolute values more than 0.3 are bolded

No	Multicolor perceptual feature	DS	GP	CW	LD	LH	SH	TT	FN	SS
1	Dynamic–static, DS	1.000	.789	−.732	.593	.422	.691	.158	−.488	.757
2	Gaudy–plain, GP		1.000	−.849	.536	.363	.757	.023	−.473	.816
3	Cool–warm, CW			1.000	−.654	−.530	−.875	−.169	.349	−.935
4	Light–dark, LD				1.000	.868	.794	.698	−.160	.738
5	Light–heavy, LH					1.000	.738	.763	−.023	.611
6	Soft–hard, SH						1.000	.418	−.240	.899
7	Transparent–turbid, TT							1.000	.159	.248
8	Far–near, FN								1.000	−.366
9	Swell–shrink, SS									1.000

The rotated factor loading matrix is shown in Table 10, accounting for 90.589% of the total multicolor perceptual features. Factor I is strongly correlated with "cool/warm", "swell/shrink", "gaudy/plain", "soft/hard", and "dynamic/static", which can be called the color vitality perceptual factor (CVPF). Factor II is strongly correlated with "transparent/turbid", "light/heavy", and "light/dark", which can be called the color energy perceptual factor (CEPF). Factor III is strongly correlated with "far/near", which can be called the color space perceptual factor (CSPF), which indicates the difference between single-color perception and multicolor perception.

Table 10 The factor loading matrix after rotation

Multicolor perceptual feature	The principle component		
	CVPF	CEPF	CSPF
Cool–warm, CW	−0.939	−0.194	0.106
Swell–shrink, SS	0.904	0.303	−0.149
Gaudy–plain, GP	0.899	0.031	−0.278
Soft–hard, SH	0.836	0.469	−0.040
Dynamic–static, DS	0.754	0.191	−0.412
Transparent–turbid, TT	−0.024	0.957	0.072
Light–heavy, LH	0.392	0.868	0.027
Light–dark, LD	0.537	0.786	−0.098
Far–near, FN	−0.253	0.076	0.947

The mathematical model for each factor is given by:

$$CVPF = 0.122DS + 0.286GP - 0.327CW - 0.017LD - 0.056LH + 0.23SH - 0.251TT$$
$$+ 0.243FN + 0.264 \tag{6-2}$$

$$CEPF = -0.015DS - 0.173GP + 0.133CW + 0.302LD + 0.36LH + 0.031SH + 0.516TT$$
$$- 0.098FN - 0.055SS \tag{6-3}$$

$$CSPF = -0.233DS + 0.021GP - 0.206CW - 0.077LD - 0.004LH + 0.182SH - 0.137TT$$
$$+ 1.012FN + 0.117SS \tag{6-4}$$

where "cool/warm" is the variable most closely related to the CVPF, "transparent/turbid" is the variable most closely related to the CEPF, and "far/near" is the variable most closely related to the CSPF.

Figure 10-12 are some examples of the multicolor samples. Fig. 10 shows the difference between the top eight samples with a large value of CVPF and the bottom eight samples with a low value of CVPF. Fig. 11 shows the difference between the top eight samples with a large value of CEPF and the bottom eight samples with a low value of CEPF. Fig. 12 shows the difference between the top eight samples with a large value of CSPF and the bottom eight samples with a low value of CSPF.

Scan the QR code to see colorful figures

Fig. 10 The examples of the multicolor samples. The upper part of the figure shows the top eight samples with a large value of CVPF, and the bottom part of the figure shows the bottom eight samples with a low value of CVPF

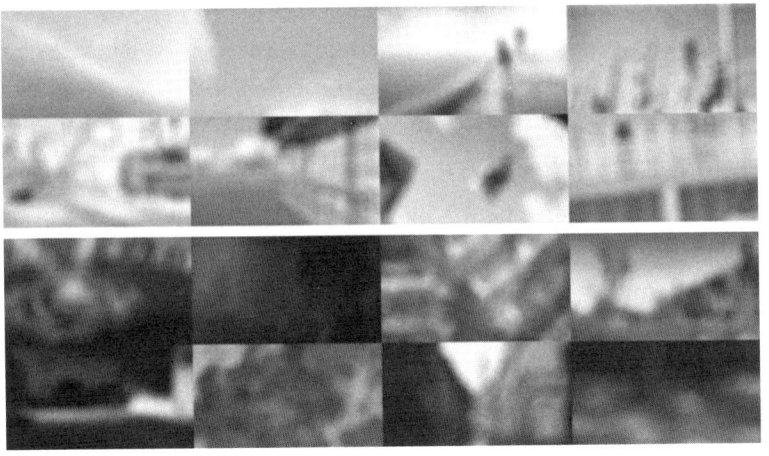

Scan the QR code to see colorful figures

Fig. 11 The examples of the multicolor samples. The upper part of the figure shows the top eight samples with a large value of CEPF, and the bottom part of the figure shows the bottom eight samples with a low value of CEPF

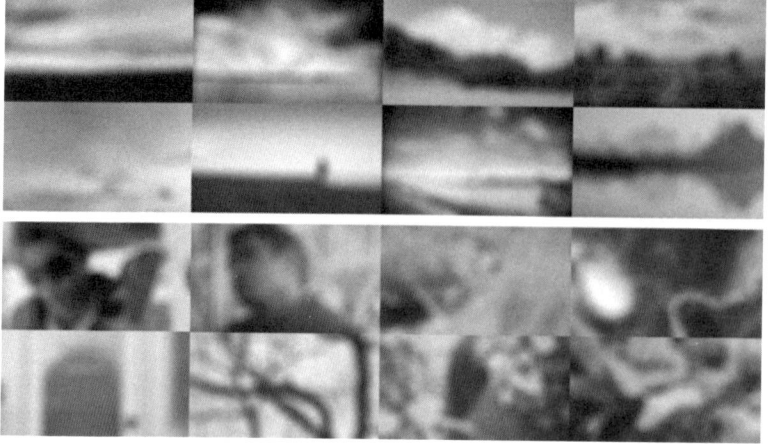

Scan the QR code to see colorful figures

Fig. 12 The examples of the multicolor samples. The upper part of the figure shows the top eight samples with a large value of CSPF, and the bottom part of the figure shows the bottom eight samples with a low value of CSPF

6.5 Sensitiveness Analysis to Different Smoothing Degrees

A subjective evaluation experiment was carried out to determine whether the multicolor perception is sensitive to the difference between different smoothing degrees or not. Thirty new subjects took part in the experiment and were evenly divided into five groups. As the evaluated samples, twelve images collected in Section 3.2 were smoothed respectively with the smoothing degree $n = \{10, 30, 50, 70, 90\}$. Each group was asked to evaluate one smoothing degree.

The samples with $n = 50$ were taken into the control group, and the correlation coefficients between them and other samples are shown in Fig. 13. In general, when the smoothing degree is more than 50, the evaluation results of all multicolor perception are close to the samples with $n = 50$. Therefore, under the premise that the edge information is smoothed, the multicolor perception is insensitive to the difference between different smoothing degrees. For "soft/hard" and "far/near", when the smoothing degree is lower than 50, the evaluation results are quite different from the samples with $n = 50$. The possible reasons are as follows. The samples with obvious edge information can make people feel hard, thus affecting the judgment of "soft/hard". In addition, when edge information is abundant, people tend to confuse the basic knowledge of "the farther the object is, the blurrier it is; the nearer the object is, the clearer it is" with "far/near".

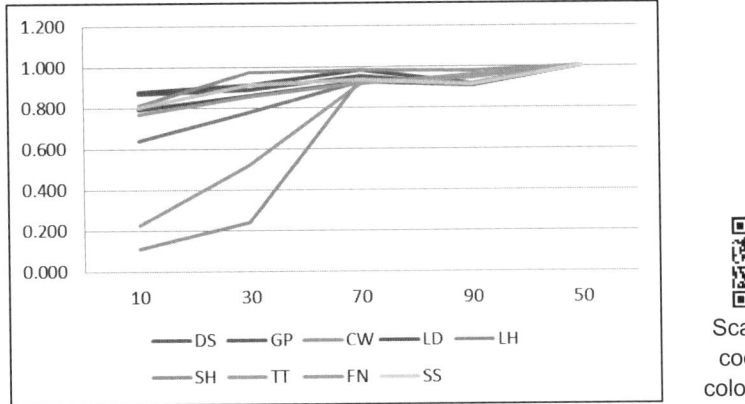

Scan the QR code to see colorful figures

Fig. 13 The correlation coefficients between the samples with the smoothing degree of 50 and other samples with the smoothing degree of {10,30,70,90}. The horizontal axis represents the smoothing degree; the vertical axis represents the correlation coefficient

7. CONCLUSIONS

This paper models multicolor perceptual features to investigate human perceptual responses to multiple colors. The salient contributions of this work are as follows. Firstly, establish the accurate mathematical model of nine multicolor perceptual features, namely "dynamic/static" "gaudy/plain" "cool/warm" "light/dark" "light/heavy" "soft/hard" "transparent/turbid" "far/near", and "swell/shrink" by the SVR algorithm. Secondly, analyze the relationships between the multicolor objective features and nine multicolor perceptual features in detail. Thirdly, based on the study of nine multicolor perceptual features, three multicolor perception factors are extracted, namely color vitality perception factor (CVPF), color energy perception factor (CEPF), and color space perception factor (CSPF), which indicates the difference between single-color perception and multicolor perception.

In future work, two aspects will be focused on. On one hand, in order to improve the reliability and universality of the model, the existing image set will be supplemented to expand the variety and quantity of the samples and the machine learning algorithm will be improved. On the other hand, the applications of the mathematical model of multicolor perceptual features will be explored, such as visual communication design and image information retrieval. At the same time, the corresponding computer system will be developed, such as the computer-aided design system and the perception-based image retrieval system.

REFERENCES

[1] Gibson J J. The perception of the visual world [M]. Boston, MA: Houghton Mifflin Harcourt Company, 1950.

[2] Luo Q M, Liu A M. Colors, emotions & packages [J]. Packaging engineering, 2002, 23(1): 73-75.

[3] Wang K. Theories and methods of computer aided color design [D]. Xi'an, China: Northwestern Polytechnical University, 2006.

[4] Gao X P, J H X. Investigation of human's emotional responses on colors [J]. Color Res. Appl., 2006, 31(5): 411-417.

[5] Li L T. Color composition [M]. Wuhan, China: Wuhan Fine Arts Publishing House, 2002.

[6] Qiao X L. The construction of color perceptive domain of digital printing image [J]. Printing quality & standardization, 2014, 9: 23-24.

[7] Liu X S, Ning Y J, Wang F M. Light performance and colors perceived appearance of polyester textiles [J]. International textile introductory newspaper, 2013, 41(10): 48-51.

[8] Yan M, Chan C A, Gygax A F, et al. Modeling the total energy consumption of mobile network services and applications [J]. Energies, 2019, 12(1): 184.

[9] Machajdik J, Hanbury A. Affective image classification using features inspired by psychology and art theory [C]. ACM International Conference on Multimedia, 2010: 83-92.

[10] Sivik L. Colour combinations and associated meanings-semantic dimensions and colour chords [M]. Gothenburg: University of Gothenburg, 1992.

[11] J X, K Cheng, G Taylor, et al. Cross-regional comparison of colour emotions part I: qualitative analysis [J]. Color Res. Appl., 2010, 29(6): 451-457.

[12] Osgood C E. The cross-cultural generality of visual-berbal synaesthetic tendencies [J]. Behav Sci., 1960, 5(2): 146-169.

[13] Wang W N, Yu Y L, Jiang S M. Image retrieval by emotional semantics: a study of emotional space and feature extraction [C]. IEEE International Conference on Systems, Man, and Cybernetics, 2006: 3534-3539.

[14] Jiang W, Wang S, Su Y N, et al. A study of color-emotion image set construction and feature analysis [C]. 18th IEEE/ACIS International Conference on Computer and Information Science, 2019: 99-104.

[15] Krishna K, Murty M N. Genetic k-means algorithm [J]. IEEE transactions on systems, man, and cybernetics: part b, 1999, 29(3): 433-439.

[16] Weiying M, Zhangjiang. Benchmarking of image features for content-based retrieval [C]. The Thirty-Second Asilomar Conference on Signals, Systems & Computers, 1998: 253-257.

[17] Beucher S, Meyer F. The morphological approach to segmentation: the watershed transformation [M] // Mathematical Morphology in Image Processing. New York: CRC Press, 2018: 433-481.

[18] Ou L C, Luo M R, Woodcock A, et al. A study of colour emotion and colour preference Part I: colour emotions for single colours [J]. Color Res. Appl., 2004, 29(3): 232-240.

[19] Itti L, Koch C, Niebur E. A model of saliency-based visual attention for rapid scene analysis [J]. IEEE transactions on pattern analysis and machine intelligence, 1998, 20(11): 1254-1259.

[20] Itten J. The art of color [M]. Beijing, China: World Publishing Corporation, 1999.

[21] Kandinsky W. Concerning the spiritual in art [M]. Beijing, China: China Social Science Press, 1987.

[22] Dictionary editing room, institute of Linguistics, Chinese academy of social sciences. Modern Chinese Dictionary [M]. Beijing, China: The Commercial Press, 2016.

[23] Dictionary research center of the commercial press. Synonym and antonym Chinese dictionary [M]. Beijing, China: The Commercial Press, 2010.

[24] Burges C J C. A tutorial on support vector machines for pattern recognition [J]. Data mining and knowledge discovery, 1998, 2(2): 121-167.

[25] Xue W. Statistical analysis and SPSS application [M]. Beijing, China: China Renmin University Press, 2018.

[26] Platt J C. Sequential minimal optimization: a fast algorithm for training support vector machines [C]. Advances in Kernel Methods-support Vector Learning, 1998: 212-223.

第三部分

研究报告

科技进步与文化建设研究(节选)[*]

一、当前文化建设的总体状况

改革开放以来,特别是党的十六大以来,我国文化建设取得了巨大成就,文化体制改革取得了积极进展,文化事业和文化产业步入协调快速发展的良性轨道,文化建设开创了新局面。同时还要看到,文化发展的体制机制还不健全,活力还不强,与全社会快速增长的精神文化需求不相适应,与日趋完善的社会主义市场经济体制不相适应,与对外开放不断扩大的新要求不相适应,与现代科学技术和传播手段迅猛发展和广泛应用的新形势不相适应。

二、推动文化领域科技进步的战略定位与战略目标

(一)战略定位

坚持改革创新和科技进步是文化发展的根本动力,这是我们党和国家贯彻落实科学发展观、解放思想、与时俱进、在实践中总结和深化出来的对文化发展规律的基本认识之一。

今后一段时期内推动文化领域科技进步的战略定位是:把握高科技时代的特点,牢固树立"科学技术是第一生产力"的思想,正确认识科技对文化的重大影响,促进科技与文化的结合与融合,坚持文化建设全面协调可持续的基本要求,在推进文化体制机制创新的同时,积极发挥科技在文化建设中的支撑作用与引领作用,制定和落实各项文化科技政策,实施文化科技创新计划和重大文化科技专项,不断解放和发展文化生产力,推动文化事业和文化产业的发展,提高国家文化竞争力,进一步增强文化可持续发展的能力。

---

* 本文节选自中宣部"十二五"时期文化改革发展课题研究报告,成稿于2009年6月。收入本书时有改动。

（二）战略目标

文化领域科技进步的战略目标，在今后一段时期内主要体现在如下 7 个方面：

我们必须大力推进文化领域的科技进步，不断推进文化内容形式的创新，推动不同艺术门类和文化活动相互融合，积极运用科技手段加强传统文化的表现力，实现题材体裁、风格流派和表现手法的多样化，加强文化艺术的表现力；

我们必须大力推进文化领域的科技进步，积极运用现代科技手段改善传统公共文化设施，催生与发展新的公共文化服务形态，提高公共文化产品的供给能力，大力提升公共文化的服务能力；

我们必须大力推进文化领域的科技进步，积极运用现代科技手段实施文化遗产的保护与管理，大力开发和利用民族文化资源，加快构建与完善优秀民族文化的传承体系；

我们必须大力推进文化领域的科技进步，积极运用现代科技手段改造传统文化产业，催生新的文化业态，大力发展文化新兴产业，加快构建和完善体现社会主义核心价值观的传输快捷、覆盖广泛的文化传播体系；

我们必须大力推进文化领域的科技进步，积极运用现代科技手段实施版权管理与保护，完善文化艺术领域的技术、服务、管理标准化体系，推动与促进文化信息化工作；

我们必须大力推进文化领域的科技进步，在促进文化发展繁荣的同时，积极运用现代科技手段实施文化内容、文化服务、市场流通的监管与执法，进一步加强科学有效的文化管理，确保文化健康有序发展；

我们必须大力推进文化领域的科技进步，积极推动中国特色的艺术学科体系和文化产业学科体系的研究与重构，进一步调整文化艺术领域的人才培养学科布局，促进文化系统内外的科技资源整合，加强文化创新人才队伍建设。

三、运用科技推动文化发展繁荣的对策建议

（一）树立"科技进步是文化发展第一动力"的观念

加强宣传、更新观念，在全社会统一"科技进步是文化发展第一动力"的认识。通过党中央领导、政府主导、全社会参与等方式，推动经济建设与文化建设的结合，促进科技与文化的融合，提高文化发展的社会化与产业化程度，在推进文化体制机制创新的同时，积极发挥科技在文化建设中的支撑作用与引领作用。

（二）制订 2010 年—2020 年的文化科技发展规划

配合中宣部、发展改革委、科技部、财政部、教育部等部门，研究提出文化科技发展的指导思想、发展原则、发展目标、重点领域和保障措施，制订到 2020 年的文化科技发展规划。

（三）改善文化科技法制环境

根据科技推动文化发展的战略定位和发展目标，按照法制统一与创新突破相结合、成功经验与文化科技现状相结合的原则，制订《文化科技促进条例》，制订相关配套文件。

（四）在国家层面整合与调整支撑文化发展的学科布局

我国的学科设置与分类目前是以科技部和教育部颁布的学科目录为导向的，其确定的重要原则之一是结合我国的产业实际。当前的文化建设和文化繁荣，特别是文化产业的兴起，与我国现行的学科设置之间存在着不适应、不协调等矛盾。这个矛盾已经成为制约科技支撑文化发展的要素之一，成为制约文化科技人才培养与使用的要素之一。

建议重点探讨与研究能够发展公共文化科技基础、文化资源和事关文化事业与文化产业发展战略的高新技术，整合与调整能够支撑我国文化大发展、大繁荣和新成就的发展目标，至少在未来二十年内保持相对稳定的学科布局。

（五）实施文化科技创新计划和对接国家重大文化科技专项

深入分析国家"十一五"和"十二五"社会与经济发展目标、科技重点布局和各类科技计划，充分发挥文化系统内外的综合优势和社会科技的作用，积极承担文化领域高技术研究发展计划、科技支撑计划和政策引导类科技计划等科技任务，同时积极组织一批符合文化科技发展战略目标的国家科技重大专项。

（六）争取并承接国家重大文化科技基础设施建设

根据科技推动文化发展的需要，结合文化建设和文化发展的学科领域布局，按照科技战略目标相对一致、研究领域相近、支撑条件易于共享的原则，积极探索与系统内外相关高等院校、骨干文化企业和地方的合作形式，以文化和旅游部直属研究机构、相关高等院校、骨干文化企业和地方为依托，建立4—8个开放的、跨学科或跨地域的国家文化科研基地，建设若干个国家文化科技基础设施，使之成为科技推动文化发展的主要力量。

（七）实现信息技术与文化的联姻

结合时代要求，以信息技术装备文化艺术研究与创作，加强民族文化原创力，促进信息技术与人文技术的全面结合，通过内容创新，创造与开发符合市场需求的文化产品，提高信息文化与网络文化的内容供给能力和服务能力。

（八）支撑重大文化服务工程

通过技术集成创新，形成支撑重大文化服务工程的关键技术，包括：移动多媒体广播（CMMB）技术、下一代广播电视网（NGB）技术、有线数字电视网络整合技术、直播卫星技术、地面数字电视广播技术、"村村通"工程支撑技术、数字电影制作基地支撑技术、农村电影放映工程支撑技术、动漫制作基地支撑技术、文化信息资源共享工程支撑技术、流动文化服务支撑技术、农家书屋工程支撑技术、国际印刷复制基地支撑技术。

（九）研发文化科技领域的核心技术

高技术的发展，已改变传统文化的形态与业态。通过数字技术和文化艺术专有技术的集成创新与应用创新，支持研发一批文化科技领域的核心技术，支持文化建设的可持续发展。

（十）促进文化产业"产学研用"结合，积极进行文化产品创新

促进科技、教育、文化产业企业之间的联系与合作，加强"产、学、研"结合，特别是鼓励教育的产、学、研相结合。教育（特别是高等教育）利用自己的科研优势，去发展高科技文化产业，并以良好的经济效益来支持与发展文化和科技。在发展过程中，又要坚持因地制宜、分类指导的原则，鼓励各地区根据地方实际科技水平提出符合本地情况的文化产业发展模式。加大地方政府对当地文化产业发展的统筹权，开拓多形式、多渠道发展的路子，满足社会对文化消费多样式、多层次的需求，促进文化产业更好地为现代化建设服务。

（十一）全面实施"文化科技"行动计划

1. 在国家文化创新工程的框架内，安排"科技文化"行动计划并组织实施。

2. 在公共文化科技基础研究、文化资源科学与技术、文化创意、文化战略高新技术等领域，集中支持一批产学研用相结合的重大项目，努力实现一批关键、核心技术突破和成果产业化。

3. 加速推广一批有利于增加国际需求、扩大内需的技术和文化消费产品。对具有我国优秀民族文化自主知识产权并能够带动形成新的文化消费市场需求的技术和产品，加大产业化、商业化和规模化应用力度。大力推广适用于文化建设和文化发展的高新技术。

4. 支持公共文化事业和文化企业研发中心的建设与发展。围绕文化科技发展所确定的重点领域，鼓励高等院校、科研院所承担国家级研发机构建设，不断增强文化科技创新能力。

（十二）大力支持文化企业提高自主创新能力

1. 支持文化企业承担国家和文化和旅游部重大科技攻关任务，加强文化企业研发能力建设。

2. 支持建立产学研用相结合的文化产业技术创新战略联盟，加强大中小文化企业的创新合作，加速先进技术向文化企业的技术辐射与转移。

3. 促进中小文化企业的兼并重组，扶持和壮大一批具有创新能力和自主知识产权的中小文化企业。

（十三）实施"文化科技人才聚集"计划

1. 在国家文化创新工程的框架内，安排"文化科技人才聚集"行动计划并组织实施。

2. 积极吸引从事前沿文化科技研究的专家学者，积极吸引掌握核心或关键技术的专业技术人才，支持文化科技研发团队，聚集一批文化科技领军人才，研究并出台支持文化科技高端领军人才的政策。支持高校毕业生参与文化科技创新和自主创业。

3. 引导部分高校积极开设具有文化科技特色的专业，协同教育部研究并出台支持文化科技特色专业的政策。

（十四）支持科研院所、高校和文化企业开展文化科技协同创新

促进科研院所、高校的科技成果向公共文化事业单位和文化企业进行转移，推进文化科技产学研用创新体系的建设。对产学研用四位一体联合提出的科研项目，在文化和旅游部科技计划中优先安排。

（十五）支持文化产业技术联盟等新型产业组织的发展

1. 鼓励文化企业联合科研院所、高校等各类创新主体，成立产学研用结合的标准联盟、技术联盟和产业联盟，开展关键共性技术的合作研究，建立科技资源开放共享平台。

2. 进一步促进文化科技协会组织发展。支持协会开展战略研究和分析，参与编制发展规划，制定文化行业标准，提升文化科技协会在文化产业和区域内的代表性和影响力。

（十六）推进文化知识产权战略和技术标准战略

1. 加速推进中华民族优良文化中自主知识产权的收集、整理、申报、注册、登记和保护工作，促进文化知识产权和专利成果的转化。建立健全文化知识产权服务体系、专利经营体系和正版文化产品流通示范体系，建立实时高效的文化知识产权侵权预警和风险防范机制。

2. 支持对文化建设和文化发展有带动作用的文化产业集群技术标准体系建设，支持以文化产业链为纽带形成的标准联盟，推进文化领域整体标准化建设。

四、运用科技推动文化发展繁荣的相关举措

（一）加快构建面向国内国际、覆盖广泛、技术先进的现代传播体系

1. 加快传统媒体与新兴媒体的融合发展；
2. 以牢牢占领互联网等新兴电子媒介的文化阵地为出发点，促进先进文化信息与手机等个人或特定群体的多媒体终端播放器的融合；
3. 促进三网融合，加强适用于文化信息传播的新型互联网等电子媒介传播技术的研发；
4. 加强博物馆、纪念馆、图书馆、文化馆、美术馆、剧院及文化信息资源共享工程等公共文化设施支撑技术的应用与研发；
5. 加快建设文化信息资源共享工程，立项建设体现国家水平、在国际国内具有重要影响力的网络博物馆、网络纪念馆、网络图书馆、网络文化馆、网络美术馆、网络剧院；
6. 实施现代传播体系内技术、管理、服务等环节的标准化。

（二）加快数字技术、信息技术和网络技术与文化内容的对接和深入融合

1. 加快提高互联网等新兴电子媒介的文化内容或文化产品与服务的供给能力；
2. 推动我国优秀创意文化作品或产品的数字化、网络化；
3. 加快中华民族文化资源的数字化、信息化的进程；
4. 加强支撑文化艺术创作、文艺表现、文艺表演、文化创意、艺术展示的新技术、新材料、新工艺等关键技术与设备的应用与研发；
5. 加强支撑动漫与游戏等数字媒体内容开发的新技术、新手段的共性技术与设备的应用与研发；
6. 推动文化内容供给在设计、制作、生产、流转等方面的技术、管理、服务等环节的标准化。

（三）推进公共文化领域新技术、新模式与新形态的应用与发展

1. 加强支撑文物保护与修复、文献保护与修复、藏品陈列与展览、非物质文化遗产保护与传承的新技术、新材料、新工艺等关键技术与设备的应用与研发；
2. 加强支撑流动放映、流动演出、图书流动借阅（包括自助图书馆）、手持多媒体文

化移动终端等新型服务模式的关键技术与系统研发；

3.加强支撑虚拟博物馆、虚拟图书馆、虚拟美术馆、虚拟文化馆、虚拟纪念馆、虚拟剧院等新型服务形态的关键技术与系统研发；

4.加强支撑文化知识产权保护、文化传播内容审查、文化市场监管、低俗与不良文化监控等的政府管理的新技术应用与系统研发；

5.支持有明显区域文化特色和广泛用户群基础的文化信息共性服务中的新技术应用与系统研发；

6.发展公共文化领域内技术、管理、服务等环节的标准化。

（四）深化文化体制改革，进一步解放和发展文化生产力

配合国家科技体制改革，整合文化系统内外科技资源与力量，深化促进科技进步的机制改革，提高管理水平，推进劳动人事制度和分配制度改革，使各种创造才能竞相展现，生机活力充分激发，增强自我发展能力。

文化科技创新活动的评价、评估与统计问题研究[*]

一、本课题主要研究内容

本课题研究内容主要包括四个方面：

一是研究文化科技创新活动的内涵，厘清文化科技的内涵和创新活动的边界，并提炼出参与文化科技创新活动的主体性要素，归纳文化科技融合创新的发展阶段，为文化与科技融合的特征识别和成效评价夯实理论基础；

二是研究文化与科技融合的关键识别特征，为国家和施政部门对包含文化与科技融合特征的产业园区、实体企业与企业产品（含服务）进行特征识别提供识别根据，并为国家扶持与资助文化与科技融合项目提供扶持与资助的判别依据；

三是研究文化与科技融合的成效评测指标，为国家与地方有关部门对文化与科技融合影响政治、经济、文化、社会的成效进行评测提供可行标准；

四是对文化与科技融合的识别特征与成效评测标准进行归一化与模态化构建，并在此基础之上设计开发评价系统，通过构建评价模型及开发评价应用系统，使文化与科技融合的特征识别和成效评价工作得以客观、高效进行。

二、主要研究结果

（一）明晰文化科技创新活动的内涵

文化科技创新活动是围绕文化科技发展及其创新而开展的一系列有利于促进文化和科技创新要素的有效互动和结合，有利于切实发挥科技创新对文化发展的支撑、引领、驱动作用，有利于实现我国精神文明和物质文明的共同繁荣和发展的研究实践活动，以服务于文化建设和满足人民群众的精神需求为根本任务，其着力点在于文化与科技的融合创新。文化与科技融合创新，本质上是高新技术向文化领域的选择性切入，重点在于

---

[*] 本文系科技部发展改革专项《国家文化科技创新战略研究》子课题研究报告，成稿于 2013 年 10 月。收入本书时有改动。

充分利用已有的现代科技成果和技术积累，加强技术集成创新，提升文化领域的科技含量与技术水平，强化发展模式、服务模式、管理模式的创新。

1. 文化科技创新活动的主要内容

从文化科技创新的形式来看，文化科技创新活动主要包括文化与科技融合创新和文化科技的自主创新两个方面：

一是文化与科技融合创新，即面向文化领域的实际需求，充分利用已有的现代科技成果和技术积累，通过技术集成创新和模式创新实现文化与科技的无缝连接和高度融合。

二是文化科技的自主创新，通过对文化各重点领域重大科技需求的分析凝练，结合实际应用，开展技术创新，突破文化领域的共性技术瓶颈和关键技术瓶颈，切实解决制约文化发展的技术难点。

从文化科技创新活动的面向来看，主要有文化事业和文化产业生产两个方面：

一是面向文化事业，提升服务能力。通过工具创新提升公共文化服务能力；加强文化资源数字化关键技术研究和应用，以及高新技术与传统工艺结合的文物保护和修复方法研究，使得文物保护的手段、目标及效果更加积极有效；通过发挥相关技术门类的应用作用，不断提高文化行政管理效率并改善文化执法科技手段。

二是面向文化产业，促进产业发展。通过文化科技创新活动加强文化领域技术集成创新和模式创新，推进文化与科技互相融合，促进传统文化产业优化升级，推动新兴文化产业培育发展。

2. 文化科技创新活动的主体性要素

文化科技创新活动的主体性要素包括政府、企业、大学、科研机构、金融机构、中介机构等，各主体性要素间互相联系而形成网络系统，各主体性要素的完备程度以及之间的联系互动能力、资源流动效率影响着文化科技创新活动的效率和质量。根据各主体性要素在文化科技创新活动中的作用分为推动者、执行者和支撑者三类。

3. 文化科技创新活动的总体特征

文化科技创新活动的总体特征包括：第一，文化科技的功能和作用必须是有助于意识形态的。第二，文化科技必须依托相应物质化的文化载体，而不能孤立存在。第三，文化科技对非强制、非结构化意识形态的物质形式产生作用。

4. 文化科技创新活动的阶段性

（1）基本融合创新阶段。即科技在文化企业、行业范围内得到应用，文化装备、软件、系统研制和自主发展得到先进技术的支撑，生产效率和生产效益不断得到显著提高。重点行业及新兴业态技术装备水平得到提高，文化产业发展方式开始发生转变，文化产业整体实力和竞争力得以加强，初步形成文化产业集群。

（2）全面融合创新阶段。文化科技从"选择性介入"走向"整体融合"，文化科技共性支撑技术取得重要突破，科技对文化产业的带动作用明显提高，以文化和科技融合示范基地为主体的产业化载体建设全面推进，文化事业科技服务能力显著增强，文化行政管理科技手段明显改善，文化科技创新体系初步建立，重点文化领域科技支撑水平显著提升，推动文化产业逐步成长为国民经济支柱性产业。

（3）深度融合创新阶段。文化和科技深度融合，科技创新成为文化发展的核心支撑和重要引擎。文化科技发展环境不断完善，文化科技创新充满活力，高素质文化科技人才队伍发展壮大，文化科技创新体系得到完善，文化和科技融合示范基地成为文化产业的重要载体，基本形成带动文化产业发展、推动文化事业进步、规范文化市场秩序的文化科技支撑体系。文化产业成为国民经济支柱性产业。

（二）确定文化科技创新活动评价的目的、对象和视角

1. 文化科技创新活动评价的目的

开展文化科技创新活动评价、评估工作，总体目的是准确了解与把握文化科技融合创新的发展现状和总体进展，重点考量文化科技的融合创新对文化发展的成效，为相关决策者（各级政府等）制定相关政策、措施、目标和规划提供依据；使相关参与者及时了解自身的发展水平和发展潜力，通过对比明确自身的优势，清醒认识自己的劣势，激发文化科技融合创新的积极性，并借鉴他人的先进经验实现自身的快速成长和跨越式发展。

2. 文化科技创新活动的评价对象

文化科技创新活动是一个多层次、多主体、多视角的综合体系，各主体性要素存在巨大差异性，评价对象的选择具有多样性，在文化科技创新活动内涵和评价目的的基础之上，选取"文化科技融合产品（含服务）""文化科技创新项目（科技类项目或课题）""文化科技融合示范基地"和"文化科技创新型企业"四个评价对象展开文化科技创新活动的评价、评估研究。

3. 选取以成效为主的评价视角

文化与科技融合是一个长期的发展过程，对其评价主要包括资源视角、应用视角和成效视角三个角度。由于现代科技对文化是一柄双刃剑，科技恰当介入为文化发展提供重要支撑、引领作用，而科技的滥用也给文化的发展带来消极影响。在文化与科技融合的过程中，要正确处理文化与科技的关系，避免走入"文化科技化"的误区。因此，对文化科技创新活动的评价不能单纯地以资源视角、应用视角、成效视角均等化地展开，应以成效视角为主，从更有利于服务文化建设、更有利于满足人民群众精神文化需求的角度出发构建评价指标体系。

（三）构建文化科技创新活动评价指标体系

评价是指通过评价者根据评价标准和评价指标对评价对象的各个方面进行量化和非量化的测量过程，最终得出一个可靠的并且具有逻辑的结论。评价具有诊断功能、导向功能和激励功能。评价的本质是价值判断。评价指标是描述评价对象所处状态和特征的科学语言，表明评价对象某一特征的概念及其数量表现，是评价的标准和尺度，是衡量、比较事物的基本依据。评价指标体系是根据评价任务和目标的需要，全面系统地评价对象的一系列较为完整的、相互之间存在有机联系的评价指标集合。评价指标体系是一个信息系统，是反映评价对象全貌的信息集合。

构建文化科技创新活动评价指标体系是在准确理解把握文化科技创新活动内涵和评价目标的基础之上，主要通过成效评价视角对评价对象进行系统分析，研究评价的维度，以及每个维度下的评价因素（多个），明确具体的评价指标；并通过评价指标的合理组合形成一个系统的、完整的评价指标体系架构。针对文化科技创新活动的特殊性和评价对象的差异性，分别构建了"文化科技融合产品（含服务）评价指标体系""文化科技创新项目（科技类项目或课题）评价指标体系""文化科技融合示范基地评价指标体系"和"文化科技创新型企业评价指标体系"。

（四）构建基于 AHP 模糊综合评价法的评价模式

本评价系统在反映文化与科技融合创新的特征和成效的指标中，存在大量定性指标，简单的线性数学模型不能很好地描述各指标之间的关系，易产生较大误差使评价结果失真。此外，一些内在的因素的度量很难通过数学统计方法进行的，需要通过评价者的主观判断，不同的人对这些因素的评价是具有模糊性的，鉴于此，本课题采用 AHP 模糊综合评价法构建评价模型。

AHP (Analytic Hierarchy Process) 层次分析法，是一种使人们的思维过程和主观判断实现规范化、数量化的方法，可以使很多不确定因素得到很大程度降低，不仅简化了系统分析与计算工作，而且有助于决策者保持其思维过程和决策过程原则的一致性。模糊综合评价应用模糊关系合成的原理，从多个因素对评价对象隶属等级状况进行综合评价，不仅可以根据模糊平价集上的值按最大隶属度原则评定对象所属等级，而且可以按综合分值的大小进行评价和排序。优点是可对涉及模糊因素的对象系统进行综合评价，将一些边界不清、不容易定量的因素定量化，从多个因素对被评价事物隶属等级状况进行综合性评价，广泛地应用于经济、社会等领域。

（五）开发基于 web 的在线评价系统

文化科技创新活动评价工作不仅要处理大量数据，而且对流程的设计、不同主体的分工有较高要求，传统的评价方法效率低下、评价能力不足，已经无法满足现代评价工作的需求。随着网络技术的快速发展，网上评价已经成为现代评价工作的一种新手段和方法，建立一套系统完善、界面友好、反应灵敏、结构严谨、安全准确的信息管理系统，可有效促进文化科技创新活动评价工作的准确、高效开展，拟开发一套在线评价系统，基于 Web 的评价系统采用 B/S 架构，HTML 标记语言生成前端网页，数据库管理系统采用 SQL Server2000，同时采用 ASP 进行脚本程序编写。客户端可通过浏览器直接登录和访问系统，便于系统的维护和管理。

三、对有关重点问题的分析

（一）文化科技的内涵与外延

文化科技在学术研究领域是一个不断发展的概念，其内涵与外延与国家在一定时期的经济和社会发展背景密切相关。理解其内涵首先要正确认识文化科技概念提出的时代背景，其次要考虑我国基本国情、技术发展水平和战略目标，再次要把握不同层级政府的职责定位、公共文化服务和文化产业的特点。总的来说，文化科技的本质是一种服务于社会意识形态的特殊工具（手段）。其特殊是因为它具有动态特点和时代特色，不同时代表达不同的文化，其作用不同，服务对象不同。

如果说文化科技是一种服务于社会意识形态的特殊工具，那么我们可以从文化科技服务或研究的对象来介绍文化科技的外延。根据文化科技的相关的国家政策以及国家文化发展战略，我们认为文化科技应该主要关注社会文化和精神文化两个层面的相关科学技术，而不是将文化科技的着力点放在物质文化这个更为物化和宽泛的层面上进行考虑。而在社会文化的层面上，我们也不应该重点考虑诸如法律、政策、政府机构等具备强制性色彩的社会架构所带来的各种文化物化产物。因此，我们认为，文化科技所关注的对象就是"服务于意识形态，有助于意识形态，特别是有助于非强制、非结构化的意识形态的表现、表示、表达、传播、影响、传递、认知、理解、认同相关的物化文化形式及内容发展的各类科学技术"。

（二）文化科技创新概念的辨析

1. 关于文化科技创新的争议

文化科技是一种服务于社会意识形态的特殊工具，文化科技创新则是以更好地发挥文化科技服务社会意识形态的工具性作用、促进文化建设为目的的。开展文化科技创新活动评价首先要搞清文化科技创新的概念，目前，对于文化科技创新的概念一直存在争议，争议的焦点主要有以下三点：一，对文化科技创新中所使用的"科学技术"的界定。对创新活动中哪些是技术性的，哪些不是技术性的，人们的认识并不一致，由此导致对文化科技创新在概念与定义上的差别和争论；二，文化科技创新对科技变动的强度有无限定以及在什么程度上限定。争论的焦点在于，增量性改进即技术上的渐进改进导致规模效益增长是否属于技术创新范围；三，既然各种科技创新都需要通过在市场上的成功实现而表现出来，不成功的不能称之为科技创新，那么，对具体的文化科技创新而言，"成功"的概念和标准是什么？文化科技创新成功指的是商业盈利、市场份额还是技术优势，抑或其他效益？文化科技创新成功的效益判据中，经济效益、社会效益、文化效益哪个更具优先级？

对于文化科技创新中"科学技术"的界定，建议采用广义上的概念，即人类在科学实验和生产活动过程中认识和改造自然所积累起来的知识、经验与技能的总和。在文化科技创新体系中所应用的文化科技主要包括认知科学、系统科学、计算科学、信息科学、材料科学以及一系列前沿性交叉科学，以及物联网技术、云计算技术、虚拟空间技术、图像传输技术、数字转换技术、监测技术、仿真技术、防护技术等一系列开发前景广阔的应用技术。文化科技在文化管理、文化创意、文化生产、文化展示、文化传播、文化交流、公共文化服务、文化遗产保护等领域，发挥着解放文化生产力和改变文化发展方式的巨大作用。

在"文化科技创新对科技变动的强度有无限定以及在什么程度上限定"的争论上，如果对文化科技创新中"科学技术"的理解达成共识，那么自然就会得出科技创新对科技改进的强弱和多少不应有所规定的结论。事实上，它与市场的销售量及市场份额、产品或服务的收益率有很大关系，由此可见，科技改进在创新中的应用是极其重要的。

对"成功"的界定应该有新的价值标准。在一般的科技创新的讨论中，学者们普遍认为当期经济利润的增长并非是评判科技创新成功与否的唯一标准。应从科技创新成功的整体概念出发，科技创新应当以正常平均利润为基点，有一个波动范围，其盈利在一段时间内可能小于、等于或大于平均利润。这样科技创新成功就表现为：一是直接获得当期超额利润；二是当前盈利不满足上述的波动范围，而在其他方面能取得较高期望收益。由于文化产品和服务的特殊性，其不仅具有经济属性，还具有意识形态方面的文化属性，因此文化科技创新活动所产生的效益不仅包含一般意义上的经济效益，还包括特有的社会效益和文化效益。由此，对文化科技创新成功的界定必须将社会效益和文化效益纳入其中，并置于优先考虑地位。

2. 文化科技创新内涵

就宏观层面而言，文化科技创新活动就是通过将各类文化元素、内容、形式和服务与科学技术的原理、理论、方法和手段的有机结合，提升有关产品（含服务）的价值与品质，形成新的内容、形式、功能与服务，更好地满足人民文化需求。

从中观层面来讲，发展文化科技的主要手段是有效实现文化与科技的融合。应根据文化与科技在不同应用领域的需求和特点，遵循文化与科技创新的一般规律，通过开展相关目标产品开发等基于应用目标的创新活动的模式，更有效地实现创新要素的集成，促进相关先进技术、前沿技术的有效应用与发展，促进相关基础性问题的发现和研究，使先进文化理念和民族优秀文化传统获得更为有效的传播、传承载体和形式。

（三）文化科技创新活动的着力点在于文化与科技融合创新

从文化科技创新的形式来看，文化科技创新活动主要包括文化与科技融合创新和文化科技的自主创新两个方面：

一是文化与科技融合创新，即通过技术集成创新和模式创新实现文化与科技的无缝连接和高度融合。面向文化领域的实际需求，充分利用已有的现代科技成果和技术积累，通过技术集成创新，加强科技在文化产品创作、生产、传播和消费等各个层面和关键环节中的渗透和融合，提升文化作品的科技含量和技术水平，促进发展模式、服务模式、管理模式的创新。

文化科技创新活动的着力点在于促进文化与科技融合。当前，文化科技已从"选择性介入"走向"整体融合"，成为文化创新驱动力的坚实基础。文化与科技融合本质上是高新技术向文化领域的选择性切入，其切入路径是"技术集成"，目标是"模式创新"，重点在于充分利用已有的现代科技成果和技术积累，加强技术集成创新，提升文化领域的科技含量与技术水平，强化发展模式、服务模式、管理模式的创新。

二是文化科技的自主创新，即以需求为导向，应用为驱动，市场为牵引，通过自主科学技术创新突破文化创新的科技瓶颈。通过对文化各重点领域重大科技需求的分析凝练，结合实际应用，开展技术创新，突破文化领域的共性技术瓶颈和关键技术瓶颈，切实解决制约文化发展的技术难点问题，提高文化领域技术装备水平和高端系统装备的国产化水平，降低文化产品制作成本，提高文化服务效率，提高文化产业核心竞争力。

文化科技的自主创新是文化科技创新活动的重要组成部分。文化的发展不断对科技提出更高的诉求，科技发展在文化领域寻找到广泛的应用空间，文化科技整体融合在推进文化创新的同时，不仅形成对文化科技基础研究和科技创新的倒逼机制，而且为文化创新发展提供可持续驱动力量。

广义上的文化科技创新活动应既包含文化与科技的融合创新应用，也包含文化科技的自主创新研究，鉴于本课题的主要研究目的，本课题主要研究和关注的对象是前者，即文化与科技融合创新。

（四）文化科技创新活动的主体性要素

1. 推动者

推动者是指中央和各级地方政府，其通过各种行政手段和政策工具为文化科技创新活动的有序开展和顺利实施提供保障和推动力。在宏观层面上，推动者参与文化科技创新活动的手段主要包括：依托现有基地、平台等建设一批各具特色的文化科技融合示范基地，加强文化科技产业集群建设；通过把文化科技重大项目纳入国家相关科技发展规划和计划，予以持续稳定支持，开展文化科技创新；综合运用资助、贷款贴息、政府购买服务等财政投入支持方式，通过政府资金引导，带动社会资本、金融资本参与文化科技相关领域的研发和产业化；依托国家各类人才计划，注重对高端文化科技人才的引进，培养造就专业化、复合型的人才队伍与团队，为文化科技创新的可持续发展提供人才支撑。

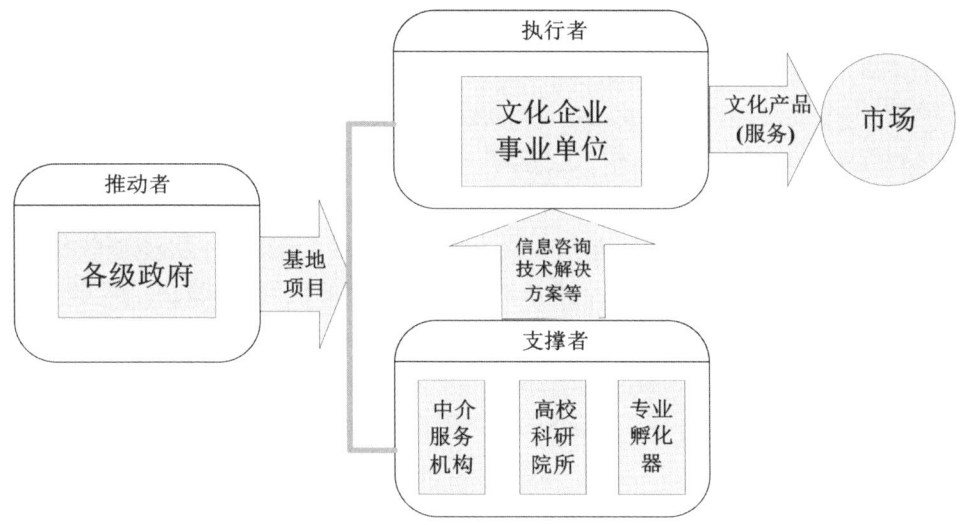

图 1　文化科技创新活动主体性要素

2. 执行者

执行者是指文化科技创新活动中文化科技的直接创新者和应用者以及文化产品和服务的直接创造者和生产机构，主要包括公益性文化单位和经营性文化单位。根据国家统计局《文化及相关产业分类（2012）》，使用是否执行企业会计制度作为区分经营性文化产业单位和公益性文化事业单位的原则。

公益性文化单位主要是指以提供公共文化服务、文化资源保护开发和文化市场管理为主的各类文化机构，主要包括文化馆、图书馆、博物馆、美术馆、空壳机关、纪念馆、工人文化宫、青少年宫等公共文化服务单位和各级文物保护单位及文化行政管理单位。

公益性文化单位进行文化创新活动是以更好地满足人民基本文化需求为目标的，按照公益性、基本性、均等性、便利性的要求，通过加强科技在适应领域的应用和技术集成创新，改善文化基础设施建设，完善公用文化服务网络，让群众广泛享有免费或优惠的基本公共文化服务。

经营性文化单位是指各类文化企业以及转企改制的一般文艺院团、非时政类报刊社、新闻网站等。经营性文化单位进行文化科技创新活动是企业家抓住市场的营利机会（或潜在营利机会），在坚持把社会效益放在首位、社会效益与经济效益相统一的原则下，通过科技、组织、商业和金融等活动，重新组织生产条件和要素，采取新的生产工艺，建立更高效的生产经营系统，最终推出新产品、新方法，开辟新市场，获得新原料来源，或建立企业新的组织等的全过程。文化企业作为文化产品和服务的主要提供者，在市场机制下参与市场竞争，具有更高的敏感度和更强的创新动力，是文化科技创新活动的主体，在研究开发投入、技术创新活动、创新成果转化应用等环节中起着主导作用。

值得注意的是，在构建公共文化服务体系的过程中，通过采用市场机制的方式，在政府采购、项目补贴、定向资助、贷款贴息、税收减免等政策措施鼓励下，越来越多的企业参与到公共文化服务之中。文化企业以公共文化服务为载体，在参与公共文化建设中实现自身价值，在获得收入的同时推动了文化事业的发展，实现文化事业与文化产业的协调发展。例如，获得第四届文化和旅游部创新奖、由江苏省文化厅推荐、由无锡市新区管理委员会社会事业局和艾迪讯科技（无锡）有限公司共同完成的《公共图书馆数字化建设与创新管理》项目就是政企合作打造优质公共文化服务的典型代表。

3. 支撑者

支撑者指为文化科技创新活动提供资源、信息、技术、整体解决方案等支持，依托中介服务机构、高校科研院所、专业孵化器等形成的文化科技创新服务体系。中介机构提供资源协调、投融资、人才培训、公共服务、展示交易、行业服务等。高校、科研院所为企业开展文化科技创新活动提供信息、技术、整体解决方案等支撑和服务，如满足文化产品设计、生产、传播、运营、体验、交易等环节的科技需求，开展关键及共性技术攻关、技术集成创新等，实现产学研用的紧密结合，提高文化科技创新及应用能力。专业孵化器促进文化科技成果转化和创新创业人才培养，培育和扶植文化科技类中小企业快速成长。

（五）文化科技创新活动的总体特征

在对文化科技创新概念的辨析以及文化科技创新活动主要内容和主体性要素的理解把握的基础上，我们展开对文化科技创新活动总体特征的研究。总的来说，文化科技创新活动的研究对象有着以下三点特征：

第一,文化科技的功能和作用必须是有助于意识形态的。这就意味着直接的物质文化中所蕴含的科技,由于其最终的功能或并非弘扬意识形态,因此可能并不是文化科技所需要进行研究和处理的对象。比如,任何工业产品的制作其实也蕴含了相应的文化成分,形成独特的工业产品文化,但是这种文化往往是从实用角度、消费角度进行考虑,并没有同上层建筑的意识形态有明显的关联,即使在其中添加了很多新的科技元素和科技成分,这种产品所关注的科技依然不能够看成是文化科技的组成部分。但是,在文艺演出、电影、网络文化的创作、演出、制作中,内容明显传递着创作者、制作者和管理者的思想,同整个社会环境中的价值观念、审美观念、思维方式、道德伦理紧密关联,而科学技术的运用能够明显改善其中蕴含的意识形态元素在表现、表示、表达、传播、影响方面取得的效果。此时,我们从目的论的角度看,是否是文化科技,首先要看其是否有助于意识形态的传播和产生影响。

第二,文化科技必须依托相应物质化的文化载体存在,不能孤立存在。由于科技是个实际存在,是改造自然世界的方法,是形而下的;而文化本身则是来自人文世界和精神世界的东西,是形而上的,物质只是文化的一种表象。那么文化科技就必须首先符合科技存在的客观规律,存在具体的物质形式,这样才可以避免将文化科技的着力点转入形而上的领域。由此,对于艺术形态的系统论等科学理论体系的梳理和建立,并不应属于文化科学需要主动研究的范畴,只有当艺术形态的方法论能够指导艺术内容创作的物化和最终实体化时,这种科学理论才能够成为文化科技的主要研究内容。因此,文化科技的对象研究还主要是针对"物"或"实体"的研究,而不是针对更深层次的形而上的研究。

第三,文化科技对非强制、非结构化意识形态的物质形式产生作用。意识形态的物化形态有很多种,政府体制和结构就是属于结构化的意识形态的物质化表现,而法律就是意识形态的强制部分,各类法律的物化形式,比如法具、刑具、警具的科技化,则不属于文化科技需要研究的对象和范围。而像国家机关、行政机构、管理体制等物质存在,虽然其属于意识形态的物质化表现,但是由于其已经相对系统化、结构化,也不属于文化科技所研究的部分。文化科技所涵盖的文化领域,应该是文学、艺术、科学、旅游、新闻、出版等意识形态相对宽泛的领域,而不是类似法律、行政之类的已经强制化、结构化的东西。

(六)评价对象:产品、项目、基地、企业

通过以上对文化创新活动主体性要素的研究,我们可以清晰地看到文化科技创新活动是一个多层次、多主体、多视角的综合体系,评价客体的选择具有多样性。结合文化科技创新活动评价的目的,选取"文化科技融合产品(含服务)评价""文化科技创新项

目（科技项目）评价""文化科技融合示范基地评价"和"文化科技创新型企业"四个评价客体，对其展开文化科技创新活动的评价、评估研究，是国家层面在当前形势下的重要关注点，是政府了解与把握文化与科技融合发展的客观需要与新要求。

1. 文化科技创新产品（含服务）

文化科技创新产品（含服务）主要指以文化为核心内容，为直接满足人们的精神需要而进行的创作、制造、传播、展示等的物品和服务；重点关注那些既有文化附加值又有科技创新驱动含量的综合型产品。

对文化科技创新产品（含服务）的评价重点，在于通过对文化科技创新产品和服务的评估，了解文化产品是否通过运用合适的技术使原有的创意和内容有了更多的表现形式和表现手段，使艺术创造有更丰富的题材和手段，使产品的文化品质得到提升，传播效果得到改善，更好地满足了某类人的文化需求，产生了更好的文化效益。

2. 文化科技创新项目（科技类项目或课题）

文化科技创新项目的评价主要针对由国家或地方公共财政支持，被纳入国家科技计划、国家文化科技提升计划、国家文化科技创新工程以及部门和地方文化科技创新项目等的文化科技类项目或课题，主要面向文化发展的科技需求，针对文化内容创作、生产、管理、传播与消费等文化产业重点环节，开展共性关键技术研究以及文化领域标准规范的建设，真正解决文化发展遇到的实际技术难点问题，以增强文化领域共性技术、关键技术支撑能力，提高文化领域科技的支撑能力并引导规范产业健康有序发展。文化科技创新项目包括文化科技战略研究、文化科技基础科研项目、文化领域重要核心技术、关键技术和集成技术攻关项目、文化行业技术标准制定研究以及先进适用技术转化推广等。

通过对文化科技创新项目的评估，主要了解文化科技创新项目（科技项目）是否解决具有前瞻性、全局性和引领性的重大科技问题，是否推动文化科技创新成果的运用和推广，是否发挥科技项目对文化发展的支撑、服务和引领带动作用，更好地满足文化建设的科技需求。

3. 文化科技融合示范基地

文化科技融合示范基地是文化企业及相关机构的集聚区域，其中集聚着各类文化和科技融合型企业，一大批文化科技复合型人才，以及专业孵化器、中介服务机构、科研院所等相关机构，是探索文化科技产业集群式发展、创新链和产业链互动集合的新模式的重要载体，能够产生集约效应和集聚效应。

文化科技融合示范基地作为文化产业的重要载体，在促进传统文化产业的优化升级、推动新兴文化产业的培育发展、提高文化事业服务能力和改善文化行政管理科技手段等方面具有很强的代表性；同时，文化科技融合示范基地作为各级政府一项重要的政策手段，是国家的政策工具，对文化科技融合示范基地的评价定位于"政策评价"，强调目的性，强调其对国家导向目标的实现程度和实际融合产出效果。

通过对文化与科技融合示范基地的评估，从区域层面对文化科技创新活动发展水平进行了解和把握，明确开展文化科技创新活动的切入点和关键环节，从而为各地推进文化科技融合提供方向性指导。

4. 文化科技创新型企业

企业是文化产品和服务的主要提供者，也是开展文化科技创新活动的主体。文化企业开展文化创新活动主要是以市场为导向，准确把握市场需求，在新思想或新方法的指导下，创造性地运用文化科技新知识，实质性改进技术、创意产品（服务），经过研究开发和技术组合对既有存量资源进行整合，提供新产品、新工艺或新服务，在技术集成创新的同时开展发展模式、服务模式、管理模式等模式创新，最终为企业创造利润、获取经济效益，同时产生文化效益和社会效益。

对文化科技型企业的评价主要是衡量企业开展文化科技创新活动的基础条件、应用水平和产出成效，对企业文化科技创新活动水平进行全面综合分析。通过对文化科技型企业的评估，对同行业内企业的文化科技融合水平形成比较，为企业加强文化科技融合提供努力方向和工作要点，从而实质性推进文化科技创新活动的进程。

（七）评价视角：以成效评价为主

文化与科技融合是一个长期的发展过程，需要分阶段推进，在辨明了文化科技内涵和外延，理解了文化科技创新活动的着力点和根本任务的基础之上，进一步讨论开展文化科技创新评价的视角。文化科技创新活动的着力点在于文化与科技的融合，通过技术集成的手段实现高新技术向文化领域的选择性切入，其成功与否取决于"切入点"的基础条件发育程度、"切入路径"的应用成熟度，以及"切入"之后的融合效果。由此，评价的视角主要包括资源视角、应用视角和成效视角三个角度。

资源视角主要从文化科技创新活动的资源就绪程度出发，主要包括基础设施和环境建设状况，衡量文化科技创新活动环境发育程度和保障水平；应用视角主要从科学技术在文化创作、生产、传播等过程中的应用情况出发，衡量科技与文化的融合的广度和深度，文化领域科技的应用水平以及文化与科技实质结合的紧密程度；成效视角关注文化科技创新活动对经济、文化、社会发展的贡献，尤其是对文化本身的成效，衡量文化科技融合对文化创造力、表现力、传播力的实质影响。

文化科技的融合使得文化的生产方式、表现形式和传播方式因科技发展而更加多元化、技术化、高效化。但是，现代科技对文化发展也是一柄双刃剑，科技的恰当介入为文化发展提供重要支撑、引领作用，而科技的滥用也给文化的发展带来消极影响。具体而言，科技给文化发展带来促进作用。从创作角度看，科技为文化提供了物质技术手段；从传播角度看，科技为文化创造了前所未有的传播手段；从审美角度看，科技造就了文化产品的实用性和审美性合一。另一方面,科技对文化也产生了消极影响。首先,科技的标准化、平均化导致文化创作中艺术个性的消解;其次,科技的滥用造成了受众艺术感的钝化;最后,科技的发展使文化走上平庸化、大众化、快餐化的道路。

科技对文化的发展有利有弊,不能一概而论,既要肯定科技进步对文化发展的积极作用,也要警惕科技滥用对文化造成的不利影响。文化与科技融合创新活动的本质是促进文化的发展,在文化与科技融合的过程中,要正确处理文化与科技的关系,避免走入"文化科技化"的误区。因此,对文化科技创新活动的评价不能单纯地以资源视角、应用视角、成效视角均等化地展开,要通过评价体系树立正确的导向。

从更有利于服务文化建设、更有利于满足人民群众精神文化需求的角度出发,在深刻理解文化科技创新活动内涵的基础上,通过对文化科技创新活动特点的分析,重点以成效视角为主,研究评价的维度,以及每个维度下的评价因素(多个),给出文化科技创新活动成效指标体系的架构,明确具体的评价指标,构建评价指标体系。

(八)文化科技创新活动的成效评价指标体系

1. 文化科技创新产品(含服务)评价指标体系

国家统计局最新颁布的《文化及相关产业分类(2012)》提出了"文化产品"和"文化相关产品",其中"文化产品"指以文化为核心内容,为直接满足人们的精神需要而进行的创作、制造、传播、展示等的货物和服务;"文化相关产品"指实现文化产品生产所必需的辅助产品、作为文化产品实物载体或制作(使用、传播、展示)工具的文化用品、实现文化产品生产所需的专用设备。还对"文化产品"和"文化相关产品"的定义和范围进行了详细的阐释,具体来说是从其内在的本质(内涵)和外在的表现形式(外延)两个方面进行了论述。广义上的文化产品包含直接满足人们精神需求的产品和服务,也包含各类文化相关产品。从受众群体角度,文化产品主要有两个面向,一个是面向人民群众的精神需求,即狭义上的文化产品;一个是面向文化建设的自身需求,即相关文化产品。本课题所关注和研究的重点在于前者。

文化科技创新产品主要指以文化为核心内容,通过将各类文化元素、内容、形式和服务与科学技术的原理、理论、方法和手段的有机结合,提升有关产品(含服务)的价值与品质,形成新的内容、形式、功能与服务,更好地满足人民精神文化需求而制作、生产、传播、展示的文化产品(包括货物和服务)。文化科技创新产品主要有图书、报纸、期刊等出版产品,唱片、录像、CD、DVD等音像制品,广播、电视、电影等视听节目,演唱会、话剧、戏曲曲艺、魔术杂技等文艺表演,雕塑、金属、漆器等工艺美术品,以及广告服务、多媒体、动漫游戏等软件服务,房屋建筑、室内装饰、风景园林、包装装潢等设计服务,以及各类文化休闲娱乐服务等。

属性上,文化产品既具有意识形态属性,又具有商品属性。意识形态属性又可以理解为政治属性或宣传属性。文化产品具有很强的意识形态色彩，这与创作者的身份是分不开的。文化产品是以"内容为王"的"软产品"，文化产品的生产者作为内容的创作者，在生产、制作过程中其价值观不可避免地会产生影响。意识形态色彩在文化产品的生产和消费过程中都有充分的体现。文化产品的商品属性主要体现在它以消费的需求为导向，这一属性体现在以经济效益为导向的生产和销售过程中。

形态上，文化产品分为生产性文化产品和服务性文化产品两大类。生产性文化产品的典型代表，是书籍、文物或邮币卡产品、音像产品等。在多样化的物化形式中，其本质在于，生产性是由其为社会提供了直接的物质财富而赋予的。服务性文化产品的典型代表是文艺演出、文博展览以及旅游休闲等。在这类文化产品的消费中，人们无法对任何一种产品对象实行占有，仅仅是在欣赏或在获取精神满足的意义上获得了使用权。因此，服务性文化产品的存在，并不取决于产品的实物或非实物形式的区别，它的根本性特征是塑造了在非占有关系下的文化产品的消费关系和消费模式。

文化科技作为文化内容的表现手段和途径，在文化与科技的融合创新中具备丰富的文化艺术的表现形式，可以增强表现力和感染力，而且能加速文化产品的传播。本课题通过基于产品形态体验性的表现力研究、基于传播模式的传播力研究、基于新产品开发的创造力研究、基于市场导向的市场竞争力研究构建了"文化科技创新产品（含服务）评价指标体系"。

表1 文化科技创新产品（含服务）评价指标体系

目标层	准则层	评价意见		
表现力（30）	审美性	美观有趣	一般	不够美观、有趣
	解读性	容易被用户理解	不太容易被用户理解	晦涩难懂
	协调性	与整体协和度高	与整体协和度较高	在整体中显得突兀，与整体矛盾
	互动性	互动性强	一般	缺少互动性
传播力（30）	传播时效	准确迅速	比较准确迅速	不太准确迅速
	传播覆盖面	广泛	比较广泛	不够广泛
	传播效果	显著	一般	不太显著
创造力（30）	新奇性	新颖独特	比较新颖独特	不够新颖独特
	效用性	为用户提供的价值高	为用户提供的价值较高	为用户提供的价值不高
市场竞争力（10）	产品销售额	销售量×平均销售价格		
	市场占有率	一种产品或品牌的销售量/该产品或品牌的行业销售量		
	出口创汇率	（成品出口外汇净收入－原料外汇成本）/原料外汇成本*100%		
	用户满意度	用户感受/期望值		

2. 文化科技创新项目（科技类项目或课题）评价指标体系

通过对文化科技创新项目的顶层设计和专家咨询机制，统筹开展文化科技创新项目的组织、实施、管理、推广、转化及应用，主要包括文化科技基础性、前沿性、关键技术研究，持续增加科学研究积累，解决具有前瞻性、全局性和引领性的重大科技问题，并推动文化科技创新成果的运用和推广，切实发挥科技项目的引领带动作用。

通过对文化科技创新项目的评估，主要了解文化科技创新项目是否解决具有前瞻性、全局性和引领性的重大科技问题，是否促进文化科技创新成果的运用和推广，是否发挥科技项目对文化发展的支撑、服务和引领带动作用，更好地满足文化建设的科技需求。

对科技项目的评价指标体系是从决策功效、研究绩效和项目成效三方面来考察科技项目研究成果。决策功效是从决策者的立场提出来的指标，用以衡量成果符合决策者的价值标准的程度，具体通过课题的重要性和迫切性、实施的可行性、成果的实用性和推广意义及效益的现实性和时间性来考察。研究绩效指标是通过学术创新度、学术水平、研究的科学性、研究的深度和难度及成果的表述水平来具体考察的。项目成效主要是项目的实施所产生的直接或间接的效益，主要包括文化效益、经济效益和社会效益。

表2 文化科技创新项目（科技类项目或课题）评价指标体系

目标层	准则层	指标解释
总目标（20）	重要性和迫切性	是否属于当前文化建设的重点研究领域
	与文化创新结合程度	是否与文化创新紧密结合
	实施的可行性	技术系统的完整性和成果实际应用的可靠性，技术的政策环境、自然条件、资源条件、技术开发能力等方面的生产适应程度及经济合理性
总目标（20）	风险分析与控制	技术风险和市场风险分析的全面性和控制能力
	技术路线完备性	技术路线设计是否完备
	推广意义和效益	指创新成果推广的现实性和时间性
运行管理（10）	承担单位选择条件	承担单位的科研能力和专业性
	产学研结合情况	创新所需生产要素的资源配置和有效组合情况
	配套措施落实情况	创新环境和硬件设备的就绪情况

续表

目标层	准则层	指标解释
学术技术价值（10）	科学性指标	研究设计严密、分析论证符合逻辑、实验条件符合有关标准、统计处理正确、提供数据真实可靠
	创新性指标	研究方法、设计思想、工艺技术特点及最终结果等是否属于国际、国内或省（自治区、直辖市）内首创，或有无实质性的突破、改进和补充等
	先进性指标	解决该领域的技术难题或行业的热点问题的情况，与同行业相比较达到国际、国内或省内何种水平
实用价值（10）	创新成果水平	科技成果的新颖性、先进性、成熟性、适用性
	知识产权指标	知识产权的保护方式、法律状态、类别、数量
	市场效果指标	指市场的占有程度、竞争能力、年销售量和销售趋势，以及成果应用的广泛性和推广的迫切性来表征
文化效益（30）	创造力	有助于提高新奇性与效用性
	表现力	有助于增强审美性、解读性、协调性、互动性
	传播力	有助于提升传播时效、扩大传播覆盖面、改善传播效果
经济社会效益（20）	创新收益	收入构成和获取利润中直接源自技术创新成果的部分，直接反映通过创新实现经济效益的情况
	成本减低率	成本降低额与按上年实际平均单位成本计算的本年累计总成本的百分比
	社会效益	促进科技、经济与社会协调、可持续发展的效果

3. 文化科技融合示范基地评价指标体系

文化科技融合示范基地是文化企业及相关机构的集聚区域，其内集聚着各类文化和科技融合型企业，一大批文化科技复合型人才，以及专业孵化器、中介服务机构、科研院所等相关机构，是探索文化科技产业集群式发展、创新链和产业链互动集合的新模式的重要载体，能够产生集约效应和集聚效应。

文化科技融合示范基地的特征：

（1）具有产业集群的基本属性，如地理集聚性、产业一致性、本地根植性和相互协同性等。在空间布局上，文化科技融合示范基地基本呈现"一区多园"的形态，注重区域文化氛围的培育和品牌建设，不同园区拥有各自的主导产业和特色产业，由此形成巨大的文化产业动力，对区域的文化产业发展起到强有力的推动作用。

（2）具有平台托举功能。各地兴建的一批文化科技产业园区，尽管类型不同、规模有别，但普遍具有综合服务平台与公共技术平台支撑功能，依托这些支撑功能，资金、技术、人才、项目以及创意环境等关键性要素程度不同地获得了聚集效果，一批拥有高水平创意人才和核心技术支撑的新型文化企业正逐渐成为中国文化产业发展版图上富有朝气的产业生力军。

文化科技融合所形成的平台托举功能，使文化创新跃升至协同推进发展阶段，协同创新意义上的诸如信息共享平台、在线交互平台、技术孵化平台、创意衍生平台、大数据与云计算平台、跨文化传播平台以及生产分工平台等，使文化创意、文化生产、文化消费、文化传播、文化贸易获得强大的平台托举支撑，获得超过预期的协同效应、聚集效应、漫溢效应、提升效应以及优化配置效应。

在对大量区域评价办法和理论的研究基础之上，充分考虑文化科技融合示范基地运作方式及特征，形成文化科技融合示范基地发展水平评价指标体系。

表3　文化科技融合示范基地发展水平评价指标体系

目标层	准测层	指标层
融合环境（20）	基地建设	基础设施建设
		基地管理体制和监管能力
		基地发展规划
		公共服务平台建设
		人才队伍建设
	产业结构	特色产业集聚度
		主导产业首位度
		每百户单位中文化科技企业数
		每百户单位中科技服务机构（中介机构）数
		与高校共建研究中心（研究所、实验室）数
融合深度（30）	创新投入	每百户企业拥有研发机构数
		每千人拥有研发人员数
		研发经费支出占园区生产总值的比重
		文化科技企业孵化器面积
		在孵文化科技企业数

续表

目标层	准测层	指标层
融合深度（30）	创新成果	发明专利数
		省级以上名牌产品数
		重大文化科技创新项目实施数量
		拥有著名、驰名商标数
		文化新产品年产出量
融合成效（50）	经济效益	基地技工贸总收入
		总资产利润率
		单位面积的资产总额
	文化产业提升度	文化产业产值利税率
		文化产业总产值
		文化产业增加值占地区GDP比重
	文化科技融合度	文化科技产品销售收入占产品总销售收入的比重
		基地内文化科技型企业的发展水平和趋势
		科技贡献率
	文化建设贡献度	对文化产业的带动作用
		文化事业服务能力
		文化领域共性关键技术研究贡献
		对传统文化产业优化升级的促进作用
		对新兴文化产业培育和发展的推动作用

4. 文化科技创新型企业评价指标体系

企业是文化产品和服务的主要提供者，也是开展文化科技创新活动的主体。文化企业开展文化创新活动是以市场为导向，准确把握市场需求，在新思想或新方法的指导下，创造性地运用文化科技新知识，实质性改进技术、创意产品（服务），经过研究开发和技术组合对既有存量资源进行整合，提供新产品、新工艺或新服务，在技术集成创新的同时开展发展模式、服务模式、管理模式等模式创新，最终为企业创造利润获取经济效益，同时产生文化效益和社会效益。

当前，企业通过高度的文化科技融合自觉性，加强文化领域高新技术应用，加大技术要素在收入分配中所占比重，从产品的创意设计、研究开发、生产制作、营销传播等关键环节促进文化与科技融合，加快生产和营销的集约化、规模化，优化管理部门资源，节约单位成本，提高生产效率和经济效益。通过文化与科技融合改造传统文化企业运作方式，推动文化生产方式、营销方式、传播方式的创新，拓展新型文化产品和服务，扩大企业发展的新空间。企业通过文化与科技融合创新，研发具有自主知识产权的核心技术、关键技术、共性技术，加快科技创新成果的转化，切实增强技术创新的动力和活力，逐渐形成自己的核心竞争力。

对文化科技型企业的评价主要是衡量企业开展文化科技创新活动的基础条件、应用水平和产出成效，对企业文化科技创新活动水平进行全面综合分析。通过对文化科技型企业的评估，对同行业内企业的文化科技融合水平形成比较，为企业加强文化科技融合提供努力方向和工作要点，从而实质性推进文化科技创新活动的进程。

表4　文化科技创新型企业评价指标体系

目标层	准则层	指标层	指标解释
就绪度（20）	宏观环境（10）	区域战略谋划	反映区域决策者对文化科技融合认知程度和把握能力
		政策工具配置	反映政府政策性资源的稳定性和支持力度
		管理体制机制	反映区域内文化科技融合的行政效率和资源配置能力
		公共平台建设	反映区域对企业的孵化培育能力
	企业基础（10）	业绩和声誉	反映企业自身综合实力和融合创新的基本能力
		企业战略规划	反映企业对融合的重视程度和战略落实情况
		知识产权管理	反映企业对知识产权的重视程度和管理水平
		创新文化建设	反映企业整体文化氛围及对创新的分配激励能力
		创新投入强度	反映企业对融合创新的投入力度，体现了企业的资源配置导向
成熟度（30）	前端驱动（10）	研发机构建设	反映企业开展文化科技融合的基础设施和硬件保障能力
		知识产权成果	反映企业原始创新能力
		标准化建设	标准化作为专利技术的最高体现形式，反映企业在行业内创新的水平
	中端驱动（10）	二次创新投入强度	反映企业对二次创新的重视程度和能力
		科技成果转化能力	反映企业运用科技创新产品的能力
		产学研结合度	反映企业配置生产要素、提高创新效率的能力
	后端驱动（10）	市场竞争能力	反映创新成果适应市场的能力
		商业模式创新	反映企业利用商业模式促进文化科技融合的能力
		国际竞争能力	反映企业文化产品的国际化水平和国际竞争能力

续表

目标层	准则层	指标层	指标解释
贡献度（50）	经济效益（10）	创新收益强度	反映文化科技融合对企业提高利润的成效
		成本降低率	反映文化科技融合对企业降低生产成本的成效
		全员劳动生产率	反映文化科技融合对企业提高生产效率的成效
	文化效益（30）	丰富文化生产要素	科技是文化生产的核心要素之一，反映科技对提高文化生产力的成效
		改善文化存储效果	反映科技对文化存储稳定性增强、存储容量扩大、效率和质量提高等的成效
		增强文化传播能力	反映科技对文化传播时效提高、范围扩大、消耗降低、受众增加等的成效
		提升文化构成品质	反映科技对文化呈现形式的质量以及所蕴含理念、价值观念提升等的成效
		转变文化体验方式	反映科技对文化的表现形式及体验感受改变的成效
		激活文化原始创新	反映科技对激发文化创意和原始创新方面的成效
		催生文化新兴业态	反映科技与文化融合而衍生的与文化产品和服务有关的文化业态的贡献
		扩大文化消费需求	反映科技对培养文化热点和消费新需求的成效
	社会效益（10）	社会责任承担力	反映企业文化科技融合创新对社会发展的促进和有益影响的程度
		促进公民享有文化权益	反映企业在保障人民享有文化权益方面做的努力和贡献
		社会风尚引领力	反映企业对人的思想道德、价值观念、科学素质和审美情趣等方面的贡献

（九）AHP 模糊综合评价的评价模型

1. 指标权重设计方法

评价体系内各评价指标赋权值的大与小，反映了国家在导向与激励方面的意志，是一个非常关键的参数，关系到评价结果的有效性。

确定权重的方法有主观赋权法和客观赋权法两类，主观赋权法的原始数据主要由专家根据经验判断得到，客观赋权法的原始数据由各指标在评价中的实际数据形成。主观赋权法的特点是专家可以根据实际问题合理确定各指标权系数之间的排序，应该说有客观的基础，但主观随意性较大；客观赋权法不需要征求专家的意见，切断了权重系数主观性的来源，系数具有绝对的客观性，但一个不可避免的缺陷是确定的权系数有时与指标的实际重要程度相悖。

层次分析法（AHP）其基本原理就是把所要研究的复杂问题看作一个大系统，通过对系统的多个因素的分析，分出各因素间相互联系的有序层次；再请专家对每一层次的各因素进行较为客观的判断后，相应给出相对重要性的定量表示；进而建立数学模型，计算出每一层次全部因素的相对重要性的权值，并加以排序；最后根据排序结果进行规划决策和选择解决问题的措施。它由于具有坚实的理论基础、完善的方法体系而深受人们的欢迎，经过深入分析，本课题拟采用层次分析法。

2. 综合评价方法

综合评价是决策科学化、民主化的基础，是实际评价工作的重点环节。综合评价模型是评价指标体系内在逻辑关系和数学关系的表达。综合评价的方法有很多，按照评价与所使用信息特征的关系，可分为基于数据的评价、基于模型的评价、基于专家知识的评价等。根据各评价方法所依据的理论基础，现代综合评价方法分为：（1）专家评价方法，如专家打分综合法；（2）运筹学与其他数学方法，如层次分析法、数据包络分析法、模糊综合评价法；（3）新型评价方法，如人工神经网络评价法、灰色综合评价法。

数据包络法是完全基于指标数据的客观信息评价，剔除了人为因素带来的误差，可以评价多输入多输出的大系统，并可用"窗口"技术找出单元薄弱环节加以改进，缺点是只表明评价单元的相对发展指标，无法表示出实际发展水平。

人工神经网络评价法是一种交互式的评价方法，可以根据用户期望的输出不断修改指标的权值，直到用户满意为止。基于人工神经网络的评价方法具有自适应能力和可容错性，能够处理非线性、非局域性的大型复杂系统，但缺点是需要大量的训练样本，精度不高，应用范围是有限的，评价模型的隐含行也是其应用障碍之一。

灰色综合评价法是从被评价对象的各个指标中选取最优值作为评价的标准，实际上是评价各被评价对象与此标准之间的距离。灰色综合评价法可以较好地解决评价指标难以准确量化和统计的问题，排除了人为因素带来的影响。缺点是要求样本数据具有时间序列特性，而且只能对评价对象的优劣做出鉴别，并不反映绝对水平，具有"相对评价"的全部缺点。

模糊综合评价应用模糊关系合成的原理，从多个因素对评价对象隶属等级状况进行综合评价，不仅可以根据模糊平价集上的值按最大隶属度原则评定对象所属等级，而且可以按综合分值的大小进行评价和排序。优点是其评价方式与人们的正常思维模式很接近，用程度语言描述对象，数学模型简单，容易掌握，对多因素、多层次的复杂问题评判效果比较好，可对涉及模糊因素的对象系统进行综合评价。

综上所述，根据本课题的评价目标和评价对象的复杂性，选择模糊综合评价法是最高效、最高质的，具有别的数学分支和模型无可比拟的优越性。

四、研究方法与过程

(一)研究方法

1. 理论与实际相结合的方法

文化与科技的融合对应了文明进程与经济繁荣,研究过程中把文化与科技看作是相互作用的两个客体,重点是寻找它们之间内在的关联性以及融合后对文明进程与经济繁荣的贡献,并注重将文化与科技的关联性建立在对当下中国文化科技发展实践的实时观测与全息把握之上。本项目研究拟通过比较研究、问卷调查、专题调查以及归纳提炼等具体方式,把握我国文化科技的发展现状与未来趋势,在此基础之上构建切实可行、富有前瞻性的评价体系。

2. 系统分析法

系统科学认为,世界上一切事物无不处于一定的系统之中。系统是指由相互联系、相互制约的若干要素组合而成的具有特定功能的有机整体。用此定义来审视文化科技创新活动,就会发现系统性是普遍存在的,比如文化科技创新体系中推动者、执行者、支撑者是相互联系、密不可分的一个整体,文化科技创新链更是一个环环相扣的系统。所以,本课题对文化科技创新活动进行研究需要运用系统分析法,探寻文化科技创新体系中各因素之间的互动关系。

3. 哲学方法

哲学方法是指辩证唯物主义和历史唯物主义的世界观和方法论,这是我们认识世界、改造世界、从事任何科学研究都必须遵循的最根本的方法。"文化科技创新活动评价体系"的构建,是建立在对"文化科技创新内涵和机制"的把握之上,而对"文化科技创新内涵和机制"的把握问题,需要深入把握文化建设的独特规律,并从文化创新与科技推动之间的互动关系来加以解决,需要我们用唯物主义的哲学方法辩证客观地认识和分析,因此,哲学方法必不可少。

4. 文献分析法

文献研究就是对文献进行查阅、分析、整理,从而找出事物本质属性的一种研究方法。本研究对文化科技创新实践活动、文化与科技融合进展等相关文献进行了细致的查找、收集与整理,并在此基础上进行了深入的分析。

5. 静态分析与动态分析相结合的方法

静态分析是截取事物发展过程中的一个时点对其横断面进行剖析,动态分析是随着时间的推移来考察事物的变化。本课题对文化科技本身以及文化科技创新活动的界定是从静态和动态两个方面结合进行的,从而使我们不仅能从文化科技创新活动的某一环节

来认识它，而且能够动态地把握它的变化。

6. 定性分析和定量分析相结合的方法

任何事物都同时具有质和量两个方面，是质和量的统一体。因此，对事物的认识既需要定性认识，也需要定量认识。对于任何科学研究领域来说，定性分析和定量分析都是两种最基本的分析方法，也是两种相互补充的分析方法。定性分析是对事物性质和本质的分析，定量分析是对事物的运动速度、规模大小和发展程度的规定性进行分析，二者的结合能够更加全面地认识事物的特征。对文化科技创新活动的实际产出效益方面的衡量，基于本课题对文化产品兼具经济价值属性和意识形态属性的认识，不仅需要在量上分析其经济价值的大小，更需要定性分析其价值观的表现及文化效益价值形态。

（二）研究过程

1. 确定评价对象

确定评价对象就是根据目标和任务确定评价的边界条件。在确定评价对象时，认真领会决策者的决策意图，以使最终的评价结果能为决策者提供有效的服务。同时，认真剖析评价对象的内外层次关系，因为在不同层次的活动中，不同领域的知识和技术、不同阶段的内涵和形式、不同类型的构成要素和运作机制构成了评价活动内部错综复杂的层次关系。本研究在确定评价对象的过程中做了大量的研究工作和反复讨论，在对文化科技创新活动的内涵和运作机制达成共识的基础上，根据文化科技创新活动主体对象的差异性选取了4个层级的评价对象，即"文化科技融合产品（含服务）""文化科技创新项目（科技类项目或课题）""文化科技融合示范基地"和"文化科技创新型企业"。

2. 明确评价目标

评价目标不同，所考虑的因素也有所不同。为了进行科学评价，本研究反复了解每次评价的目标及为此目标应注意的具体事项，熟悉评价方案，进一步分析和讨论了考虑到的因素。

3. 资料信息的搜集与分析

根据评价目标，集中搜集有关的资料和数据，并在此基础上，抓住影响评价对象的主要因素，分析因素之间的各种关系，为构建指标体系奠定基础。

4. 确定评价指标体系

根据评价指标设计原则，采用科学恰当的构建方法，比如层次分析法、频度分析法、理论分析法、专家调查法等初步形成指标体系，然后通过分析法、综合法、交叉法、指标属性分组法等初选方法对指标体系进行初选，使评价指标体系科学地、客观地、尽可能全面地反映各种因素。

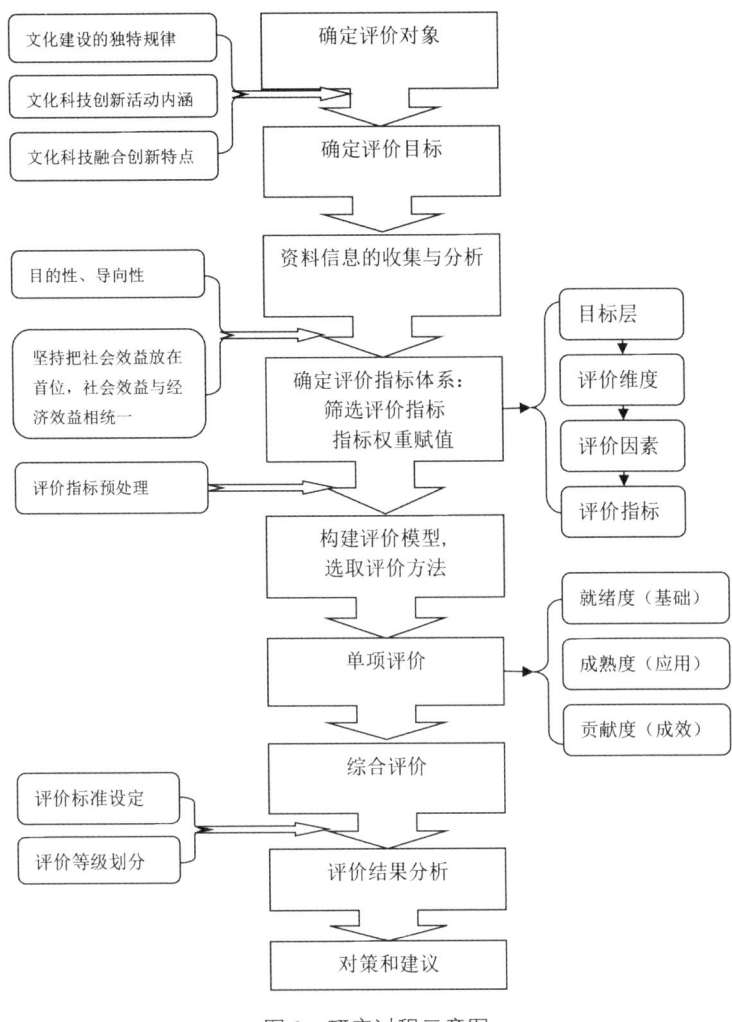

图 2　研究过程示意图

5.选择评价方法构建评价模型

评价方法根据评价对象的具体要求不同而有所不同，总的来说，要按系统目标与系统分析结果恰当选择成熟、公认的评价方法，并使评价方法与评价目的相匹配。

参考文献

[1] 中共中央. 中共中央关于深化文化体制改革推动社会主义文化大发展大繁荣若干重大问题的决定 [Z]. 2012–02.

[2] 中共中央国务院. 国家"十一五"时期文化发展规划纲要 [Z]. 2012–02.

[3] 科技部. 国家文化科技创新发展纲要 [Z]. 2012–05.

[4] 中共中央国务院. 关于深化科技体制改革加快国家创新体系建设的意见 [Z]. 2012-09.

[5] 文化和旅游部. 文化和旅游部"十二五"文化科技发展规划 [Z]. 2012-09.

[6] 文化和旅游部. 文化产业倍增计划 [Z]. 2012-02.

[7] 中国科学技术协会学会学术部. 我国科技发展的文化基础 [M]. 北京：中国科学技术出版社，2008.

[8] 李凤亮. 文化科技蓝皮书文化科技创新发展报告（2013）[M]. 北京：社会科学文献出版社，2013.

[9] 陈名杰，孟景伟. 海淀区文化和科技融合发展报告（2013）[M]. 北京：社会科学文献出版社，2013.

[10] 向勇，陈名杰. 北大讲坛文化创新战略，创意与科技 [M]. 北京：北京联合出版公司，2013.

[11] 吴和成，华海岭. 工业企业科技活动效率评价实证研究 [M]. 北京：科学出版社，2010.

[12] 任丽梅. 现代文化技术的本质与特征 [J]. 自然辩证法研究，2009，25(5)：49-53.

"十三五"时期科技与文化融合发展的新趋势及其对文化发展的影响*

一、绪论

当前文化与科技融合发展正处在一个新的历史起点上,文化科技创新在国家发展全局中的战略地位更加突出,文化科技事业迎来了一个空间更加广阔的发展机遇期。中央高度重视文化科技创新,可以从三个方面来理解:一是全球新科技革命和产业变革的"大势"与我国转方式调结构的"大事"形成历史性交汇,对文化科技工作提出了更高的要求;二是文化科技不仅是推动新形势下文化发展的重要动力,也成为促进全面深化改革的重要力量;三是从文化科技自身发展来看,我国文化科技创新呈现领跑、并跑、跟跑"三跑"并存格局,建设社会主义文化强国需要进一步提升自主创新能力。

二、"十二五"以来文化科技发展概况

(一)基本情况

科技进步已经成为文化发展的重要引擎。"十二五"以来,在党和国家的战略决策下,文化与科技融合在广度、高度、深度、跨度四个维度上实现了跨越性的进展,取得了较为丰硕的成果。文化科技创新能力不断增强、体制机制逐步完善、国际影响日益扩大,为"十三五"文化科技发展奠定了坚实的基础。文化科技发展处于新的起点。

文化科技已成为支撑驱动文化发展的主要力量。"十二五"以来,适应人民需要的文化产品不断丰富,公共文化网络覆盖面持续扩大,文化产业整体实力显著增强,推动中华文化走向世界的文化开放格局进一步完善。以先进技术支撑的一批公共文化服务设施、渠道、装备和软件系统被广泛应用,形成一批面向需求的系统化集成解决方案和网络化运营服务平台,数字技术引领公共文化内容呈现形式、数字空间载体建设、互联共享的

---

* 本文系文化部"十三五"时期文化改革发展规划前期研究课题研究报告,成稿于2015年3月。收入本书时有改动。

作用凸显。以技术创新、业态创新、内容创新和模式创新为主导的文化信息传输服务、文化创意和设计服务等新兴文化产业占比大、增长快，传统文化产业和文化相关产品生产继续保持增长，高新技术引领高端文化专用装备的作用明显。文化产品和服务的生产、传播、消费的数字化与网络化进程加快，与相关产业跨界融合发展呈常态，对外文化贸易的进出口结构得到进一步优化。数字技术在物质和非物质文化遗产保护传承领域的开发应用得到持续推进，民族文化资源和特色文化资源的开发利用途径得到进一步拓展。

探索中国特色文化科技发展道路取得重要进展。"十二五"以来，立足提高文化科技自主创新能力，构建文化技术支撑体系，实施国家文化科技创新工程和国家文化科技提升计划等科研专项，有效引导和支持文化科技创新要素向文化建设集聚。立足形成推动文化科技创新合力，提高科技成果转化应用水平，遴选与认定34个国家级文化与科技融合示范基地，有力推动新兴文化业态的形成和发展，促进区域产业结构调整和优化升级。立足提升文化创新能力，遴选与认定3个国家文化创新研究中心、6个文化和旅游部重点实验室，支持成立1个文化科技创新服务联盟，开展文化科技领域应用基础研究，发展我国文化科技服务力量。

（二）未来发展趋势与基本判断

数字科技引领的新浪潮，将全面影响文化发展的路径。全球已经融入大数据、工业4.0、网络智能化三大潮流中，信息通信技术、计算机技术、视听表达技术、仿真技术、新材料技术、节能环保技术是推动潮流发展的六大技术。这些技术为文化发展植入了创新基因，将对当今及未来的生产生活方式产生革命性影响，加速了文化生产方式及发展模式的变革，开始了文化传播传承方式的新革命，促进了文化消费与接受方式的新变革。以科技为核心竞争力的一大批新兴文化业态必将应运而生，革命性地改变我们所处时代的日常文化存在形态，将全面助推文化服务运营和文化产业链整合的大繁荣。

文化与科技融合呈现加速推进态势，将有力驱动文化创新。我国文化科技将从"选择性介入"走向"整体融合"，为文化创新驱动力奠定坚实基础。文化发展不断提出更高的科技诉求，科技发展在文化领域找到广泛的应用空间，文化科技整体融合在推进文化创新的同时，不仅形成对文化科技基础研究和科技创新的倒逼机制，而且为文化创新发展提供可持续驱动力量。经过多年持续积累，我国文化科技实力实现整体跃升，与发达国家差距明显缩小，呈现领跑、并跑、跟跑"三跑"并存格局。文化与科技融合发展在文化管理、文化创意、文化生产、文化展示、文化传播、文化交流、公共文化服务、文化遗产保护等领域，将越来越发挥出解放文化生产力和改变文化发展方式的巨大作用。

文化科技的杠杆倍增功能和平台托举功能，将加速驱动文化创新向协同发展迈进。我国文化科技的跨越式进步将助推各级文化行政管理部门积极深化文化科技体制改革，加快实施创新驱动发展战略，加快转变政府职能，不断提高政府文化行政治理效率，推进文化制度运行和文化政策落实的长效化、规范化、精密化和可操作化。以科技创新和模式创新为核心竞争力的各类文化平台将大量涌现，使文化创意、文化生产、文化消费、文化传播、文化贸易获得强大的平台托举支撑力，资金、技术、人才、信息、项目以及创意环境等关键性要素将获得超过预期的协同效应、聚集效应、漫溢效应、提升效应以及优化配置效应。文化科技的引擎牵引功能将进一步放大，在协同创新的文化发展道路上充分显示其主动性、能动性、导向性和可持续性，以源源不断的牵引力量带动中国文化建设的各个具体领域。

三、文化科技发展目前存在的关键问题与面临的挑战

（一）主要问题

文化科技顶层理论体系建设不完善，文化科技融合基础理论研究不充分，对于定义、内涵、外延、融合方式和路径等基本概念存在认识差异，难以保障文化科技相关政策制定的全面性、普遍性、权威性和连续性。

文化建设与文化科技创新的工作方向脱节问题依然没有完全解决，文化科技创新尚无法对接文化大繁荣大发展的具体工作，文化科技创新中的市场化机制尚未完善，部分创新成果转化渠道不畅。

文化科技领域原始创新能力和核心关键技术突破能力依然不足，文化科技企业的核心科技竞争力较差，自主创新能力依然偏低。

文化科技融合主要体现在高科技企业对于文化行业的选择性切入，传统文化企业的科技转型动力依然不足，技术创新能力差，技术基础薄弱。

文化科技小微企业的相关扶植政策环境有待完善，现行文化科技促进政策与文化科技领域"小团队、轻资产、重创意、新模式、强整合"的创新特征难以完全匹配，文化科技领域大众创业、万众创新的氛围未能形成。

文化科技复合型人才匮乏成为制约文化科技创新的重要因素，急须建立高等院校的完整学科培养体系。文化科技人才认定缺乏相应标准和政策指导，降低了创新载体的人才吸引能力。

（二）面临挑战

十八大明确提出实施创新驱动发展战略，强调科技创新是提高社会生产力和综合国力的战略支撑，必须摆在国家发展全局的核心位置。十八届三中全会对深化科技体制改革做出具体部署。

 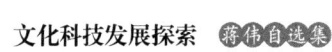

习近平总书记对实施创新驱动发展战略进行了系统阐述，明确提出"五个着力"要求，强调要推动以科技创新为核心的全面创新，抓好创新驱动发展战略的顶层设计和任务落实。

李克强要求强化科技在经济社会发展中的全局性、战略性地位，强调通过科技创新实现经济提质增效升级。

中央经济工作会议要求更多依靠人力资本质量和技术进步推动经济增长，让创新成为驱动发展新引擎。刘延东九次召开国家科改领导小组会议，部署推进科技体制改革重点任务。

新形势下，对照党和国家对文化发展和科技创新的新部署，文化科技目前尚不能满足建立公共文化服务体系、现代文化管理体系、现代文化市场体系的技术要求，与之相配套的技术支撑体系尚未建立，尚无法满足建设社会主义文化强国的科技要求。以科技为重要载体的新一轮文化发展竞争，已经开始引发各类模式创新、技术创新、业务创新、服务创新的爆发式增长，正处在新业态的孕育期与发展期，亟须文化科技政策的重点切入和支持。

四、"十三五"文化科技工作的基本思路、原则及目标

紧紧围绕实施创新驱动发展战略，落实科技体制改革任务，引导和支持创新要素向文化领域集聚，进一步构建完善以企业为主体、市场为导向、产学研结合的文化技术创新体系，着力加强文化科技创新体系建设，精心组织实施文化科技创新工程和文化科技重点专项，促进科学技术在文化领域的应用与创新，进一步提高文化资源和文化内容形式的协同运用能力，完善文化领域基础、技术和服务标准，推动文化与科技融合向纵深发展。

（一）指导思想

以邓小平理论、"三个代表"重要思想、科学发展观为指导，贯彻落实党的十八大和十八届三中、四中全会精神，贯彻落实习近平总书记系列重要讲话精神，按照建设社会主义文化强国和增强国家文化软实力的总体要求，牢固树立以人民为中心的工作导向，发挥科技对文化创新的驱动作用，加强文化与科技融合，深化文化科技体制机制改革，促进创新资源的合理配置，培育创新主体，增强创新动力，优化创新环境，切实提高科技对现代文化市场体系建设、现代公共文化服务体系构建和文化开放水平提升的驱动支撑能力，推动社会主义文化大繁荣大发展。

（二）基本原则

需求牵引，持续提升。文化是民族凝聚力和创造力的重要源泉，以面向人民需求和面向市场需求为牵引，充分发挥政府在文化科技创新体系和文化技术支撑体系建设中的积极作用，有效聚集、整合和利用相关创新要素资源，推进文化与科技深度融合，着力提升国家文化软实力。

系统规划，统筹推进。加强文化科技创新发展的顶层设计，优化配置文化资源、科技资源和人力资源，强化文化部门与科技部门的联合，统筹发展项目、基地、人才、政策以及文化科技创新体系，从主要依靠科技项目推动转向从工作层面系统全面推动文化科技创新发展。

创新驱动，融合发展。充分调动社会各方面积极性，促进技术创新、业态创新、内容创新、模式创新和管理创新，持续提升中国文化的生产力、创作力、感染力、表现力、传播力和影响力，充分发挥科技进步对文化繁荣发展的支撑驱动作用。

（三）发展目标

在文化资源领域，加速民族文化资源、文化遗产等文化资源的数字化、信息化、网络化进程，形成支持文化资源采集、加工、获取、整备、管理、保护、保存、应用的系列标准，研发与创新一批文化资源的转化技术、表现技术、呈现技术和传播传承系统，让中华优秀传统文化活起来。

在文化产业领域，研发一批共性关键技术，创新一批产品、服务、装备和模式，发展一批文化与装备制造、消费品工业设计、城乡建筑、信息服务、旅游等跨界深度融合的新型业态，提高文化产业整体实力和核心竞争力。

在公共文化服务领域，数字技术支撑文化信息资源共享、数字图书馆、数字博物馆、数字美术馆的作用更加强化，研发一批公共数字文化资源的加工、供给、分发、保护等关键技术，形成一批面向互联互通及应用的系统化技术解决方案和网络化运营服务平台，创新一批公共文化服务业务、渠道、模式，促进基本公共文化服务标准化、均等化、便捷化。

在文化科技管理领域，文化产业科技方面实现从投资驱动为主向创新驱动为主的转变，公共文化服务科技方面实现以政府投入为主向多元化投融资为主转变；技术进步方面实现以引进为主向二次创新和自主创新为主转变；管理模式方面从政府具体管理为主的格局向宏观管理为主的格局转变。

到 2020 年，基本形成推动文化事业进步、文化产业融合创新、文化管理有序的文化科技创新体系，初步形成以企业为主体、市场为导向、政产学研用相结合的文化科技术支撑体系。

（四）主要指标

——共性支撑技术取得重要突破。重点围绕文化资源互联互通、文化内容版权保护、文化安全监管、文化诚信服务等共性瓶颈技术问题，攻克20项以上关键支撑技术难题，制定30余项文化服务技术与管理标准规范，构建3—4个网络化管理和科技服务平台。

——文化科技驱动支撑作用明显强化。聚焦现代文化市场秩序和现代公共文化服务重点领域，全链条布局，有针对性地研发一批文化产品创意、生产、传播、运营、展示、消费等环节的关键技术和集成应用技术，研制一批文化专用装备，提出一批面向应用的系统化集成解决方案，形成6—7项系统软件和系统平台，构建3—4个文化科技创新服务运营平台，创新一批服务模式，发展一批新兴文化业态，在典型文化领域开展一批应用示范，打造3—5家文化服务运营品牌，扶持30家以上规模化文化科技创新型企业。

——文化科技创新体系不断完善。积极培育发展以国家重点实验室、工程技术研究中心、企业技术创新中心和技术创新战略联盟为主体的文化科技创新体系；建设2—3家文化科技领域国家重点实验室和国家工程（技术）研究中心，统筹建设一批各具特色的文化与科技融合示范基地，统筹培育一批各具特色的文化科技融合产业化基地（示范园区），加强文化科技产业发展载体建设，形成文化科技发展良好环境。

五、"十三五"文化科技发展的主要任务

（一）塑造数字文化资源新优势

支持数字文化资源在采集、加工、获取、整备、管理、保护、保存、应用、传播、表现等全过程链条中相关技术和装备的研发，构建文化资源相关技术支撑平台和基础研发平台，加速文化资源数字化、信息化、网络化进程。支持图书馆藏资源、博物馆藏资源、美术馆藏资源的数据化专用技术研发，加强现代人文艺术学科研究的基础数据支撑；支持民族文化素材的创建、描述、组织、检索、服务与长期保存的技术、标准和装备研发；鼓励记录保存展现中国传统生活文化的新方法、新手段、新模式的研究，推动传统文化生活方式在现代生活中的有效保存和二次创新；支持数字文化资源记录与保存介质材料的研发，鼓励传统文化介质的现代复原工艺研究；推动文化资源与信息产业有效对接的模式创新，加快技术层面的文化资源整合与互联互通，着力打通数字化文化资源访问的关键技术环节，实现文化价值与产业应用的有效结合。

（二）推动新型文化业态融合创新

充分运用数字技术、网络技术、智能技术、材料技术，加快文化产业重要装备、材料、工艺、系统、平台的开发和利用，加快传统文化企业的转型升级步伐；促进新兴科

技企业向文化领域的渗透，实现传统文化产业领域的颠覆式创新；推动大数据、云计算、虚拟现实、互联网+、人工智能等新兴战略科技在文化领域的创新试点，形成由点带面的示范性应用，强化文化产品（服务）的互动性和体验性，触发文化产业的深刻变革；促进众筹、众包、O2O、社交聚合等互联网成熟商业模式向文化产业领域的渗透，推动文化产业的业务融合创新；支持文化与相关产业双向或多向融合发展。

（三）拓展公共文化服务新空间

加快公共文化服务的数字化建设步伐，结合智慧城市、智慧社区、宽带中国等国家重大战略举措，建立起技术先进、覆盖广泛、方便快捷的数字化公共文化服务网络与载体；研究制定一批公共文化领域标准规范和服务模式；支持流动文化工作站、移动文化方舱、数字农家书屋等文化下乡的专用设备与装备的研发；鼓励符合我国核心价值观的公共文化内容供给的新呈现、新表现和新揭示的相关技术和标准研发；支持一站式文化服务相关技术、装备、系统与平台的研发；针对博物馆、美术馆、文化馆等重要公共文化设施，开展相应的虚拟化、数字化、智能化特种体验装备研究；鼓励公共文化服务手段创新和新兴公共文化服务业态创新。

（四）培育文化艺术新形态

推动文化艺术创作的集约化、专业化发展，鼓励创作手段创新，催生与培育文化艺术新形态；支持动漫游戏编辑制作、影视编辑、特效生成处理等专业生产工具和系统的研发；支持舞美、布景、道具、灯光、音响、机械、视效、观演互动等领域的技术与系统研发，鼓励虚拟现实、人机交互、自动控制等先进技术在演艺舞台中的集成应用；支持艺术创作与观众情感间的定量化分析研究；研发舞蹈、音乐编排数字化专用工具，鼓励拉班舞谱可视化、传统民乐音符标准化和数字化的研究，推动数字乐谱、数字钢琴、云谱台等创作工具的研发。

（五）提升政府文化行政治理效率

支持文化施政管理过程中的数据采集、交汇、存储、处理和分析等相关技术与系统的研发；鼓励文物鉴定相关标准规范、参数指标、标准物质、装置装备的研究；开展艺术品的量化估值方法研究，建设相应数据库；针对演出场所、娱乐场所、公共文化设施建设，制定相应规划、验收、评估、公共安全、运营维护等强制性技术标准；推进文化行业相关计量检测和检验技术的研究；展开文化市场监管、文化市场诚信评估、文化内容版权保护等文化管理共性技术研究；支持对文化工作统计制度、指标体系、调查方法的研究，展开文化科技领域的软科学研究。

六、"十三五"时期文化科技发展的政策措施

面对科技高速发展时代的严峻挑战，文化建设机遇稍纵即逝，必须站在国家文化发展的战略高度，统筹谋划，科学应对，努力寻求促进文化科技融合及其对文化创新驱动的制度张力，让文化创新全面释放实现"中国梦"的强大正能量。

（一）强化制度设计

强化顶层制度设计，将文化科技融合及其对文化创新的有效驱动提升到国家文化发展战略层面给予制度安排；统筹相关职能部门事权会商处置机制，在政府行政平台形成文化科技发展合力，使各级政府对文化科技融合与文化创新发展更具调控能力；把推进文化科技融合纳入各级政府议事日程，尤其纳入各级政府文化行政部门的重要工作安排，促使文化科技成为政府文化治理制度运行内容的重要组成部分。

（二）完善工作机制

进一步完善相关政府职能部门之间的联合会商制度，强化相关各方政策功能链接，实现文化科技融合进程中的信息资源共享，形成推进文化科技融合的行政合力；加强文化科技工作的顶层沟通协调，文化部门与科技部门要建立常态化的合作机制；建立文化科技领域的智库，完善行政决策专家咨询制度；将文化科技创新纳入国家科技发展专项规划，优化科技项目的组织实施机制，支持设立文化科技专业服务机构管理文化科技项目；建立健全文化领域的技术标准、服务标准和基础标准体系；完善文化科技相关数据统计制度，开展文化科技的量化分析和评价；加强文化科技的前期调研和数据整理工作，积极推进科研体制改革和科技计划管理改革。

（三）发挥科技项目示范作用

结合中央财政科技计划（专项、基金等）管理改革要求，将文化科技创新纳入科发展专项规划，深入实施国家文化科技创新工程。有序安排公共文化服务体系构建、民族文化资源开发、文化产品创作生产、文化遗产保护利用和传承、文化产业与相关产业融合、文化市场监管体系构建、对外文化交流与贸易等重点领域的文化科技研发活动，探索科技项目的有效组织方式，发挥科技项目的推动与示范作用。

（四）培育创新载体

着力打造文化科技融合发展平台，彰显"文化发展"的本质要求，破解文化与科技

"两张皮"难题，形成文化科技融合战略优势；以提高文化科技创新能力为目的，整合支持一批文化、技术、经济、管理等方面力量相融合的文化科技综合研究机构，论证设立中央级的文化科技研究院，恢复或布局建设省级文化科技研发机构；加大对文化科技领域国家与部门重点实验室与工程技术研究中心的支持力度，鼓励高等院校、科研院所的实验室与研究中心向文化科技领域聚集；鼓励具有优势的文化科技企业申办工程（技术）研究中心，鼓励具有优势的文化服务运营企事业单位建立技术中心，支持相关创新主体依托技术中心建立技术创新联盟及创新平台；鼓励发展一批文化科技领域的大学科技园、创业孵化中心等创新载体，鼓励建设一批特色鲜明的文化与科技融合示范基地网络创新服务平台；推动文化科技相关行业产业联盟、专业协会、专业学会、非营利性组织的建设。

（五）培育复合型人才

打破体制机制瓶颈，鼓励高等院校跨学科培养人才，探索文化科技复合型人才的培养模式；鼓励高校、研究院所、产业联盟（基地）、行业协会建立文化科技跨界人才培养基地、文化科技的实践实训基地，完善社会培训机制；推动文化科技领军人才的培育，加强核心人才的引进和储备，优化文化科技的人才引进机制；加强文化科技人才的国际交流和合作，促进海外高端人才的回流，探索政府奖励、社会奖励、行业奖励相结合的文化科技人才奖励机制；着力构建一支门类齐全、梯次合理的文化科技人才队伍。

（六）加大财税支持

在国家重点研发计划、技术创新引导专项等国家科技计划中，增加对文化科技领域科技项目的投入，引导社会资金投向文化科技创新；鼓励地方政府加大资金投入，支持本地区文化科技基础领域的自主创新；引导鼓励文化创投和金融机构对文化科技的科技创新投入；加大对重要文化科技创新载体的常态性经费支持，保障创新活动的持续进行；增加对文化科技人才的培养培育投入。

（七）加大舆论宣传力度

广泛开展文化科技深度融合知识普及，增强全社会对文化科技驱动文化创新的价值认同感；动员更多的媒体和专家就文化科技驱动文化创新的发展趋势、基本规律和探索实践等进行全方位讨论，营造文化科技融合与文化创新的社会氛围；解放思想，更新观念，凝聚智慧，形成合力，以理论先导推进文化自觉，以文化自觉引领文化创新。

工业和信息化部、文化和旅游部文化装备发展行动计划（2018—2020年）[*]

为支撑社会主义先进文化事业的蓬勃发展，贯彻落实《中国制造2025》和《国家"十三五"时期文化发展改革规划纲要》部署和要求，培育壮大文化装备制造业，健全文化装备制造产业体系，特制订本行动计划。

一、重要意义与当前形势

文化装备是支撑、保障和服务于文化内容生产、文化传承传播、文化服务活动的装置、设备、器具、材料、设施及其系统的总称。文化装备以先进的技术和工程手段服务于文化创作、生产、传播、服务、消费等各个环节，是国家装备体系的重要组成部分。本行动计划着力推动的文化装备主要涉及：面向文化艺术领域的演艺装备、面向公共文化领域的服务装备、面向文化遗产保护与传承领域的专用装备、面向文化娱乐消费领域的体验装备、面向文化领域的安全装备等。

文化装备以服从和服务于文化发展的需求为先导，是推动国家文化建设与文化创新的重要技术基础。文化装备为社会主义文化繁荣提供精致、准确、具有美感和高品质的执行力与服务力，是传承弘扬中华优秀传统文化、助力新时代国家文化创新与繁荣兴盛的重要物质载体。文化装备精准对接新时代社会主义文化发展新要求，是满足人民日益增长的美好生活新期待的重要支撑手段。加快推进文化装备制造业持续健康发展，对于推动社会主义文化繁荣发展、实现文化装备的有效供给、推动我国装备制造产业结构升级具有重要意义。

经过多年的发展，我国文化装备制造业已形成门类相对齐全、具有一定发展基础的特色产业体系，装备性能不断提升，应用领域日益拓展，发展模式不断创新，技术水平大幅提升，部分装备达到国际领先水平，文化装备制造"走出去"步伐明显加快，形成了若干产业集聚区。但从总体看，发展不平衡不充分的问题依然突出：供需结构性失衡

---

[*] 本文系受工业和信息化部、文化和旅游部委托而代拟的文稿，成稿于2018年3月。收入本书时有改动。

相对突出，部分文化建设领域的装备供给保障仍处于空白；自主创新能力整体偏弱，关键部件与重要功能部件依赖进口；产业生态体系不完善，系统集成和打包供给能力不足；品牌知名度不高，具有国际竞争力的优势企业相对较少，与新时代文化建设的新征程新需求相比仍有较大差距。"十三五"时期是全面建成小康社会的决胜阶段，也是促进文化繁荣发展的关键时期。新时期的文化内容、表现形式、服务方式等文化创新活动，对文化装备制造业提出了新的更高要求。

二、指导思想与基本原则

（一）指导思想

全面贯彻党的十九大精神，以习近平新时代中国特色社会主义思想为指导，坚定文化自信，贯彻落实新发展理念，坚持以人民为中心的发展思想，按照党中央关于加快建设制造强国、加快发展先进制造业的战略部署，以保障与提升文化装备有效供给为主线，以促进装备制造与文化创新融合发展为抓手，强化创新驱动，大幅提升文化装备的技术水平与质量，培育具有国际影响力的品牌和领军型企业，切实发挥文化装备对文化生产及文化消费的支撑、保障和服务作用，推动制造强国和文化强国建设。

（二）基本原则

需求引领。面向人民对文化生活的更高要求，着重补足供给侧短板，针对支撑社会主义先进文化发展的装备制造关键薄弱环节，着力化解产业化主体缺失等问题，加强重大技术研究成果的推广和应用。

创新驱动。把科技创新摆在文化装备制造业发展全局的核心位置，加强产业共性技术与核心技术研发，突破关键材料、核心零部件等瓶颈，提高自主创新能力，积极推动文化装备向智能化、高端化、成套化方向发展。

质量为本。稳步提高文化装备的可靠性、稳定性和一致性，大力提升技术标准、先进工艺和知识产权保护等基础能力。加强自有品牌培育，通过品牌建设实现文化装备产业体系的产业链和价值链升级。

开放协同。促进产学研用金的紧密结合，加强制造资源与文化资源的融合共享，促进文化装备制造产业集聚化发展。鼓励领军型企业加强在技术创新、标准制定、知识产权等方面的国际交流合作，在全球范围优化配置创新资源。

三、行动目标

到2020年，文化装备制造技术的进步与创新能力显著增强，供应保障更加完善，产品质量全面提高，品牌塑造更加深入，产业规模效益稳定增长，生态体系建设显著完善，国际化步伐明显加快。

技术进步与创新能力明显提高。 企业研发投入持续增加，全行业规模以上企业研发投入强度达到1.5%以上。突破100种以上关键工艺、核心器件、关键材料，中高端文化装备制造的引领作用进一步增强。文化装备的供给保障能力显著提升，覆盖面进一步扩大。

质量效益与产业规模效益显著提升。 文化装备质量标准提高，质量安全保障加强。打造3—5个具有国际影响力和较高美誉度的知名品牌。产业化主体进一步壮大，生产组织方式、产业形态、商业模式得到改进。

产业组织结构优化升级。 培育一批参与国际分工的"专精特新"关键零部件生产企业，大型企业对行业的发展引领作用进一步加强。形成3—5家具有国际竞争力的龙头企业。推动建立20家高端文化装备示范企业。加快公共服务平台建设。支持推进5个左右产业集群创建新型工业化产业示范基地。培育世界级产业集群。

国际化发展能力稳步提升。 推进高水平双向开放，推动一批装备、产品、标准走向国际市场。知名品牌的文化装备出口稳定增长，出口交货值占销售收入的比重力争达到10%。出口结构显著改善，中高端和成套化装备出口比重提高。境外投资规模扩大，国际技术合作进一步深化。

四、主要任务

（一）增强产业创新能力

一是完善政产学研用协同创新体系。发挥政府的引导和推动作用，营造激励创新的政策环境。强化企业技术创新主体地位，发挥骨干企业整合科技资源的作用，扶持掌握关键技术的研发型小企业发展。推动企业加强与高校、科研院所和文化机构技术协作，建立符合文化装备研发特点的投入、收益、风险分担机制，加速研发成果产业化。

二是推动创新升级。引导企业提高创新质量，培育重大产品，满足重要需求，解决重点问题，提升产业化技术水平。发展演艺装备、公共文化服务装备、文化遗产传承专用装备、文化娱乐装备，推动高端技术装备研发从仿制为主向自主创新为主转移。发展文化专用新材料，加快文化专用新材料关键技术产业化。加快文化装备核心技术和关键部件开发，提升集成创新能力和制造水平。

三是加强研发支撑。加快建设面向文化装备领域的国家级工程技术研究中心和重点实验室，优化国家级科技创新基地布局，促进科技成果转化应用。加强文化装备研发数据和公共资源建设，提高开放共享水平和专业化服务能力。发挥金融创新对技术创新的助推作用，引导社会资本设立文化装备领域创业投资基金、股权投资基金，支持早期研发项目实施和创新型企业成长。

专栏1　创新能力提升工程

文化装备制造创新中心建设。整合政府和社会投入、科研院所、高校和企业研发力量、文化机构创意创新资源、企业产业化能力等各方面资源，围绕产业发展共性关键技术问题开展合作，实现3—5项重点技术突破，提高全产业链创新能力，促进创新驱动发展。

文化装备产业创投计划。引导社会资本设立5个以上文化装备产业创投基金，总规模达到10亿元，为文化装备技术创新项目提供投融资支持。

文化装备研发数据和公共资源平台建设。依托文化装备领域的国家级工程技术研究中心和重点实验室，重点支持建设和整合一批演艺装备与娱乐体验装备的相关数据库和资源库，实现数据和资源开放共享，为文化装备制造的研发提供服务。

（二）提升供应保障能力

一是保障短缺文化装备供应。引导企业开发和生产短缺的文化装备，重点解决支撑文化艺术表达与呈现、非物质文化遗产保护与传承、中华文化资源数据库建设、中国古代典籍整理、民族民间文化典藏与传播、传统工艺振兴、文化市场监管等专用技术装备缺乏和供应保障能力严重不足等问题。

二是保障文化专用材料供应。在文化传承用的文化专用纸、传统书画美术颜料、纸质文献脱酸/防腐/固色/专用材料、艺术表现与呈现用的喷雾/喷雪/喷烟/专用材料（不含烟花）、高声学品质用的传声器/扬声器专用膜片材料、音箱箱体专用材料、演艺灯具传统光源材料、LED光源材料、舞台机械系统专用材料、传统手工艺品用的锦绣/陶瓷/漆器/雕刻/编织/专用材料等特种材料领域，引导企业开发和生产短缺的文化专用材料和品种，重点解决供应保障能力不强等问题。

三是满足多样化市场需求。鼓励企业在发展成套与高端文化装备的同时，对已有产品开展各种形式的微创新，不断丰富产品谱系，满足多层次与差别化的市场需求。

 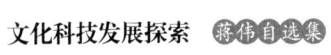

> **专栏 2　文化装备供应保障工程**
>
> **文化装备生产供需信息系统建设。**建立和完善全国统一的文化装备各细分门类有关装置、设备、器具、材料、设施等产品供求中长期预报与信息发布平台制度,引导协调企业开发生产与供应。以平台为核心,形成文化装备供需协调网络,实现文化装备生产供需信息的共享与交流,推进对文化装备生产供应的调控,为保障供应提供支撑。
>
> **短缺文化装备研发与定点生产试点计划。**针对文化发展细分领域特种技术装备的迫切需求,依托有条件的企业及科研机构,协同进行核心技术攻关与工程化,开展用量小、市场供应短缺的定点生产试点。
>
> **文化专用材料生产基地建设。**选择综合实力强与质量管理水平高的生产企业,在全国布局若干文化专用材料生产基地,增强文化专用材料的供应保障能力。

(三)提升质量水平与品牌价值

一是健全文化装备标准体系。重点支持在设计、安全、环保、质量、工艺、功能、检验检测以及知识产权、品牌建设等生产性服务标准的标准研制,形成一批强制性国家标准和行业标准。推动创新技术快速转换为标准或技术规范,提高文化装备性能稳定性、质量可靠性、操控适用性,重点提升涉及人身安全、视听安全防护等安全运行性。跟踪国际先进技术发展趋势,注重与国际标准接轨,积极参与国际标准制(修)订工作,促进自主创新产品进入国际市场。

二是完善检验检测认证体系。加强文化装备与产品质量检验检测能力建设,提高质量检测水平。建设文化演艺装备、游乐设施装备、文化互动体验装备等新型装备产品检验检测和认证机构,完善国家强制性产品认证体系。

三是培育品牌文化。针对具有较好发展基础、已实现研发制造、部分设备与设施已实现批量生产的文化装备产品,重点提升质量竞争力。支持文化装备企业开展设备产品质量品牌建设,完善包括战略管理、技术创新、流程变革、质量度量考核、闭环质量保证等在内的生产组织方式。鼓励培养以质量和信誉为核心的国产品牌意识与理念,提升文化装备国有品牌的附加值。

> **专栏 3　质量品牌升级工程**
>
> **文化装备标准化计划。**提升企业标准制度修订的积极性与参与度,推动创新技术快速转换为行业标准或技术报告。支持通过与检测、认证机构、招标单位等机构的合作,扩大标准的采信范围和领域。加快推动演艺装备领域的标准化发展进程,建立和完善演艺装备技术与服务标准体系。

续表

> **文化装备检验检测能力建设。**推动企业构建产品验证、实验、监测平台,促进提质增效。加快培育与择优遴选若干第三方认证与检验检测机构,重点发展以演艺装备、游乐设施、文化互动体验装备为主要对象的认证与检验检测服务业务,稳妥推进在线检验、基于风险的检验、无损检测等新技术新方法的应用,增强认证和检验检测能力。
>
> **中国自主品牌建设。**推动企业加大自主品牌建设投入,增强自主创新能力,追求卓越质量,提升产品品质,建立品牌管理体系,提高品牌培育能力。培养消费者自主品牌情感,树立消费信心,扩大自主品牌消费。支持自主品牌发展,助力供给结构和需求结构升级,发挥品牌引领作用。

(四)优化产业生态体系

一是拉动消费升级。催生与创造适应文化发展需要的境内市场需求,面向境外市场巩固与提升以演艺成套装备和文化互动体验成套装备为代表的生产、系统集成与供给能力,扩大和提高文化装备产品的产能、技术含量、附加值和成套水平。

二是夯实基础支撑能力。瞄准高端文化装备的成套化发展趋势和产业链瓶颈,提升产业技术基础公共服务能力,突破一批需求迫切、基础条件好、带动作用强的基础产品和技术发展瓶颈,夯实工程化与产业化发展基础,推动基础与成套系统装备的紧密结合,促进基础发展与产业应用良性互动,扭转我国文化装备制造业基础制造技术与关键零部件发展滞后的被动局面。

三是提升高端化水平。开展重点文化装备原理样机和工程样机研制,集中攻克一批长期困扰文化装备产业发展的核心技术与共性技术难题,掌握以绿色、智能、协同、服务为特征的先进设计制造技术,形成一批具有全局性影响、带动性强、满足文化发展和市场需求的重大设备与系统装备,促进重点文化装备向集成化、智能化、模块化发展,大幅提升我国文化装备制造业的创新能力。

四是培育文化装备制造产业集群。支持大型骨干文化装备企业跨行业、跨地区、跨所有制兼并重组,逐步形成具有工程总承包、系统集成、国际贸易和融资能力的大型企业集团,培育稳定的专业化零部件生产企业,逐步形成整机(系统)牵引和配套支撑协调互动的文化装备产业发展格局。

五是推动国际产能合作。落实"一带一路"建设的要求,鼓励企业利用制造优势,在适宜地区开展收购兼并和投资建厂。引进和培养国际化人才,提高研发注册、生产质量、市场销售各环节的国际化经营能力。

 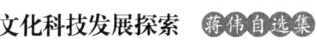

专栏 4　文化装备提升工程

文化装备制造强基计划。重点遴选50种左右重要核心基础零部件（元器件）、关键基础材料和先进基础工艺，组织开展工程化和产业化。按照小规模、专业化、精细化的原则组织生产专用核心基础零部件（元器件）和关键基础材料，重点满足终端用户的迫切需求。按照大批量、标准化、模块化的原则，组织生产通用核心基础零部件（元器件）和关键基础材料，推广先进基础工艺，重点提升产品可靠性和稳定性。

高端文化装备制造计划。培育一批技术水平高、资源整合能力强、产业规模优势突出的高端文化装备制造领军企业，形成一批技术先进、管理创新的再制造示范企业，带动行业整体水平提升。重点推进舞台机械、演艺灯光、游乐设施等领域高端制造示范企业建设，鼓励依托文化装备产业集聚区建设示范工程。

文化装备走出去计划。支持骨干文化装备企业承接国际重大文化建设工程，支持骨干文化装备企业承接海外中国文化中心建设任务。支持企业收购或投资建设境外文化装备生产基地，促进产能国际合作。鼓励企业提升国际市场运营能力，建立面向国际市场的销售渠道，培育中国制造品牌。

（五）推进智能制造发展新业态

一是推进智能制造。支持文化装备制造企业试点建设数字化生产线、车间、智能工厂，加快数字化、网络化、智能化步伐，加快文化装备制造关键技术的系统集成，促进制造工艺仿真优化、数字化控制和自适应控制的应用。推动信息技术与文化装备制造业的深度融合，积极应用工业大数据、传感器和物联网技术驱动文化装备制造的智能化。

二是提高服务化能力。支持骨干文化装备企业在工程承包、系统集成、设备租赁、提供解决方案、再制造等方面开展增值服务，鼓励有条件的企业延伸扩展创意、设计、研发、服务等业务，为文化发展提供全程化服务。推动优强企业由生产型制造向服务型制造转变，由提供装备向提供系统集成总承包服务转变，由提供设备产品向提供整体解决方案转变。

三是推动产教融合。支持文化装备制造业与高等教育进行产教合作，建立产教融合机制。鼓励文化装备制造业举办高等职业教育，突破文化装备制造人力资源匮乏的瓶颈。

专栏 5　智能制造与新业态发展工程

文化装备自动化生产车间建设。支持建设5家以上针对文化装备离散化制造特点的自动化生产示范车间，改变多数文化装备以人工组装、人工测试为主的状况，提高机械组装水平，实现自动化配送、质量检测和定制生产，系统提升文化装备的稳定性和可靠性。

续表

> **文化装备服务型制造计划。**依托骨干文化装备企业，发展文化装备远程监测、故障诊断、远程维修、趋势预测等在线支持服务业务。支持文化装备龙头企业取得资质，提供工程总承包、建设－移交（BT）、建设－运营－移交（BOT）、建设－拥有－运营（BOO）等多种服务，开展市场调研、产品设计、工程监理、工程施工、系统控制、运营维护等业务。
>
> **文化装备人才培养。**支持相关高等院校探索联合共建面向文化装备制造业的专业课程体系及专业培训的新模式。重点支持通过工学交替、订单人才培养、生产性实训等方式帮助相关高等职业学院根据文化装备行业实际需要把握办学方向，使专业设置和教学内容更加符合产业和市场的需求。

五、重点领域

按照政府引导与"制造＋服务＋应用"相结合的模式，汇聚一批科技、文化、制造、服务等资源，解决一批核心技术与共性关键技术难题。面向重点领域，遴选建立重大项目库，支持开发一批创新型文化装备，探索建立一批文化装备示范基地。

（一）面向文化艺术领域的演艺装备

推进与实现演出场所内的演出设备类、支撑新兴文化表演形式的观演互动类、支撑艺术表现与呈现类的技术系统与装备的自主化。攻克关键部件与重要功能部件有关结构、材料、工艺、软件等核心技术难关，重点实现舞台机械类、演艺灯光类、演艺音响类、演艺特效类、观演视效类、乐器类等主要设备的国内自主制造和谱系化。强化演艺装备的可靠性、稳定性和一致性，加快发展成套化与高端化演艺装备的中试熟化与制造，满足文化艺术呈现和重大文化演出活动对演艺装备的高质量高品质需求。

（二）面向公共文化领域的服务装备

推进与实现文化消费终端类、文化内容制作类、公共文化空间展陈类等公共服务技术系统与装备的自主化。攻克流动文化服务载体、"互联网＋文化服务"等一批公共文化服务领域的核心技术难关，重点实现流动文化服务可移动载体装备、基层公共文化场站专用服务装备的中试熟化制造，进一步扩大文化装备的供给覆盖面。

 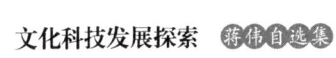

（三）面向文化遗产保护与传承领域的专用装备

推进实现文化遗产调查与发掘类、文化遗产保护与安全防护类、文化遗产记录与保存类、中国传统工艺振兴与传承类、文化遗产展示与传播类等技术系统与装备的应用。攻克规模化纸质文献脱酸装备、专用材料制备等一批文化遗产保护传承利用领域的核心技术难关，重点实现一批专用或特种技术工具与设备的中试熟化与自主制造，大力缓解专用装备、专用材料、专用器材的供给短缺状况。

（四）面向文化娱乐消费领域的体验装备

鼓励支持大众游乐类、交互体验类等文化游乐娱乐技术系统与装备的研发。攻克一批交互体验、虚实融合等核心技术难关，发展一批面向不同文化主题类型的娱乐消费装备与设施，进一步提高文化互动技术系统与成套装备的性能质量。

（五）面向文化安全生产领域的专用系统工具

攻克与掌握一批涉及人身安全、视听安全防护、设备安全运行的专门测试、检验方法与技术，发展支持演艺设施、文化游乐娱乐设施、公共文化空间、重要文化服务载体安全运行的检验、检测、监测、诊断等专用或特种仪器、仪表、设备和技术工具，满足文化安全生产领域的技术工具需求。

（六）文化装备新业态

鼓励利用数字技术、网络技术、人工智能、虚拟现实、人机交互、增材制造等现代技术手段，推动文化装备制造与相关产业双向或多向融合发展，催生一批新技术、新工艺、新产品、新服务、新模式和新业态。大力推动文化装备制造与文化创新双向融合发展，催生与培育文化新形态。

六、保障措施

（一）加强统筹组织协调

加强顶层设计，加强与有关部门的协调配合，强化部门协同和上下联动，推动建立和完善协同工作机制，有效利用中央、地方和其他社会资源，协调解决文化装备制造产业发展中的重大问题，不断完善中央和地方协同推进的产业政策体系，形成资源共享、协同推进的工作格局。

（二）营造良好政策环境

研究制订《首台（套）重大文化技术装备推广应用指导目录》，完善使用国产首台(套)装备的风险补偿机制。推动行业协会发布《文化装备制造技术进步和技术改造设备产品目录》，重点支持目录内文化装备的研制推广。不断丰富《文化产品和服务出口指导目录》内容，探索利用自由贸易试验区、海关特殊监管区域现行税收政策，开展重点文化装备配套设备和零部件加工、物流业务。支持将符合条件的文化装备企业纳入享受支持科技创新进口税收政策的国家中小企业公共服务示范平台。

（三）加大资金扶持力度

深化产融结合，鼓励地方财政、金融资本、风险投资及民间资本投入文化装备技术创新。充分发挥工业转型升级（中国制造2025）等现有资金以及先进制造业产业投资基金的引导作用，鼓励符合条件的文化装备产品及应用试点示范、支撑平台建设等通过政府首购、订购和购买服务等方式支持国内文化装备创新产品。在风险可控、商业可持续的前提下，加大对重点文化装备出口信贷支持，鼓励金融机构增加出口信贷资金投放，支持国内企业承揽国外重大文化工程，带动成套文化装备和产品出口。

（四）健全人才保障体系

加强文化装备人才队伍建设，重点培养和汇聚复合型研发设计人才、开拓型经营管理人才、高级技能人才，满足文化装备企业可持续发展需要。鼓励国内文化装备制造企业和经营企业，引进国外研发设计、经营管理等高层次人才和团队，与国外专业机构和高校加强合作，联合培养适应文化装备发展的专业技术技能人才。完善文化装备职业教育体系。支持面向文化装备安装、调试、使用、维护人员的岗位技能培训。

（五）发挥行业组织作用

发挥行业协会贴近企业优势，充分发挥相关行业协会和中介组织的桥梁纽带作用，推广先进管理模式。各相关行业协会要指导企业抓好技术创新、人才培养，及时反映企业诉求，反馈政策落实情况，积极宣传和帮助企业用足用好各项政策。支持建立文化装备产业联盟。支持行业协会、产业联盟建设文化装备综合公共服务平台、共性技术研究院以及高水平生产中心，提升服务行业发展的能力。

（六）拓展国际交流合作

坚持引进来和走出去并重，充分利用双边、多边国际文化交流与经济合作机制，抓住"一带一路"建设契机,多层次地开展技术、标准、知识产权等方面的国际交流与合作。鼓励企业、国内外科研院所、行业组织拓宽交流渠道,广泛开展合作,实现优势互补,推进文化装备制造技术在"一带一路"伙伴国家的推广应用。

七、组织实施

工业和信息化部、文化和旅游部负责计划并组织实施,加强领导,精心组织,及时解决实施过程中遇到的问题,推动各项任务和措施落到实处。

各地工业和信息化、文化主管部门要密切沟通与配合,按照本行动计划确定的目标、任务和举措,抓紧制订紧密衔接的实施方案,抓好工作落实,引导与推动文化装备制造可持续健康发展。

"十四五"城镇化与城市发展领域战略科技研究（节选）*

一、国内现状与需求分析

（一）我国城镇化与城市发展领域科技创新现状

1. 城镇化与城市发展领域科技创新应坚持以人民为中心

党的十九大报告指出，"我国社会的主要矛盾已经转化为人民日益增长的美好生活需要和不平衡不充分的发展之间的矛盾"，"坚持以人民为中心，人民健康是民族昌盛和国家富强的重要标志，实施健康中国战略，为人民群众提供全方位全周期健康服务；大力度推进生态文明建设、建立健全绿色低碳循环发展的经济体系"。城市是人类主要集聚区，承载着为人民提供美好生活环境和良好公共服务的功能。城市功能和人居环境品质直接影响到人民群众能否获得"美好生活"的幸福感。

当前我国已进入新型城镇化时代，但在城市综合功能、基础设施运行效率、资源能源利用、人居环境品质、城镇治理和管理手段等方面依然存在诸多问题，制约了城市健康可持续发展。党中央、国务院高度重视我国城镇化建设，提出要走集约、智能、绿色、低碳的新型城镇化可持续发展道路。"十九大"报告指出，加快新型城镇化建设，"坚持以人民为中心，坚持改善民生"，推进"绿色发展、高质量发展"。2017年3月，习近平总书记参加两会上海代表团审议，提出"城市管理应该像绣花一样精细。城市精细化管理，必须适应城市发展"。2019年11月，习近平总书记在视察上海时进一步指出，"无论是城市规划还是城市建设，无论是新城区建设还是老城区改造，都要坚持以人民为中心……走内涵式、集约型、绿色化的高质量发展路子"。

2. 政府对城镇化与城市发展领域科技发展工作高度重视

《国家中长期科学和技术发展规划纲要（2006–2020年）》首次将城镇化与城市发展领域作为重点领域进行独立部署，设立了"城镇区域规划与动态监测、城市功能提升与

---

* 本文节选自科技部"十四五"城镇化与城市发展领域战略科技研究报告。成稿于2020年10月。收入本书时有改动。

空间节约利用、建筑节能与绿色建筑、城市生态居住环境质量保障、城市信息平台"等五个优先主题。《住房和城乡建设部等部门关于推动智能建造与建筑工业化协同发展的指导意见》强调"以数字化、智能化升级为动力,创新突破相关核心技术,加大智能建造在工程建设各环节应用,形成涵盖科研、设计、生产加工、施工装配、运营等全产业链融合一体的智能建造产业体系"。在国家科技支撑计划、重点专项研发计划和国家自然科学基金等国家科技计划的支持下,我国在区域规划、建筑节能、城市基础设施、生态居住环境等技术领域得到快速发展。

近期,中共中央、国务院及多部门先后发布《中共中央 国务院关于建立国土空间规划体系并监督实施的若干意见》《关于实施健康中国行动的意见》(国发〔2019〕13号)、《关于全面推进城镇老旧小区改造工作的指导意见》(国办发〔2020〕23号)、《关于推动智能建造与建筑工业化协同发展的指导意见》(建市〔2020〕60号)、《关于印发绿色建筑创建行动方案的通知》(建标〔2020〕65号)、《关于印发绿色社区创建行动方案的通知》(建城〔2020〕68号)、《关于加快实施老年人居家适老化改造工程指导意见》(民发〔2020〕86号)、《关于推进建筑垃圾减量化的指导意见》(建质〔2020〕46号)等鼓励支持文件,均对城镇化与城市发展领域的发展与科技工作提出了具体要求。

3. 新型城镇化建设和城乡融合发展应重点完善文化和旅游科技创新体系建设

党的十九大报告指出"文化是一个国家、一个民族的灵魂。文化兴国运兴,文化强民族强"。2017年1月,中共中央办公厅、国务院办公厅印发《关于实施中华优秀传统文化传承发展工程的意见》,意见指出"坚持创造性转化和创新性发展,使中华民族最基本的文化基因与当代文化相适应、与现代社会相协调"。2019年2月,习近平总书记在北京慰问基层干部群众时指出,"一个城市的历史遗迹、文化古迹、人文底蕴,是城市生命的一部分,文化底蕴毁掉了,城市建得再新再好,也是缺乏生命力的"。2019年10月,《坚持和完善中国特色社会主义制度、推进国家治理体系和治理能力现代化若干重大问题的决定》指出,"推进中华优秀传统文化传承发展工程。……优化城乡文化资源配置"。2019年11月,习近平总书记在上海考察时指出,"文化是城市的灵魂。……让人们记得住历史、记得住乡愁……增强家国情怀"。2020年9月22日,习近平总书记在教育文化卫生体育领域专家代表座谈会上强调指出:"统筹推进'五位一体'总体布局、协调推进'四个全面'战略布局,文化是重要内容;推动高质量发展,文化是重要支点;满足人民日益增长的美好生活需要,文化是重要因素;战胜前进道路上各种风险挑战,文化是重要力量源泉。"

2017年3月1日起,全面施行《中华人民共和国公共文化服务保障法》,鼓励和支持发挥科技在公共文化服务中的作用,提高公众的科学素养和公共文化服务水平。2020年6月26日,国务院办公厅关于印发国务院2020年立法工作计划的通知(国办发〔2020〕18号)中明确《中华人民共和国文化产业促进法(草案送审稿)》预备提请全国人大常委会审议",该法将"科技支撑"设为独立一章共 8 条,鼓励发挥科技在文化创新发展中的作用,推动文化和科技深度融合。

各部委发布了系列政策文件,推动文旅科技发展。2019 年 8 月,国务院印发《关于进一步激发文化和旅游消费潜力的意见》,要求完善文旅科技创新体系建设、加强文旅技术研发、提升文旅装备技术水平。同月,六部委联合发布《关于促进文化和科技深度融合的指导意见》,对文化和旅游科技创新发展作出具体部署。2020 年 4 月,发改委发布《2020 年新型城镇化建设和城乡融合发展重点任务》,指出要活化利用工业遗产,发展工业旅游,实现城乡公共文化设施一体化布局。2020 年 5 月,中央文改办发布《关于做好国家文化大数据体系建设的通知》,明确文化大数据体系建设工作任务。

4. 城镇化建设与城市发展过程中应加强文物保护与传承利用研究

党的十八大以来,以习近平同志为核心的党中央站在新的历史方位,从留住文化根脉、守住民族之魂的战略高度关心和推动文化遗产保护工作,多次做出重要指示批示。党的十九大报告提出"加强文物保护利用和文化遗产保护传承"。2019 年 8 月 19 日,习近平总书记在敦煌研究院主持召开座谈会并就文物保护工作发表重要讲话,强调"文物保护靠科技","要持续加大投入,运用先进技术加强文物保护和研究",为我们做好文物科技工作提供了根本遵循和科学指引。近年来,中共中央办公厅、国务院办公厅连续印发《关于实施革命文物保护利用工程(2018-2022 年)的意见》《关于加强文物保护利用改革的若干意见》等重要文件,部署了一系列重点任务和项目,强调要"加强科技支撑""加强新型城镇化和新农村建设中的文物保护"。从新型城镇化与城市发展的角度而言,城市精神是支撑城市发展的灵魂和根基。文物以其独特价值和丰富内涵,赋予城市深厚的文化底蕴,构筑了城市形象的基础,为城镇化和城市可持续发展提供精神滋养和内在动力。

5. 我国城镇化领域绝大部分技术处在跟跑或并跑状态,少数技术处在领跑状态

科技部 2019 年组织的第六次国家技术预测工作邀请国内城镇化领域数百位专家,对 149 项由各位专家提供的重要技术进行了中外对比情况评估,针对各项技术的"三跑"情况(跟跑、并跑、领跑)、技术成熟度(实验室、中试、产业化)、各国技术领先情况、技术发展趋势等进行了问卷调研。

根据问卷调研结果,我国城镇化领域绝大部分技术都处在跟跑(44.4%)或并跑(42.3%)的状态,少数技术处在领跑(13.4%)状态。其中,建筑设计、城市治理、城市建设与维护等子领域技术以跟跑为主;在土木工程技术、城市能源系统、城市规划等子领域,技术以并跑为主。对于存在差异的技术,各子领域与国外整体差距均在 5 年以上。与上一轮技术预测相比,大部分子领域和国外技术差距在不断缩小。总体看,我国城镇化与城市发展领域的整体技术水平处于国际先进水平,某些关键科技点处于国际领先水平,总体超越发展中国家水平,但和国际领先水平仍存在差距。

(二)"十四五"城镇化发展对科技创新的战略需求

自《国家中长期科学技术发展规划纲要(2006—2020年)》实施以来,我国政府十分重视城镇化与城市发展领域科技研发,首次设立城镇化与城市发展领域,涵盖5个优先主题、25个重点研发方向,在区域发展、节能减排、人居环境、城镇功能、产业技术和重大工程等多个方面取得了90余项重大技术成果,其中大部分成果形成了工程示范,实现了产业化应用,获得了明显的经济、环境和社会效益。

"十三五"期间重点研发计划中设立了"绿色建筑与建筑工业化"一个重点专项,投入专项经费13.54亿元,领域覆盖面有所不足。"绿色建筑与建筑工业化"专项为工程建设的绿色化、工业化和信息化新技术奠定了良好基础,但距离全面支撑可持续城镇发展场景需求还存在较大差距。

"十四五"期间,我国城镇化发展将进入新阶段,呈现新特征,涌现新需求:一是城镇发展模式将从"量的增长以满足基本需求"转变为"质的提高以满足美好生活的向往",需要更高效可靠、更高品质、绿色低碳的城市基础设施系统,城市能源系统需从满足供应保增长转为改变系统方式以适应国家能源系统的低碳转换;二是我国城镇化的发展将由大规模新建逐步过渡到新建、维修、功能提升并重的阶段;三是万物互联的大数据时代使得建筑、街区、基础设施和在其之上的人流、物流、物质流的动态过程都可能实现定量感知和分析,将在很大程度上改变社会生态和城市科学范式,带来城市规划和运维的颠覆式变革;四是人口红利减退对建筑与基础设施建造智能化和工业化的需求,由此会带来从结构形式、材料到建造与维修方式的全面革命性变化;五是我国城镇化发展必须将"中华优秀传统文化融入生产生活,深入挖掘城市历史文化价值",使中华民族最基本的文化基因与当代文化相适应、与现代社会相协调;六是新冠疫情的暴发,要求城市管理的重点转向社区,建设以居住小区为基本单元的中国城市社会组织结构应对各种灾害及突发事件,需要更多"平疫结合"的健康社区和高品质建筑;七是国际形势转变对科技发展自主创新的需求,建筑信息化、高精度仪器等方面补短板任务艰巨。

为此必须通过科技创新积极应对上述"场景和需求变化",促进城镇化领域科技创新体系的改造升级,为提升城市治理能力和人民群众的获得感与幸福感提供硬核支撑。

二、国内外形势趋势分析

发达国家已进入高城镇化率发展期,城镇化增速较慢、发展较为平稳,以美、日、英、德为主的发达国家在城镇化与城市发展领域科技部署时,更加关注绿色低碳(欧洲为代表)、智慧(美国为代表)、精致建造(日本为代表)和文化名城名镇名村保护与城市特色风貌管理(欧洲、日本为代表),绿色建筑、低碳城区、既有城区和建筑改造升级、老龄社会、医养、文化、旅游、体育等第三产业发展,以及信息化等新技术在规划、运维和功能提升等方面的研究和应用。

城镇化与城市发展领域国内外科技创新发展动态,可从城市功能提升与空间高效利用、智能建造与新型建筑工业化、城镇可持续支撑系统、文化和旅游融合、文物保护与传承利用等几方面总结如下。

(一)城市功能提升与空间高效利用
(略)

(二)智能建造、智慧运维与新型建筑工业化
(略)

(三)城镇可持续支撑系统
(略)

(四)文化和旅游融合

1. 文化科技

国外运用高新技术助推文化创新发展。在智能舞台领域,欧美研发追光灯应用模式识别技术实现了智能舞台灯光操作;美国 GE 和荷兰飞利浦公司引领了高技术的照明光源创新发展;美国杜比实验室研发了分布式声场计算和电声调控等舞台音响智能化技术。在艺术科技领域,日本、美国、法国、意大利等国的艺术科学实验室在智能视觉识别、机器图形识别、绘画机器人等方面有较高水平。在文化资源保护技术领域,荷兰、德国、法国等通过三维微观特征来"标记"和识别艺术和文化遗产,开发馆藏的综合数字存档系统;耶鲁大学实现了交互式三维构建和记录技术构建遗产地模型;东京大学采用数据获取、图像配准技术对石刻大佛进行几何重建;德国斯图加特大学集成了计算机视觉、机器学习、三维建模和虚拟现实技术,生成 4D 地图以应用文物识别分析。

在我国,文化领域推进与提升文化科技创新能力的进程正在加快。文化价值挖掘/文化大数据/文化信息传播理论/数字版权服务/文化服务评测/文化服务征信/文化统计与调查/文化可信网络与计算/等为代表的文化领域基础服务技术,认知智能/语言智能/视听智能/AI创作/数据智能等为代表的文化领域智能化技术,体验科学/人机交互/混合现实/博弈对抗/虚拟仿真/艺术呈现等为代表的文化领域沉浸化技术,文化演艺/数字内容/公共文化服务/文化遗产/文化旅游/创意设计/文化装备等为代表的文化领域

 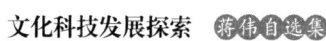

集成技术与系统,融合媒体/网络视听/知识服务/移动社交/网络直播/电子竞技等为代表的网络文化新技术新服务,已在文化领域得到初步创新应用,助推了文化发展方式的转变。

但支撑文化艺术表达与呈现、非物质文化遗产保护与传承、中华文化资源数据库建设、中国古代典籍整理、民族民间文化典藏与传播、传统工艺振兴、文化市场监管等专用技术/系统/装备仍严重缺乏;在文化传承用的文化专用纸、传统书画美术颜料、纸质文献脱酸/防腐/固色/专用材料,艺术表现与呈现用的喷雾/喷雪/喷烟/专用材料(不含烟花),高声学品质用的传声器/扬声器专用膜片材料、音箱箱体专用材料,演艺灯具传统光源材料、LED光源材料,舞台机械系统专用材料,传统手工艺品用的锦绣/陶瓷/漆器/雕刻/编织/专用材料等文化专用材料领域,相关技术与制备工艺仍处在探索发展阶段;在数字文化领域,支撑内容创作、生产、传播和交互的主要软件工具,缺乏自主知识产权并受制于国外;在文化新业态领域,数字技术、网络技术、人工智能、虚拟现实、人机交互、增材制造等现代技术手段的利用与应用还不足,新技术、新工艺、新产品、新服务、新模式的创新仍处在孕育期与催生培育阶段;总体上,亟须以体系化思维攻克文化科技的关键核心技术和系统集成技术难关,统筹文化科技基础研究与应用技术研究,统筹应用示范与成果推广。

2. 旅游科技

国外旅游科技发展迅速。大数据、互联网等新科技促进企业数字化运营,欧洲国家旅游智慧管理应用处于领先地位,通过定位设备、无线射频手腕带、智能交通管理、智能预订等技术,既满足游客便利化、安全性、舒适性需求,又结合技术应用优化运营管理。发达国家重视旅游高端装备制造和文物保护技术应用,美国、德国等在主题公园、邮轮、滑雪、文化遗产旅游等领域发展较快,开发虚拟旅游设备、VR、光影制造、可穿戴设备与虚拟场景结合的全触感空间和沉浸式空间。发达国家重视环境保护,将生态环保、人工智能技术、节能减排等技术综合用于目的地、景区、饭店和交通运营管理和资源保护,以新技术促进文化和旅游融合发展,将数字扫描、全息投影、AR等技术用于文化遗产和非遗资源的存储和展示,打造电影酒店、移动图书馆、电竞酒店、景区游戏、数字博物馆等。

我国旅游科技总体处于少数"领跑"、部分"并跑"、多数"跟跑"的位次。新一代信息技术应用最活跃的部分,人工智能旅游定制、移动支付、机器人客服等领域处于"领跑"位势;景区、酒店等旅游企业数字化运营和节能技术方面处于"跟跑"位势;旅游高端装备制造、展陈与信息技术融合集成领域处于"跟跑"位势。我国在面向散客化市场的便利化和安全服务、庞大市场的智能体验和监管、高端装备制造技术等方面劣势明显,旅游创新体系的政策支持不足。

"十四五"期间,将以物联网、人工智能等新技术提升游客体验,包括智慧酒店的游客自助导航，智能游览中的 RFID"手腕带"集中预订、收费、身份验证、智能定位等，旅游交通中的实时交通路况显示，旅游景区的游览规划等。同时，用高科技打造体验感好的科技旅游产品，运用 AR、VR、全息投影等技术打造沉浸式体验产品、夜间光影秀、数字艺术展等。

（五）文物保护与传承利用

（略）

三、指导思想和目标原则

（一）指导思想

高举中国特色社会主义伟大旗帜，全面贯彻党的十九大要求，深入贯彻习近平总书记系列讲话精神，按照"五位一体"总体部署，坚持"四个全面"战略布局和以人民为中心的发展思想，牢固树立和贯彻落实"创新、协调、绿色、开放、共享"五大发展理念，坚持"自主创新、重点跨越、支撑发展、引领未来"的指导方针，面向世界城镇化领域科技前沿、面向国民经济主战场、面向国家重点需求，围绕美丽中国、新型城镇化和生态文明建设，实施创新驱动发展战略，增强自主创新能力。

以"以人为本"为指导思想，以体系设计为着眼点，以目标导向为主线，以技术突破为手段，以场景应用为驱动，进一步整合城镇化与城市发展领域科技资源。以"加强城市规律和关键技术集成研究，提升城市功能与空间利用效率；加强创新技术应用研究，提升智能建造和新型建筑工业化水平；加强能源、韧性和生态技术支撑体系建设，提升城镇可持续发展能力；加强文化和旅游科技创新体系建设，坚守中华文化立场、传承中华文化基因，提升文化科技创新能力；加强技术转化平台建设，提升科技成果产业化水平；加强国际合作与人才队伍建设，提升科技创新能力"等为抓手，通过全创新链设计、系统部署和重点突破，着力提升城镇化领域功能和可持续发展的科技支撑能力，破解城镇化发展难题，释放经济发展新动能，开创我国城镇化与城市发展领域科技创新工作新局面。

（二）发展目标

针对城市功能、市政基础设施、人居环境、社区品质、城镇管理等制约城市健康发展的瓶颈问题，以建筑－社区－城市－城市群四方面为点线面域载体，以满足人民的居住幸福感与精神文化生活新期待和提升城市建设与治理水平为目标，通过高新技术、新

材料与工程建设技术的融合创新，围绕城市功能提升（城市诊治更新、绿色建筑、健康社区和地下空间开发）、智能建造和新型建筑工业化（数字化规划设计、智能建造、智慧运维）、城镇可持续支撑系统（城市低碳能源系统、城市生命线工程、生态诊断和生态修复）、文化和旅游融合（文化科技、旅游科技）、文物保护和传承利用等重点领域开展全链条一体化科技创新，兼顾渐进式和颠覆式创新部署重点专项和重点任务，突破120项关键技术、形成120种以上系统与专用设备，并在国家可持续发展议程创新示范区、雄安新区以及京津冀、长三角、粤港澳大湾区等重点区域完成100项重大工程示范，显著提升我国城市的功能、品质和精致程度，大幅提高人民居住获得感和满意度，为形成中国特色的可持续城镇范式提供科技支撑，确保2025年我国可持续城镇化领域科技水平和公共文旅服务或创新能力达到或部分超过美、日、英、德等国。

至2025年，城镇化与城市发展领域科技创新体系更趋完善，创新能力显著提高，科技进步对城镇化发展贡献率稳步提高，为新型城镇化提供更高质高效的技术解决方案，相关产业发展壮大，科技成果更多更好地惠及民生、服务国家城镇可持续发展、推动文旅高质量发展。至2025年，建成一批科技创新人才队伍、创新企业和科研平台。通过自主培养、积极引进等多种形式，培育形成科技领军人才、高技能人才、企业家人才、科技惠民专员和创新服务人员，培养一批城镇化领域国家级高端人才和核心队伍。积极搭建平台，推动城镇化领域科研人员成为"双创"主力军，培育一批城镇化领域科技创新骨干企业和全产业链应用示范骨干企业，推动国家科技创新基地、创新团队和产业技术创新战略联盟建设。

（三）基本原则

1. 坚持民生为先，以人为本

解决城镇化进程中人民群众最直接、最关心、最迫切的问题，坚持科技进步造福人民，科技成果惠及百姓。坚持人才是科技创新第一资源的理念，坚持在创新实践中发现人才，在创新活动中培育人才，在创新事业中汇聚人才。

2. 坚持顶层设计，系统集成

针对制约城镇化与城市发展科技创新的重大问题，探索围绕产业链部署创新链、围绕创新链配置资金链的新模式和新机制。坚持发挥不同创新主体的作用，按照功能定位、分类统筹的原则建设完善社会发展科技创新平台，营造城镇化与城市发展领域科技创新的新局面。

3. 坚持政府引导，市场为主

以新型城镇化市场需求为导向，充分发挥市场配置创新资源的作用，构建政府和社会在资金、技术和人才等方面实现多主体融合、多渠道汇集的科技创新格局，促进城镇化与城市发展领域科技创新跨越式发展。

4. 坚持创新驱动，开放协同

通过放管结合、优化服务，充分调动高校、科研院所、企业等各方面的积极性、主动性、创造性，构建开放高效的创新资源共享网络，推动科技创新与大众创业、万众创新有机结合，拓展公众参与空间，丰富公众参与载体，以协同创新牵引城镇科技发展。

四、重点任务部署

（一）城市功能提升与空间高效利用

（略）

（二）智能建造、智慧运维与新型建筑工业化

（略）

（三）城镇可持续支撑系统

（略）

（四）文化与旅游融合

1. 文旅资源保护利用

（1）文化资源保护与复原复现关键技术

研究文化资源保护基础理论和方法，制定文化资源保护重要技术标准；研发古籍善本、文献修复与保护关键技术与设备，研制民国纸质文献规模化脱酸处理成套技术装备；研究古籍文献的数字化保存、分类存储、数据恢复、检索、分类管理等技术；研发非物质文化遗产资源无损检测和新材料应用技术；研发宣纸、瓷器、丝绸等系列传统文化介质的现代复原复现技术；研发中国传统矿物颜料现代替代材料制备技术和工艺；研发中国传统陶瓷无烟柴烧窑技术；研发传统瓷器、漆艺、丝绸、金工等复原复现技艺；研发文化资源鉴定鉴证材料分析、区块链、智能合约集成技术；研发古文字、少数民族文字等中华传统语言文字识别与处理、资源采集与记录、保存、编码转换集成技术；开展重要典籍、民俗、宗教等文化资源保护以及新材料、新工艺示范；开展非物质文化遗产过程记录、修复、复制、再现和传承集成示范；开展古籍文献修复保护技术与数字化保存、分类管理集成示范；开展中华古籍文献数据平台示范；开展战略性互联网文化资源保存示范；开展甲骨文综合数据平台示范。

（2）文化资源数字化与内容挖掘集成技术

研制数字文化资源全链条相关技术和装备；研发传统文化资源的素材组织和数字挖掘技术、标准、系统与装备；研究中华文化基因的数据标识、价值挖掘和阐发理论与技术；研发海量文化资源检索、物质载体专用监控与管理技术；开发民族民间文化典藏、传统工艺等中华文化资源数据库；开展数字文化资源全链条集成技术和装备系统示范；开展中华文化基因智能挖掘标识示范；开展馆藏公共文化资源智慧管理与共享平台示范。

（3）文化资源内容创作技术

研究语言及视听认知表达、跨媒体内容识别与处理、情感关联等智能创作基础理论与方法；研究语音、声乐和乐器处理基础技术理论；研究类人视觉、听觉和感知以及视听情感表达的融合信息处理等基础理论、方法、技术；研发演艺数控系统设备、动漫游戏编辑制作与特效处理等核心关键技术和软件；研发舞蹈、音乐、美术等数字化编排关键技术及工具；开发演艺娱乐业、动漫游戏业、艺术品和工艺美术业、文化会展业、创意设计业、网络和数字文化服务业等技术装备和系统；开发基于数据智能自适配生产、智能创作生产应用技术和系统；开展舞美、布景、灯光、音响、机械、视效、观演互动等领域的智能设计、制作、体验、呈现集成示范；开展智慧剧院（场）示范；开展文化艺术内容可视呈现、互动传播、沉浸体验一体化示范。

（4）旅游资源保护开发技术与装备

研发景区地理信息网络化提升与沉浸式体验技术；开发景区、场馆、旅游酒店等场所的节能减排装备；开发高端休闲体验类、旅游运动类、基础设施类旅游装备和系统软件；开发国家文化公园、旅游景观的保护监测及评估装置核心关键技术和装备；开发旅游资源数据服务平台；开展旅游资源动态管理及智能规划和智能推广集成示范；开展旅游资源与交通、教育、康养等融合提升示范；开展红色旅游、乡村旅游基础资源和服务智能规划示范；开展长城、大运河、长征等国家文化公园资源评价、检测和生态保护示范。

2. 公共文旅服务

（1）公共文化服务共性关键技术

研发馆藏公共文化内容大数据处理、内容传播、安全与隐私保护技术与标准；研发公共文化资源以及服务效能大数据处理技术；研发物理形态和数字形态文化资源的备灾存储关键技术与系统装备；研发基础文化设施智能化技术和装备；研制智能化公共文化服务网络、一站式文化服务系统和流动公共文化服务装备；开展线下线上展演、展映、展播、展览等公共文化内容供给新型呈现示范；开展新兴网络文化形态的信息传播技术及前沿引导集成示范；开展公共文化服务效能分析和评估示范；开展智慧图书馆、美术馆、文化馆、博物馆、纪念馆、科技馆、社区文化活动中心等智慧公共文化设施示范；开展中国海外文化中心和"一带一路"文化交流场馆等海外文化设施建设和对外文化传播示范。

（2）全域旅游智慧发展与公共旅游服务集成技术

研究基于大数据、云计算、人工智能的旅游公共文化服务场所布局、精准管理等理论和关键技术；研发城市旅游多业态综合信用自动监测与信用管理技术；研发游客流量智能监测与服务技术；研发旅游推广服务可视化、场景化呈现技术；研发区域游客承载量多维测算技术；研发旅游公共服务智慧化设施和技术装备；开发大数据公共管理决策支撑系统；研发节能减排、景观保护装备和环境评估装置。开展全域旅游"智慧大脑"公共服务云平台集成示范；开展多媒介融合旅游行为数据汇聚与挖掘示范；开展旅游目的地数字化宣传推广集成示范。

3. 文化和旅游行业治理能力提升共性关键技术

（1）文化行业治理与安全保障技术

研究文化市场管理、信用评估、综合执法中的数据采集、交汇、存储、分析、评估和行为预测理论和关键技术；研究文化场所安全保障基础理论，制定文化领域安全技术标准。研发文化消费行为需求预测模型；研发文化领域舆情监测、信息分类、识别与预警等关键技术；研发执法电子证据生成技术及系统；研发文化行业大数据统计与分析集成技术和系统；研发演艺场所、文娱场所等专用计量、测量与安全检验检测技术与装备。开展公共文化场所应急处置集成示范；开展文化装备质量评测检测示范；开展文化市场综合运营监管智慧平台示范。

（2）旅游行业治理与安全保障技术

研究旅游统计调查和征信服务基础理论；研究国家旅游大数据体系理论与关键技术。研发旅游危机管理与应急处置集成技术。研发旅游景区、休闲街区、主题园区等安全检验检测技术和装备；开发动态公用旅游信用平台和不文明游客数据平台。开展游客行为综合监管与市场治理集成示范；开展境内境外旅游安全防控及预警系统示范；开展旅游大数据治理集成示范；开展基于地理信息系统的可视化疫情管控示范；开展预约服务、流量管理、分流疏导的旅游综合治理示范。

（五）文物保护和传承

（略）

五、改革和保障措施

（一）完善体制机制，激励自主创新

完善科研经费管理机制和科研评价体制，坚持分类评价与政策激励相结合，使科研项目和资金配置更能满足既有建筑诊治领域重大需求。提倡科研经费包干制度，充分发挥科研人员的积极性和创造性，切实提升自主创新能力。

以科研平台促进研究成果共享与落地。完善制度规则，搭建信息平台，推进土木工程行业重点科研平台、大型仪器设备和科学基础设施的开放共享，加强文物领域国家和行业两级科研基地（平台）建设，提升平台的国际性和开放性，加大对国际标准、技术的跟踪、评估和转化力度。完善平台运行管理机制，加强行业平台间的合作交流。充分发挥行业平台在重大工程建设、重大研发任务中的技术支撑保障作用。完善平台发展政策，支持平台开展科研基础条件建设，不断提高研究实验水平。

（二）加强政策扶持，创新投入机制，推动产业发展

利用现有政策和资金渠道，增加中央财政投入，着力支持既有建筑诊治关键技术研发、成果产业化、应用示范、创新能力建设等。鼓励地方各级政府加大财政扶持力度，强化对城市更新产业投入的引导和带动作用，建立以政府扶持为引导、企业投入为主体、多元社会资金参与的创新投入机制，推动城市更新产业高质量发展。加大对文物保护与传承等公益性科研活动的支持力度，在国家自然科学基金等设立相应学科，建立稳定支持和竞争性支持相结合的资金投入机制。

注重科研成果的创新性、系列性、系统性和完整性，坚持科研工作源于工程、服务工程、高于工程、指导工程、引领工程，创新"出大成果、出系统成果、出专家"的管理机制，完善同行评议和考评机制，充分发挥专家作用，弱化行政干预，简化项目申请程序和考评环节。

（三）加强对学者与团队的鼓励与支持

着力实施创新人才推进计划和领域科研杰出人才培养计划，加快培养领域科技领军人才和创新团队。完善人才激励机制和评价体系，以国家科技计划项目为纽带，重点培养中青年科研骨干。

重点支持青年科技人才持续发展，建设行业专家智库。支持青年科技人才承担重大科研项目，开展独立性和原创性研究。充分发挥专家在行业新技术跟踪与预测、科技规划计划编制和实施评估、行业科技服务等方面的指导和咨询作用。

（四）大力开展典型工程试点示范

在基础条件好和需求迫切的重点领域，围绕城市功能提升与空间高效利用、智能建造、智慧运维与新型建筑工业化、城镇可持续支撑系统、文化和旅游融合、文物保护与传承利用等方面，开展新模式、新技术、新产品试点示范，形成有效的经验和模式，遴

选标杆企业和产品进行推广和移植。

(五)积极开展国际交流与合作

在标准制定、知识产权等方面广泛开展国际交流与合作,不断拓展合作领域。支持国内外科研机构、企业及行业组织间开展技术交流与合作,做到引资、引技、引智相结合。鼓励跨国公司、国外机构等在华设立相关领域研发机构。围绕"一带一路"等国家战略,提升科技支撑能力和国际竞争力。

第四部分
讲话发言

开创"十二五"文化科技发展新局面的相关考虑[*]

一、深刻认识文化与科技融合的重大意义

目前文化建设"十二五"规划正在制订过程中,要实现新阶段文化发展目标靠什么?最根本是依靠两大动力,一要靠坚定不移地推进文化体制改革与机制创新,二要靠文化科技进步和文化创新的有力支撑。

推进文化与科技的融合,是更加自觉、更加主动地推动社会主义文化大发展大繁荣的客观要求,是实现新阶段文化发展目标的必由之路,是文化科技工作的核心。

因此,从长远来看,文化行业内生的自主创新能力和科技进步动能若不能发展起来,文化发展的动力将面临衰竭的危险,文化建设的可持续性将受到影响。所以,推动与加速文化与科技的融合,大幅度增加文化创新的有效供给,提升中国文化的软实力,是文化科技服务国家战略和促进地方经济社会文化发展的历史重任。

二、当前文化科技工作取得的成就与面临的不足

当前及今后一段时间如何推动与加速文化与科技的融合,需要我们从国情出发,认清我国文化科技发展的优势、不足和潜力。

(一)取得的成就

1. 文化科技的地位与作用得到空前提升,方向进一步明确

毛泽东同志、邓小平同志、江泽民同志、胡锦涛同志分别提出"为社会主义服务、为人民服务""科学技术是第一生产力""积极进行文化创新""推动社会主义文化大发展大繁荣",为我国文化指明了前进方向。李长春同志指出:"改革创新和科技进步是文化发展的根本动力。"刘云山同志指出:"要从战略高度审视科学技术在文化发展中的重要地位

---

[*] 本文系 2010 年 8 月 15 日在文化和旅游部相关座谈会上的发言,收入本书时有改动。

和作用,积极推动文化与科技的融合。"蔡武同志指出:"我国当前文化科技工作的重点,首先是加快构建有利于科技与文化融合的体制机制;其次是积极运用现代科技推动与文化各领域的融合,用先进的生产手段和表现形式,增强文化产品的感染力和影响力,拓展文化产品的消费方式和传播能力。"文化科技的地位与作用从来没有像今天这样重要,文化科技发展的紧迫性从来没有像今天这样突出,当前及"十二五"期间,文化科技工作的方向进一步明确。

2. 文化科技支撑体系的作用进一步凸显

科技与文化融合的体制机制创新正在不断被探索和进一步推进;以企业为主体、市场为导向、产学研用相结合的文化科技创新体系初步形成;以文化领域各专业标准化委员会为主体,推进文化服务、技术、管理和基础标准化进程为目标,企业、高校、科研机构、行业协会共同参与的文化标准体系建设取得实质性进展;以落实和完善文化科技进步的政策环境、实施国家文化创新工程、实施国家文化科技提升计划和文化和旅游部科技创新项目、谋划国家文化科技重大专项、凝聚文化科技力量、吸纳和推广科技成果、进行文化创新奖励等为主要架构的文化科技管理体系发挥了应有的作用;文化科技支撑体系的作用进一步凸显。

3. 文化科技拉动相关文化服务与文化经济的作用成效显著

在传统领域,图书馆、博物馆、美术馆、展览馆、文化馆以及剧院等公共文化设施的主体技术已被基本掌握,主要装备已基本实现国产化,部分装备技术已经达到或接近国际先进水平;大型文化活动与文化娱乐场所综合应用科技手段的能力显著提高;舞台灯光、音响等消费电气电子器材的生产能力和产量跃居世界首位,并大量进入国际市场;文化设施与娱乐场所的工程设计及建设进军国际市场。

在新兴领域,围绕数字文化资源处理、网络文化传播、舞台艺术表现、电子娱乐体验和文化监管等的文化科技成果不断丰富,科技手段和科技含量显著提高,文化科技贡献率逐年提高,推动和拉动了相关文化服务、文化消费和文化产业的快速发展。

4. 文化科技领域进一步拓宽,文化科技工作进一步丰富

公共文化资源的数字化、网络化技术的应用得到跨越式发展,为文化传承与传播提供了新的内容表现形式与支撑手段;以内容创意为特征的动漫游戏等数字媒体技术得到快速发展与推动,形成新的文化形式与文化业态;随着三网融合的推进,网络已经成为大众文化传播的主要渠道之一,支撑网络文化发展的技术研发与应用以及支撑网络文化发展的内容与生产技术已形成当前文化科技的热点之一;适应文化事务与文化市场新时期管理与监控需求的科技手段正在成为文化科技研究的新领域;文化科技已经形成了多层次、宽视野、跨行业的研究领域新格局,文化科技工作进一步丰富。

（二）面临的不足

1. 科技与文化融合的体制有待进一步改革完善

文化科技工作还不能适应新时期文化建设的形势和需要，国家科技与文化分割的体制性问题还没有从根本上解决，科技与文化建设之间脱节的问题虽有所改善但也尚未根本改变，科技成果转化为文化生产力与文化竞争力的渠道不畅，无论是科技体制还是文化行业内部体制，都有待进一步改革完善。

2. 尚未形成文化科技促进与提升文化持续健康发展的长效机制

文化科技与现代科学技术的迅猛发展及广泛应用还不相适应，文化科技竞争力相对较弱，文化和旅游部及各级文化部门缺乏新时期战略层面的科技发展规划和组织、引导的调控手段，科技队伍整合、科技资源和成果共享问题没有很好解决。

3. 文化领域关键技术自给率和科技成果转化率较低

科技与文化的融合程度还不能适应文化发展的需求，关键技术自给率和科技成果转化率较低；公共文化事业与文化产业中的高新技术比重较小，具有自主知识产权的核心技术的数量和质量都落后于其他行业，文化科技自主创新能力与核心技术供给对文化发展的贡献虽有提高但仍有限。

4. 文化科技投入总量有待大幅度提高

全国文化科技发展还处于不平衡状态，不同区域文化科技水平差别较大，科研力量分散、低水平重复现象仍较严重，文化科技创新平台的综合性、交叉性以及国际化程度普遍较低，科技转化与服务平台不够完善。各级文化部门的科技投入总量相对不足，科技资金短缺的问题依然突出，科研力量尤其是高层次创新型科技人才较少，文化科技机构可持续发展能力有待提高，吸引与凝聚全社会文化科技力量的工作有待进一步加强。

三、准确把握文化科技发展的指导方针和目标

当前及"十二五"期间，文化科技发展要确定一个怎样的指导方针？目标是什么？这是推动与加速文化与科技融合必须首先解决的根本问题。

（一）文化科技方针

结合专家的意见并经过认真思考与论证，文化科技司拟提出"面向需求，汇聚资源，引创并重，推进提升"的文化科技方针。这十六字方针，从全面推进"两大一新"全局出发，既是对以往文化科技工作的继承和发展，又体现了新时期新阶段对文化科技发展的新要求，是科学发展观在文化科技工作中的具体体现。同时，拟提出的十六字方针也改善了新中国成立以来我国文化科技方针长期缺失或模糊不清的局面。

面向需求，是十六字方针的核心。文化是民族凝聚力和创造力的重要源泉，文化创新的价值取向决定着文化创新的精神品质。以面向群众需求和面向市场需求为牵引，国家和各级政府引导，逐步完善文化科技支撑体系和市场机制，推动企业科技创新主体地位的形成，加速科技与文化的融合与协调发展，提升国家与区域文化创新能力。

汇聚资源，就是着眼于发挥民族文化资源优势。优化配置跨学科、跨部门和跨区域的文化资源、科技资源和人力资源，统筹文化部门所辖行业科技与文化系统，注重文化科技研发与应用的区域协调和阶段衔接，支持文化科技中介机构健康有序发展，逐步完善文化科技转化与服务平台。

引创并重，就是坚持多种方式并举、实现可持续发展。鼓励以应用为导向的自主创新，统筹文化科技的基础研究与应用技术研究，加大行业重大共性技术与集成技术的研发力度，注重适用科技的引进消化与自主科技成果转化应用，大幅度增加文化科技的有效供给与推广，着力推进文化标准化、文化信息化建设，增强文化科技的创新能力、文化科技的吸纳能力和文化科技的转化能力。

推进提升，就是从现实的紧迫需求出发，通过文化科技载体建设，汇聚文化科技主干力量，着力解决当前制约文化发展的重大科技问题和战略产品研发问题；通过示范带动，培育文化新业态和优势文化产业及特色文化产业，辐射带动文化产业向优势区域集聚，延伸完善产业链，整体促进文化产业可持续发展。

（二）战略目标

以十六字方针为指导，文化科技司确定了未来中长期我国文化科技发展的战略目标。

1. 推动文化科技领域的学科布局的调整与重构，进一步凝练文化科技目标，促进系统内外的科技资源整合，加强创新队伍建设，推进文化领域的科技体制机制改革与创新。

2. 推进现代科技与艺术创作（生产）的结合，开发利用民族文化资源，提升文化内容和艺术形式的表现力、感染力并进而扩大其影响力，构建与完善优秀民族文化的传承体系，构建与完善体现社会主义核心价值观的文化传播体系，促进人民群众获得精神慰藉与文化滋养的需求，促进对外文化交流和对外文化宣传工作。

3. 加快公共文化设施建设布局、文化传承与传播体系构建、非物质文化遗产保护与古籍保护、文化市场监管体系构建中的支撑技术与关键技术的研究与应用，运用现代科技手段提升公共文化服务能力，构建与完善文化领域的标准化体系，促进文化信息化工作。

4. 推动科技与文化产业的交叉融合，运用现代科技手段促进民族文化资源优势转变为文化产业优势，构建与完善现代文化市场体系，创新文化生产方式、催生新的文化业态，衍生出一批具有国际竞争力的现代文化科技企业，促进文化产业在我国经济与社会发展中战略地位的进一步提升。

实现上述目标，不仅会使我国文化科技发展水平跃上一个新的台阶，也会使文化与科技的融合程度跃上一个新的台阶。

四、明确文化与科技融合的主要任务与指标

文化科技司从切实落实"一手抓公益性文化事业""一手抓经营性文化产业"和"文化创新能力建设"的战略部署出发，对文化与科技融合的主要面向进行了认真的梳理。

回顾历史，我们可以看到，通信技术、机械电子技术、印刷技术等现代科技的进步与发展，衍生出了广播电视业、电影业、印刷出版业、演艺业等一批文化业态。反观这些业态内部的各环节与链条，其链条下游既有经济属性的文化产品（含服务），又有公益属性的公共文化服务设施，如电台、电视台、影院、图书馆、剧场等，而这些公共文化服务设施又与博物馆、美术馆、展览馆、文化馆等一起构筑成了我国公共文化服务体系，还关系到文化传播体系。在链条的最上游，无论是什么文化业态，都必须与文化资源相联系，关系到文化资源的修复、开发、加工、保存、存储、利用、传承以及保护等环节。在链条的中游，其实质是文化产品创作生产过程，关系到社会主义核心价值观。上述的业态内部环节与链条还涉及市场与政府，关系到市场监管与政府管理两大方面。同理，其他新型的文化业态也不例外，其中顺应时代而发展起来的网络文化业，可以看成是上述若干具体业态的一个集合，同时也可以看成是公共文化服务体系中一个非物理化的公共文化服务设施。

由此可见，文化与科技融合的面向既包括公益性文化事业和经营性文化产业，同时也包括文化创新，涉及纵横立体交叉的文化建设各个领域，量大面广。因此，如何明确推进文化与科技融合的总体思路，以及如何明确其主要任务与指标，是文化科技司近期主要思考与研究的重大主题之一。

（一）总体思路

定位上，在确保一定的基础科学研究作为必要的战略储备的前提下，重点关注文化与科技融合的效率和效益。

路径上，在若干优势领域内聚焦有限目标，通过开展原始创新、集成创新和引进消化吸收再创新，持续增强文化科技自主创新能力。

抓手上，将文化科技基地建设、文化新业态和优势文化产业及特色文化产业的示范带动作为文化与科技融合的两个重要突破口。

载体上，将企业作为技术创新的主体，产学研用相结合。

（二）主要任务与指标

围绕我国文化科技发展的中长期战略目标，当前及"十二五"期间文化与科技融合的主要任务与指标拟定如下：

1. 文化科技体系建设方面。打破条块分割，整合文化科技资源，促进产、学、研结合，逐步建立适应新时期文化发展和科技自身发展规律的新型文化科技体制；至"十二五"期间，基本形成国家和企业相结合的文化科技投入机制，科技投入大幅度增加，设立并实施"国家文化科技基础条件平台建设"专项，科技基础设施和条件平台明显改善；现代信息技术全面应用，文化标准化体系基本完善。

2. 文化与科技融合的效率和效益方面。当前至"十二五"期间，文化与科技的融合对国家和区域经济增长及发展方式转变的贡献率有显著提高，公共文化服务与文化产品供给基本满足人民群众的需求，传统文化产业改造、新型文化业态培育得到有效推进，科技的引进消化与自主科技成果转化应用率明显提高，基本满足文化事务管理与文化市场监管业务的需求；设立并实施"文化科技成果转化与服务平台"专项，协同实施"国家文化创新工程""国家文化资源数字典藏与应用计划""全国传统工艺美术资源普查""全国文艺基础资源抢救修复计划""中国当代艺术家基础档案数据库建设"等关联项目；示范带动1—2个文化新业态和优势文化产业及特色文化产业项目。

3. 文化科技项目攻关方面。当前至"十二五"期间，行业重大共性技术与集成技术的研发能力大幅度提升，攻克30—40项关键技术难关；基本掌握数字文化资源处理、网络文化传播、舞台艺术表现、电子娱乐体验、文化监管等领域核心技术，整体技术水平达到国际中等以上；继续实施"国家文化科技提升计划"，设立并实施"文化与科技融合促进工程"专项，国家骨干文化科研院所的作用进一步发挥，建设3—5个文化科技基地。

4. 文化科技能力建设方面。当前至"十二五"期间，培养10名左右在国内外文化科技领域有重要影响的科技专家，100名左右中青年科技骨干，形成一支学术品德好、专业素质高、研发能力强、团队结构优的创新型文化科技人才队伍；对文化科技基础条件资源进行的战略重组和系统优化、文化系统科技布局进一步调整并趋合理，文化科技转化与服务平台进一步完善，文化科技中介机构健康有序发展；加大逐步进入国家级重点实验室行列的步伐，争取实现文化和旅游部所辖行业没有国家重点实验室的历史性突破；科技在基层管理、服务单位的普及应用水平大幅度提高，干部职工科技意识进一步增强。

根据文化科技工作发展及文化与科技融合的需求，强烈建议文化科技司组织专家凝练若干重点领域和几十个优先主题，以便为加快文化与科技融合进程经一步细化目标与任务。

五、落实推进文化与科技融合的政策措施建议

保证推进文化与科技融合的有效、努力开创文化科技发展的新局面需要从深化体制改革、完善配套政策、加大科技投入、加强人才队伍建设的社会环境等方面加大工作力度，采取切实措施。

（一）大力推进文化科技体制改革

文化科技体制改革是科技事业发展和推进自主创新的动力。要继续深化文化科技体制改革，加快建立与社会主义市场经济体制相适应、符合文化科技发展规律的科技体制，更大程度地发挥市场配置科技资源的基础性作用，最大限度地激发广大科技工作者和全社会的文化科技活力，不断解放和发展科学技术生产力。

1. 文化科技体制改革的关键，是建立以企业为主体、市场为导向、产学研相结合的技术创新体系。其目的之一是有效整合产学研的力量，面向群众需求和面向市场需求，加快技术创新成果的产业化；目的之二是使企业成为推进文化与科技融合的投资主体、研究开发的主体和科技成果应用的主体。

"国家文化科技提升计划"和"文化与科技融合促进工程"专项向国内企业开放；文化和旅游部重点实验室、文化和旅游部工程中心和公共科技成果，向社会特别是系统内外企业开放；逐步建立健全文化科技中介服务体系，为系统内外各类企业的创新活动提供社会化、市场化服务；支持企业建立研发机构，鼓励企业与科研部门、高校联合共建工程实验室、共性技术研发和工程化平台。推行以项目为纽带的文化科技协作攻关机制。

2. 继续推进文化科研院所管理体制和文化科技宏观管理体制等方面的改革。贯彻国家关于科研院所管理体制改革的精神，面向市场的应用技术研究开发类文化科研机构要在"十二五"期间完成进入文化企业集团或向企业化、市场化转制的过程。从事基础研究、前沿技术研究和文化公益研究的文化科研机构要在"十二五"期间完成现代院所制度的建立。加大对中国艺术科技研究所等中央级公益性文化科研机构的建设力度，为适应文化与科技融合的需要，"十二五"期间这些机构可考虑更名为中国文化科技研究所或中国文化科技研究院。

3. 继续完善文化科技宏观管理体制，助推文化科技司职能的转变，促进文化科技资源优化配置和高效利用，健全文化科技资源社会共享机制，提高文旅部动员和整合文化科技资源的能力。完善文旅部内部各部门间的沟通机制，加强艺术科学项目和文化科技类攻关项目的统筹规划，"十二五"期间，建议成立文旅部科学技术委员会，科技委主任

一职由分管副部长担任,建议"全国艺术科学规划领导小组办公室"独立建制。

(二)制定和实施鼓励文化与科技融合的政策措施

政府引导和推动文化与科技融合,关键是要营造良好的政策和制度环境。"十二五"期间,继续完善与出台相关配套政策及实施细则,主要包括:制订《文化科技"十二五"规划》,依法加强对文化科技发展的规范管理;完善文化与科技融合的政府采购制度,优先购买国内具有自主知识产权的高新技术装备和产品;优化文化科技成果转化的政策,制定和完善促进引进技术消化吸收再创新的政策,强化技术引进与消化吸收的有效衔接,提高技术配套和自主开发能力;加强对重大技术和装备引进的管理;完善国家知识产权保护体系,加大知识产权保护执法力度,坚决查处和打击各种违法侵权行为。

(三)进一步加大科技投入

科技投资是战略性投资,建立健全财政性科技投入稳定增长的机制。"十二五"期间财政科技投入增幅要明显高于财政经常性收入增幅。继续调整财政性科技投入的结构,重点支持文化公益研究和文化领域新产品、新技术的研发。支持文化领域重大战略产品和重大科技工程,加强文旅部重点实验室、文旅部工程中心等科技基础设施建设。科学组织文化科技攻关项目,切实加强科技经费监管,提高资金使用效益。

积极引导系统内外企业和社会增加对文化与科技融合的投入,营造政府、企业、社会多元化、多渠道的科技投入格局,努力形成政府财政性科技投入结构在原始创新、集成创新和再创新的比例大致为2:6:2,以此带动全社会的原始创新、集成创新和再创新投入结构趋于1:3:6。

(四)加强文化科技人才队伍建设

适应文化与科技日益融合的趋势,凝聚与建设一支掌握现代科技知识、善于运用科技手段推动文化发展的文化科技人才队伍。"十二五"期间努力营造人才辈出、人尽其才、才尽其用的体制环境和政策环境,主要包括:协同抓好全国宣传文化系统"四个一批"人才培养工程;加大高层次文化科技创新人才和高级技术管理者公开招聘力度,重点科研机构的学术带头人、重点实验室主任和其他高级科研岗位,要逐步面向系统内外公开招聘;加大文化科技人才培养使用力度,重点加强对具有科技创新素质和技术经营能力的复合型人才的培养,逐步解决人才队伍规模素质结构不适应文化科技发展需要的矛盾。加强项目-基地-人才一体化建设,依托重大科研和重大工程项目、重点科研基地、国际学术交流合作项目,培养一批中青年专家,形成一批骨干科技创新团队。联合教育部门逐步建立文化科技类人才培养渠道。

文化与科技融合涉及文化领域的方方面面，我们必须高举邓小平理论和"三个代表"重要思想伟大旗帜，贯彻落实科学发展观，以高度的责任感和紧迫感，抓住新一轮文化体制改革和文化建设带来的机遇，努力开创文化科技发展的新局面，为实现文化的大发展大繁荣而努力奋斗！

对接国家新需求，推动科研迈向文化科技领域*

各位老师：

10月15日至18日，中国共产党第十七届中央委员会第六次全体会议在北京举行，审议通过了《中共中央关于深化文化体制改革，推动社会主义文化大发展大繁荣若干重大问题的决定》。

《决定》提出建设社会主义文化强国的宏伟目标和战略任务，为我们指明了文化建设的奋斗目标，描绘了文化发展的美好蓝图，指明了前进的方向。我们必须全面准确地把握党的十七届六中全会的基本精神。

全会认为，当前和今后一个时期，推进文化改革发展，需要着力研究解决以下几个问题：一是进一步深化对推进文化改革发展重要性和紧迫性的认识，增强全党全社会的文化自觉。二是加强社会主义核心价值体系建设，巩固全党全国各族人民团结奋斗的共同思想道德基础。三是促进文化创作发展，更好地满足人民的精神文化需求。四是加快文化事业和文化产业的发展，提高我国文化的总体实力。五是完善文化的体制机制，增强文化发展的动力活力。六是加大文化人才培养的力度，壮大文化人才队伍。七是加强和改进党对文化工作的领导。

这次全会虽然没有规定建成社会主义文化强国的时间表，但是根据实现全面建设小康社会的奋斗目标，提出了到2020年文化改革发展的七大目标。这七个目标是：1、社会主义核心价值体系建设深入推进，良好思想道德风尚进一步弘扬，公民素质明显提高；2、适应人民需要的文化产品更加丰富，精品力作不断涌现；3、文化事业全面繁荣，覆盖全社会的公共文化服务体系基本建成，努力实现基本公共文化服务均等化；4、文化产业成为国民经济的支柱性产业，整体实力和国际竞争力显著增强，公有制为主体、多种所有制共同发展的文化产业格局全面形成；5、文化管理体制和文化产品的生产经营机制充满活力、富有效率；6、以民族文化为主体，吸收外来有益文化，推动中华文化走向世界的文化开放格局进一步完善；7、高素质文化人才队伍发展壮大，文化繁荣发展的人才保障更加有力。

围绕上述七大目标，《决定》做出了若干部署，将"推动文化科技的创新"专门作为

---

* 本文系2011年11月16日在信息工程学院学习贯彻落实十七届六中全会精神大会上的讲话，收入本书时有改动。

一节。这是党和共和国历史上第一次明确"文化科技"的地位与作用。文化科技界的同志们说：这是文化科技的春天来了。

当前及今后一段时期文化科技工作的核心是"发挥文化和科技的相互促进作用，深入实施科技带动战略，增强自主创新能力"。

我结合目前科技部、文旅部、财政部正在着手的有关文化科技工作，介绍一下几方面概况：

一、努力推动各地区各区域形成文化科技提升文化持续健康发展的长效机制

1. 积极实施文旅部与科技部的部际会商机制；
2. 研究与起草《关于促进文化与科技融合发展的指导意见》；
3. 研究与起草《国家科技与文化融合联合行动计划（2011年—2015年）》。

二、进一步加强文化科技创新能力建设，构建与完善以企业为主体、政产学研相结合的文化技术创新体系

1. 积极推动文化企业科技创新主体地位的形成，研究与起草《文化与科技融合示范基地认定办法》《文化与科技融合示范企业认定办法》；
2. 积极汇聚文化科技主干力量，研究与起草《文化科技国家与部级重点实验室（研究中心）认定办法》；
3. 加强与优化文化科技支撑体系结构与布局研究，建设一批重点实验室（研究中心），适时启动相关认定工作；
4. 联合教育部逐步建立文化科技类人才培养渠道，支持与扶持高等院校优化专业结构，培养一批掌握文化科技的专门人才与复合型人才。

三、进一步加强科技项目的实施力度，推进成果转化与产业化

1. 在大力实施国家文化科技提升计划项目、文旅部科技创新项目、国家文化创新工程项目的同时，积极谋划与组织实施国家科技计划中涉及文化科技领域的相关重点项目；
2. 联合科技部适时启动国家科技与文化融合联合行动计划项目；
3. 预计明年推出《文化与科技融合建设工程》；

4. 加快推进文化领域标准化和信息化进程；

5. 凝练与部署一批科技项目，重点支持数字技术、信息技术、网络技术在网络文化建设与管理、文化传播渠道及体系构建、文化传承体系建设、新兴文化业态与新型文化产业领域中的集成应用与创新。

四、进一步谋求扩大文化科技发展在文化建设公共财政中的投入比重

1. 与财政部积极沟通，争取新增中央财政支持文化科技专项经费；
2. 力争文旅部成为使用公益性行业科研专项经费的国务院所属行业主管部门；
3. 在设立的国家文化发展基金中，将文化科技的基础研究和应用基础研究项目纳入其主要资助领域；
4. 扩大国家文化科技提升计划项目、文旅部科技创新项目、国家文化创新工程项目的财政资金规模；
5. 努力推动各地区各区域公共财政对文化科技发展投入的增长幅度高于财政经常性收入增长幅度；
6. 支持各地区各区域设立文化科技专项经费。

各位老师，我们学院的定位与文化科技密切相关，我们应牢牢抓住和把握时机，主动对接国家的新期待、新要求、新需求，共同努力把我院的工作更加向前推进一步。

文化阵地的新载体与新服务*
——论云文化馆的新担当与新征程

主持人好!

各位嘉宾、各位朋友,很高兴能够来参加这次的论坛!

今天我主要是谈谈对云文化场馆的一些认识与观点。

我的核心观点是,云文化场馆与后疫情时代是没有关系的,云文化场馆这种文化服务形式,是时代发展的必然的产物。

从国家视角出发,我认为云文化场馆是文化阵地的新载体,在这个新载体上应该有相应的新服务。云文化场馆是高技术发展和时代发展背景下,文化服务特别是文化服务中的新的载体形式,当然也有着新担当。

20世纪90年代有人说过:当你控制了粮食,就控制了人;当你控制了石油,就控制了国家;当你控制了货币,就控制了世界。时代已经进入了21世纪20年代,这里,我试着引出几个问题,供大家思考。试问:当一个民族的文化、一个国家的文化,丧失其民族文化的本体或失控时,会发生什么?如何守住与发展文化阵地?特别是如何守住与发展基层文化阵地?在高新技术特别是信息技术与网络技术推动下,我们的文化阵地在哪里?文化阵地的形态是否适应我国新时代新征程的新趋势与新要求?

回到我的主要观点,即云文化场馆是文化阵地的新载体。我所理解的云文化场馆,不仅仅是指狭义上的云文化馆,当然也包括其他的云文化场馆,比如说云美术馆、云图书馆、云博物馆等等。这里面我就"云文化馆"谈几个观点。

第一,云文化馆是按照一定标准规范提供数字文化公共服务的平台、资源和服务的总称。云文化馆是数字公共文化服务的新载体,同时又是数字公共文化服务的新渠道,当然也是我们物理意义上的文化馆建设的有机组成部分,两者形成了一个共同体。

我的第二个观点是"数字文化资源是云文化馆服务的主要内容"。在这个方面,我认为数字文化资源主要由三个维度来决定:一个是政府评估准入,因为资源与内容是为全体人民服务的,所以对于资源与内容应该有准入的要求。第二个是个人、企业或者是用户来进行竞争,因为资源与内容涉及全体人民的精神家园,是要守正有序的。第三个是用户自主选择,这一点就不多谈了。我认为,数字文化资源主要包括如下几类:一是各

---

* 本文系2020年12月22日在2020世界城市文化论坛(上海)上的发言,收入本书时有改动。

类数字文化内容，这是最主要的；二是文化创作生产工具软件；三是文化消费的工具软件；四是在线服务应用系统。因为云文化馆的用户也要产生内容，所以提供各类适宜的软件工具也是一种资源，包括供给侧与需求侧软件工具，此外云文化馆平台运营所需的各类在线服务相关的运营系统，从某种意义上讲，也是一类资源。

我认为，把握好数字文化资源内容，要关注几个要点：一是文化资源的配置；二是面向区域的特色文化资源的供给；还有一个要点是面向垂直领域或者是按照分众兴趣的专业数字文化的供给。

围绕这三个要点，我认为有四个方面的难点：第一个难点是数字资源的有效供给。过去国家在实施数字文化共享工程时已经产生了大量数字文化资源，但是这些数字文化资源基本上还属于传统性的资源，这些传统性的文化资源需不需要？也需要的，但是我认为在今后它可能未必是最最主要的。第二个难点是创新性的数字文化资源的供给。这种所谓的创新性的文化资源，其主要的特征是交互实时的，即在服务和交互过程中产生的资源，这与现在的技术进步与迭代是分不开的。第三个难点是数字文化资源的内容审核。不是所有的资源和内容都可以放进云文化馆当中的，因为是文化阵地，因为不能文化失控，所以要对内容负责任，所以要内容审核，如何面对海量的内容审核，将是一场大考。第四个难点是数字资源的版权保护，包括确权、追踪等等，有一系列问题需要面对，时间关系，这一点就不展开了。

我的第三个观点是"服务是云文化馆的永恒主题"。我认为需要把握好服务的三大核心：第一个是文化资源整合服务和内容服务及其拓展；第二个是服务模式的创新与迭代；第三个是服务的区域化与服务的本地化。特别是服务模式的创新与迭代，这是有别于不同类型云文化馆的根本体现，也是决定各类云文化馆生命力的命脉。服务的区域化与本地化，体现了面向不同区域、不同民族的需求，也就是体现特色。我认为今后不同的云文化馆，都可以在某一方面找到自己的特色，彼此之间走差异化与特色化发展之路。其中，服务模式创新、服务区域化与服务本地化，也是难点。此外，孤立地就云文化馆谈云文化馆的发展，是不合适的，需要与物理意义上的实体文化场馆建设协同发展，故如何实现线上服务与线下服务相结合，也是难点之一。

如何发展好服务业务？我认为需要把握好六个要点：一是文化艺术普及服务及拓展；二是大众文化活动共享服务及拓展；三是非物质文化遗产和工艺美术技艺培训服务及拓展；四是与实体文化场馆共享服务及拓展；五是相关文化产品展示服务及拓展；六是个性化推荐和撮合服务及拓展。围绕这些要点可以拓展出很多很聚集的服务业务，时间关系，这里也不展开了。

我的另外一个观点是"运营是云文化馆的生命线"。这个运营的核心是互联互通，用户统一，共治共享，协同服务。因为是云文化馆，"互联互通"在网络空间中当然是互联互通的，在当今技术条件下，这已经不是障碍。"用户统一"今后将有可能成为难点，无论是从国家安全还是从平台运营,还是各类运营的便利等角度来看,今后的愿景应该是每个人都有统一的账户,不管在平台上还是各个平台之间的转换,每个人应该有唯一的账户,以便今后可以实现全网范围内的有序管理。"共治和共享"主要是指政府、平台、用户的共治和共享。那"协同服务"也是与"共治共享"同理的。围绕云文化馆运营的要点有两个,一个是通过网络的形式提供文化服务,一个是信息技术环境下的文化服务的模式。这里的"运营模式"需要不断地与"文化服务模式"进行匹配,难点主要是三块:一是运营模式的创新与迭代,这个运营模式的创新迭代时时刻刻都需要我们进行思考和创新迭代;二是共治共享,需要不断地平衡政府、个人/企业用户、平台主体之间的社会责任;三是如何提高消费者或者是用户的活跃度和平台的黏度。时间关系,这里也不展开了。

我的第五个观点是"强化云文化馆的担当与责任",这个观点与我的主要观点是一脉相承的,即守住基层文化阵地、发展基层文化阵地、助推文化场馆的数字化建设进程。"坚持文化自信、坚持为人民服务、坚持为大众百姓服务"是发展云文化馆的初心与使命。云文化馆要承担特有的社会责任,国家对文化类平台是有要求的,要点是"把握正确导向,弘扬和践行社会主义核心价值观,树立正确的历史观/民族观、国家观/文化观"。云文化馆还要担负特有的道德责任,要点是"反映中国人民审美追求,维护国家文化安全、维护社会公共利益、维护社会公序良俗"。

我想强调的是,云文化馆的举办主体可以是政府、企业,也可以是混合制的新兴主体。如何是政府举办的,这里不再赘述;如果是企业举办的或新兴主体举办的,追求经济效益将是不可回避的现实问题。未来,企业举办或新兴主体举办云文化馆,将可能是一个大趋势。从这个视角出发,围绕上述的使命、担当与责任,云文化馆运营的难点主要包括两方面:一是"社会效应与经济效应的有效统一",平台的运营总是要赚钱的,但是赚钱和社会效应如何进行有机统一?二是"商业运行与公益服务的并行互惠",这个"并行互惠"可能会倒逼政府在相关机制上进行相关突破。只有这两个难点解决好,云文化馆才能可持续地发展。

综上,发展云文化馆面临着许多的机遇和挑战。总之,要坚持用先进技术支撑云文化馆的可持续发展,要坚持用先进技术引领云文化场馆发展方式的转变,要坚持服务模式与运营模式的不断迭代,倒逼相关服务业务与相关技术的不断创新与迭代。我相信,云文化馆的前景是广阔的!是美好的!

以上是我个人的主要观点,供大家一起交流!也欢迎批评指正,谢谢各位!

数字体育专业委员会工作任务及聚焦方向的一些考虑*

各位委员，大家好！

今天，"中国技术经济学会数字体育专业委员会"成立了！这是中国技术经济学会的一件大事。

根据中国技术经济学会2021年12月《关于设立中国技术经济学会数字体育专业委员会的决定》（中技经发〔2021〕56号）文件，本专业委员会的工作任务是：团结全国在相关领域从事科学研究、政策制订、产业运营管理的科技工作者，研究并促进数字技术与体育产业的深度融合，赋能体育产业的转型升级，助力健康中国、体育强国、数字中国建设。

基于对工作任务的理解，我提炼了四个主要"关键词"，即"体育""数字体育""科技""技术经济"。这四个"关键词"可大致反映出本专业委员会的工作任务的指向。

体育与科技相互促进、融合发展是体育行业高质量发展的最重要特征，是新时代体育发展的重要引擎。体育和科技融合是在现代产业经济环境下体育、科技、服务模式、商业模式等多种要素综合的体育发展方式变革，是体育力量和科技力量的有机融合。

近年来，适应人民需要的数字体育产品不断丰富，数字公共体育服务覆盖面持续扩大，数字体育产业整体实力显著增强，以数字技术支撑的一批公共体育服务设施、渠道、装备和软件系统被大量应用，形成一批面向需求的系统化集成解决方案和网络化运营服务平台，数字技术引领公共体育内容呈现、数字空间载体建设、互联共享的作用凸显；以技术创新、业态创新、服务创新和模式创新为主导的新兴体育产业占比大、增长快；传统体育产业数字化和数字体育相关产品生产继续保持增长，数字科技引领高端体育专用装备制造的作用明显；体育与相关产业跨界融合发展呈常态，体育资源的开发利用途径得到进一步拓展。

数字科技在体育领域中的综合创新应用，极为深刻地影响并改变着体育发展的环境、业态、格局。体育为体、科技为酶。近些年来，数字科技已经全面融入体育综合业务管

---

* 本文系2022年7月24日在中国技术经济学会数字体育专业委员会成立大会上的发言，收入本书时有改动。

理、全民健身公共服务、竞技体育服务、体育产业服务等数字体育的全链条中。

体育与科技融合呈现加速推进态势，正有力地驱动数字体育创新。体育发展不断提出更高的科技诉求，科技发展在体育领域寻找到广泛的应用空间。经过多年持续积累，我国以数字科技为代表的体育科技实力实现整体跃升，与发达国家差距明显缩小，呈现领跑、并跑、跟跑"三跑"并存格局。体育数字化、数字体育产业化、体育产业数字化正在成为更加广泛的共识。

技术经济作为经济学的一个重要分支，主要关注科技领域的经济活动规律，主要关注经济领域的技术发展规律，主要关注技术发展的内在规律。就我们专业委员会而言，就是要面向"数字体育"领域，发展与丰富技术经济的评估、论证、评价等科学方法，并对应用与实践开展具体指导工作。具体包括：采用系统分析、综合分析的研究方法和思维方法，对数字技术的研发、应用与发展进行估计；通过一套经济效果指标体系，对完成同一目标的不同技术解决方案的计算、分析、比较等进行论证；对技术解决方案的经济效果、社会效果等进行评价；等等。

"数字体育"的内涵丰富、领域宽广。体育行业已经基本树立了"数字技术引领体育供给，新算力赋能体育竞技，新融合驱动体育产业，新视角传播体育文化，新智能优化体育决策，新模式重塑体育管理"新发展理念；以企业为主体的社会力量早已经主动融入"数字体育"，技术创新的引领支撑作用明显，产学研用深度融合，一批综合技术解决方案应运而生。

可以看出，上述的这些现状，已经为本专业委员会开展"数字体育"领域的技术经济活动提供了丰厚的土壤与广阔的空间。

在中国技术经济学会的领导下，在各位委员的支持和努力下，本专业委员会拟聚焦以下几个方面，开展相关工作：

一是推进体育资源的数字化与数据化。支持健身场地、体质测试、体育组织、赛事活动、科学训练、体育行业人员等基础数据库的建设，推动数据归集、治理、共享和开放方面实现无缝对接，进一步消除数据孤岛，推进数据共享开放，探索开展数据开放创新应用。

二是促进各类体育数字化业务应用服务。将各类数据形象化、直观化、具体化地按主题进行交互展示，对不同维度的数据进行组合分析，满足不同应用场景和决策分析的需求。

三是促进体育公共服务的数字整合。推进集全民健身、训练管理、赛事服务、体育产业为一体的高质量特色服务平台建设，支撑群众参与健身锻炼、体质测评、科学训练、赛事活动等一站式服务供给。

四是推进体育赛事文化创新发展。借助现代信息技术，推动数字体育内容呈现、赛事直播、融媒体中心等方面建设与发展。

五是推进体育公共场馆智慧化改造。推动"数字孪生"技术在智慧场馆建设中的应用,支持大中型公共体育场馆智慧化场景体验覆盖,支持运动健身基础设施"线上线下"融合支持全民健身进社区、进乡村。

六是推进体育训练管理数字赋能。支持训练管理和备战智慧化发展,提升训练效果,提高伤病预防和运动康复水平。

七是引导体育赛事管理与服务向数字化发展。推进体育赛事与信息化的深度融合,全面提升体育赛事管理与服务效能。

八是推动体育产业核心业务数字化应用迭代升级。推进数字体育新产品、新服务和新业态的培育,推进数字体育建设示范区、示范点、产业集聚区。

九是推动数字体育与实体经济融合发展。推进体育装备制造的智能化与"互联网服务+"化,推进数字体育与文化和旅游融合发展,推进传统体育产业的数字化转型升级。

十是推动新型基础设施建设。推进信息网络基础设施建设,推进云网协同和算网融合发展,推进数字体育产业技术创新基础设施建设。

上述的十个方面,仅是初步的考虑,还需要进一步丰富与论证。

各位委员,我们的专业委员会,生逢其时、使命光荣、责任重大!我愿意与大家一起,共同开创这项伟大的事业!

谢谢大家!

推进文化与科技的融合，把握好研发团队的建设[*]

党的二十大报告指出，加快建设社会主义文化强国、科技强国是全面建设社会主义现代化国家的应有之义，而文化和科技融合正是文化强国和科技自立自强两大战略的重要交汇领域。全面提升文化科技创新能力，对于转变文化发展方式，推动文化事业和文化产业更好更快发展，更好地满足人民精神文化生活新期待，增强人民群众的获得感和幸福感，有着重要的支持引领作用。

新发展格局为文化科技创新提供了广阔的空间和场景，在"发展积极健康的网络文化、推进媒体深度融合、加强国家重大文化设施和文化项目建设、传承弘扬中华优秀传统文化、实施文化数字化战略、创新推进国际传播"等重点领域，亟须通过基础理论和共性关键技术研究，为行业科技发展奠定理论、方法和技术基础；亟须以科学技术推动文化艺术的形式创新、内容创新、模式创新、呈现方式创新，提升文化艺术创作效率能力与艺术的表现力、感染力；亟须利用先进科技支撑中华优秀传统文化传承发展，开展文化遗产保护与文物活化利用技术与创造性转化技术研究，推动传统文化"活起来"；亟须通过文化公共服务内容和手段的科技创新，丰富服务供给，创新服务形式，提升文化和旅游公共服务效能；亟须围绕实施文化产业数字化战略，以科技创新提升文化生产和内容建设能力，提高文化产业数字化、网络化、智能化发展水平；亟须强化大数据技术在"互联网＋监管"中的运用，提高文化治理效能，推动实现文化治理体系和治理能力现代化；亟须以科技支撑对外文化交流方式和方法创新，提升对外文化交流传播的效能和效果，向世界讲好中国故事，传播好中国声音。

构建与加强研发团队建设，是完善文化科技创新体系的最基础的要求之一，是文化科技创新载体的最基本单元。

视听技术与智能控制技术文旅部重点实验室、现代演艺技术北京市重点实验室是国家战略科技力量的组成部分，是由信息与通信工程学院发起与精心培育起来的一支研发团队，团队主要成员来自信息与通信工程学院。该团队在中国传媒大学高速腾飞和政治生态风清气正的大背景下，坚持聚焦文化科技领域，近几年取得了跨越式的发展。

该团队坚持丰富并支撑文艺演出的表现形式和手段，以提升演出内容的艺术表现力、

---

[*] 本文系 2023 年 9 月 8 日在中国传媒大学首届"三牛奖"颁奖典礼上的发言，与蒋玉暕合作撰写。收入本书时有改动。

感染力、影响力和受众欣赏体验与消费传播为主旨，重点聚焦演艺灯光、演艺音响、演艺机械、演艺特效、演出协同与控制、观演环境控制以及演艺资源数字化、视听融合信息处理等领域的关键技术与系统装备，形成了独有的研究领域特色和优势，承接了多项国家重大科技任务，累计获得科研到账总经费超过 5000 万元，取得了一批高水平研究成果，研发了一批高新技术核心装备，引领了演艺视听技术的迭代发展，促进了文艺演出服务业与演艺装备制造业的技术进步。团队的整体技术水平与研发创新能力，基本处在全国同行"领跑者"地位。

该团队 2008 年组建、2014 年获得北京市和文旅部相关重点实验室的认定，经过十几年的建设与发展，形成了一些可借鉴可参考的经验做法，大体上有三大方面。

一、坚守重点实验室初心

心系"国家事"，肩扛"国家责"，始终牢记"国家队""国家人"职责使命，坚持研发团队的使命定位与目标愿景不动摇。

1. "抱团作战"才能形成科技创新的合力。有了合力，才能"谋事""干事"和"干成事"。

2. 研发团队必须要有明确的使命定位与目标愿景。"使命定位"决定了团队未来的"地位与高度"，"目标愿景"决定了"往什么方向走和走多远"。

3. 设定一个"跳一跳，够得着"的团队目标。必须要有一个努力蹦与拼命跳，才能"够得着"的目标，才是一个"好目标"或者是一个"合适的目标"。

4. "使命定位与目标愿景"是团队"抱团作战"成功的前提。这个前提是团队成员"共同价值认同"与"共同事业追求"的基石。同时，也是团队成员"优胜劣汰"与"吐故纳新"的基线。

二、坚守科研阵地

凝神聚力，坚持稳定的重点领域，在任务布局方面注重战略性、把握规律性、体现创新性、突出实践性，十几年如一日地聚焦与坚守重点实验室的重点领域与任务布局不动摇。

1. 重点领域：意味着团队的研究领域，是聚焦的，是"有限边界"的。"重点"这两个字，意味着"有限范围"，而不是"大而全"。要有"经得住诱惑和耐得住寂寞"的坚强意志，要长期坚守"重点领域"。

2. 任务布局：是研究领域范围内的子集。任务布局也可理解为主要研究方向的设置。

3. 稳定："稳定"意味着不会轻易变化。稳定的重点领域与任务布局，必须是基于"团队目标愿景"基础上的。

4. 坚持与明确主要产出与核心指标不动摇，主要包括到账科研经费、国家级重点科研项目、省部级科研项目、"三高"学术论文、申请或授权发明专利、登记软件著作权、政策咨询建议专题报告、科技成果转化，等等。

5. 系统研判团队在"人无我有、人有我优、人优我特"三个维度上的态势。没有比较，就没有差距。只有通过比较，才能挖掘出团队发展的增长点。

6. 打造"文化与科技融合"学术交流阵地。建好团队的"学术交流朋友圈"，并尽量争取当好"群主"。

三、坚持有组织的科研

统筹创新人才高地，强化团队的特色和优势，提升团队整体竞争力。

1. 注重人才质量提升与队伍结构优化。以更加积极开放的姿态广泛吸纳优秀青年人才，制订并实施一系列的青年骨干成长计划。

2. 为年轻教师的"快速成长"提供机遇和路径。通过积极申报与承担国家重大科技任务，助推团队的年轻教师自我加压与主动加压。

3. 强化团队的特色和优势。集聚校内校外、重点实验室内外、团队内外的优质创新资源，努力保持团队特色与优势的稳定与光大。

4. 着眼于提升"七大能力"。始终保持清醒的头脑，针对团队发展中可能存在的"观念钝化""知识老化""能力弱化"的现象，长期坚持提升"七大能力"，主要包括：学习研究能力、创新思维能力、科学决策能力、沟通协调能力、团结协作能力、工作实践能力和攻坚克难能力。

我们有理由相信，我们中传人、我们中传信通人、我们中传信通团队，一定会对接服务于国家战略需求，顶天立地干实事、出成效，在相关文化科技细分领域实现高水平科技的自立自强，开拓创新，再展宏图！

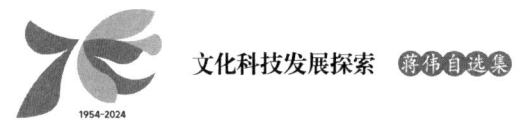

数字化赋能与激发文化创新*

各位领导、各位专家,大家下午好!

围绕今天座谈会的"数字化赋能文化改革发展、激发文化创新创造活力"(以下简称"数字化赋能")主题,我主要谈谈我个人的一些基本认识、考虑及建议。

一、对"数字化赋能"的基本判断

文化与科技相互促进、融合发展是人类文明发展的最重要特征。新一轮科技革命正在深度影响和重构文化的形态、结构和价值追求,是新时代文化创新性转化和创造性发展的重要引擎。当前主要呈现出如下五个基本状态:

1. 数字科技已成为支撑驱动文化发展的主要力量之一。

2. 数字科技在文化领域中的综合创新应用,极为深刻地影响并改变着文化发展的环境、业态、格局。文化为体、科技为酶,数字科技已经全面融入文化创作、生产、传播、服务、消费以及文化服务与模式创新、文化内容与形式创新、文化产业升级与业态创新、文化市场监管与服务创新等全链条中。

3. 数字科技引领的新浪潮,正在深刻地影响文化发展的路径,为文化的发展植入了创新基因,对当今及未来的生产生活方式产生了革命性的影响,加速了文化生产方式及发展模式的变革,开创了文化传播传承方式的新革命,促进了文化消费与接受方式的新变革。

4. 数字文化已经成为当今社会文化的一种新文化存在形态。数字文化在现实社会文化的延伸和多样化呈现的同时,也形成了其自身独特的文化行为特征、文化产品特色和价值观念和思维方式的特点,革命性地改变着我们所处时代的日常文化存在形态。

5. 文化数字化、数字文化产业化、文化产业数字化,是赋能文化改革发展与激发文化创新创造活力的三大主要领域。

---

* 本文系 2023 年 2 月 16 日在中宣部文化数字化专家座谈会上的发言,收入本书时有改动。

二、在"数字化赋能"须遵循的主要原则方面的考虑

1. 坚持价值导向，特别是文化价值导向。坚持将持续发展的价值效益作为核心评判依据，有效平衡、兼顾实效性价值与中远期发展价值，建立覆盖数字化赋能重大投资决策、应用决策、成效评价及绩效考核的建设与治理体系，不断激发文化企事业单位的动力和活力。

2. 坚持深化改革。把握好生产力和生产关系协同优化、持续变革的规律和趋势，同步推进新一代数字技术应用和组织管理机制变革，突破传统业务发展的瓶颈，加速推进业务数字化改革试点和最佳实践复制，为新技术、新产品、新服务、新模式、新业务的发展完善环境、留足空间。

3. 坚持数据驱动。将数据作为新的生产要素，深化数据资源的开发利用，促进以数据为核心的新型产品与服务创新，以信息流带动技术流、资金流、人才流、物流，在更大范围加快各类资源汇聚和按需流动，带动提高全要素生产率和创新水平。

4. 坚持创新引领。加强数字时代核心能力建设，推进新一代数字技术及其应用产品集中攻关，推动和支持创新成果和能力的输出，不断加强技术和产品与服务迭代优化和创新。聚焦本质安全需要，推动实现从企业到完整产业链、从服务到完整服务链的安全可靠。

5. 坚持统筹推进。导入先进的系统化管理体系，做好数字化赋能蓝图与推进路线图的顶层设计与过程把控，以应对数字化赋能带来的高度复杂性与风险性，确保战略、业务、技术等的一致性和协调联动，促进整体协同效应的发挥。

6. 坚持开放合作。树立开放、包容的发展理念，加强文化资源和能力开放共享，有效利用先进技术与实践，补齐发展中的能力短板，加快基于平台的能力社会化输出，构建互利共赢的合作生态，又好又稳地加快数字化能力建设。

三、在"数字化赋能"落地层面的主要建议

（一）提高三个基本认识

1. 数字化赋能是一项涉及数据、技术、流程、组织等的复杂系统工程，要注重深化对数字化赋能文化发展与创新艰巨性、长期性和系统性的认识，加强战略性统筹布局；

2. 数字化赋能当前的工作重心是充分发挥数据要素驱动作用，打通全产业链、全价值链、全创新链、全服务链，共建数字化赋能生态，获得价值增量发展空间，要强化数据驱动、集成创新、合作共赢等数字化赋能理念，加强多线条协同并进；

3. 数字化赋能不仅是一把手工程，更是涉及全员、全要素的创新活动，要充分激发基层创新活力，营造勇于、乐于、善于数字化赋能文化发展与创新的氛围，强化上下一盘棋。

（二）夯实四个赋能基础

文化企事业单位要从技术、管理、数据、安全四个方面，加强对标，夯实数字化赋能的基础。

1. 技术基础。数字化赋能本质是新一代数字技术引发的系统性变革，新一代数字技术作为通用使能技术，需要不断强化其技术赋能作用，及与其他专业技术融合。

2. 管理基础。数字化赋能不仅仅是技术渗透和融合的问题，更是一项优化管理模式以适应技术变革的问题，要导入系统化管理体系，有效获取预期的成效。

3. 数据基础。在数字时代，数据已成为第五大生产要素，要充分发挥数据要素驱动作用，打破传统要素有限供给对增长的制约。

4. 安全基础。安全是发展的前提，要加强安全可靠和信息安全两方面基础工作，强化本质安全。

（三）把握四个赋能方向

文化企事业单位要从产品、生产运营、用户服务、产业体系四个方面系统推进数字化赋能。

1. 产品与服务创新数字化。与价值创造的载体有关，要加强产品和服务创新及产品研发过程创新，以不断提高产品附加价值，缩短价值变现周期。

2. 生产运营智能化。与价值创造的过程有关，要加强横向纵向全过程贯通，实现全价值链、全要素资源的动态配置和全局优化，提高全要素生产率。

3. 用户服务敏捷化。与价值创造的对象有关，要以用户为中心，实现全链条用户服务，最大化为用户创造价值，提高用户满意度和忠诚度。

4. 产业体系生态化。与价值创造的生态合作伙伴有关，要加强与合作伙伴之间的资源、能力和业务合作，构建优势互补、合作共赢的协作网络。

（四）突出三个赋能举措

文化企事业单位及社会科技力量要站在服务于文化改革发展与激发文化创新创造活力的高度，勇于担当，加强核心技术攻关和资源能力的社会化输出，提升整个经济社会的数字化赋能价值。

1. 新型基础设施建设。积极开展新型基础设施投资和建设，带动产业链上下游及丰富应用场景。

2. 关键核心技术攻关。加快攻克核心技术难题，着力构建国际先进、安全可控的数字文化技术体系。

3. 发展数字文化产业。合理布局数字文化产业，培育行业领先的数字化服务龙头企业。

（五）部署三个实施策略

文化企事业单位要构建以能力为主线的数字化赋能战略布局和实施体系，加强数据、流程、组织和技术四要素统筹和协同创新，有效推进数字化赋能工作。

1. 加强顶层规划。开展数字化赋能，首要任务就是要制订数字化赋能战略，并将其作为发展战略的核心内容。条件成熟的文化企事业单位，数字化赋能战略和发展战略可合二为一。发展战略制订要加强竞争合作优势、业务场景和价值模式等分析，加强诊断分析，发现问题，找准方向。

2. 强化协同推进。开展数字化赋能、新型能力建设是贯穿始终的核心路径，通过能力建设、统筹规划、科技、信息化、流程等管控条线，支持业务按需调用能力，以快速响应社会与市场需求变化。

3. 做好资源保障。开展数字化赋能，还应建立相匹配的治理体系并推进管理模式持续变革，以提供资源和管理保障，包括领导机制、管理机制、资金机制、人才机制等。

以上是我个人的观点，供参考。